MW00826863

OPENING KAILASANATHA

OPENING

Kailasanatha

The Temple in Kanchipuram Revealed in Time and Space

PADMA KAIMAL

UNIVERSITY OF WASHINGTON PRESS

Seattle

Publication of *Opening Kailasanatha* has been aided by a grant from the
Millard Meiss Publication Fund of the College Art Association.

This book was made possible in part by a grant from
the McLellan Endowment, established through the generosity of
Martha McCleary McLellan and Mary McLellan Williams.

Additional support was provided by grants from the Colgate University Research Council,
Office of the Provost and Dean of the Faculty, and Michael J. Batza Chair in Art & Art History.

Design by M. Wright
Composed in Adobe Text, typeface designed by Robert Slimbach

25 24 23 22 21   5 4 3 2 1

Printed and bound in the United States of America

UNIVERSITY OF WASHINGTON PRESS
uwapress.uw.edu

LIBRARY OF CONGRESS CATALOGING-IN-PUBLICATION DATA
LIBRARY OF CONGRESS CONTROL NUMBER: 2020932709

ISBN 978-0-295-74777-4 (hardcover)
ISBN 978-0-295-74778-1 (ebook)

Interior photographs are by the author unless otherwise noted.

The paper used in this publication is acid free and meets the minimum requirements of
American National Standard for Information Sciences—Permanence of Paper
for Printed Library Materials, ANSI z39.48–1984.∞

To Andy, Sophie, and Phoebe, my darlings, my heroes

CONTENTS

Plates follow page 160

PREFACE & ACKNOWLEDGMENTS

THIS BOOK COULD HAPPEN BECAUSE MANY PEOPLE GAVE ME THEIR TIME, insights, expertise, encouragement, and funding. Listing all of those people here is a challenge I am likely to fail, and for this I am very sorry. But I am deeply grateful to everyone who interacted with me over the past twenty-five years about the Kailasanatha temple complex in Kanchipuram. All of you have helped me to think out these ideas and to have the luxury of time to write them down.

Long before conceiving this project, I received a Junior Fellowship from the American Institute of Indian Studies (AIIS) thanks to Joanna G. Williams. That gave me my first chances to visit the Kailasanatha in 1984–85. P. Venugopala Rao, head of the AIIS Madras office, and his assistant Perumal made my research year a success by gracefully navigating many bureaucratic waters for me. The invaluable support of the Hindu Religious and Charitable Endowments Board as well as the Archaeological Survey of India enabled me to photograph and study this and many other sites.

Overwhelmed on my first visit by the visual wealth of the Kailasanatha, I wandered through it for hours and wore out the patience of my bicycle rickshaw driver. I had come to look at a few potential portraits, but I left convinced that the temple complex deserved someone's sustained attention. I could not yet imagine it would be mine.

My dear friend Dennis Hudson gave me the courage ten years later to think that that someone might be me after all. His own study of the Vaikuntha Perumal temple in the same city made a convincing case for that temple having been designed as a kind of "response text" to the Kailasanatha, though exactly what this earlier building meant still remained puzzling to us both. He helped me get started. As we talked about cave temples, he taught me that directionality is the most likely principle organizing the placement of sculptures on temples in the Tamil region. And he collaborated with me to produce a pair of papers on the Kailasanatha for the 1996 symposium of the American Council for Southern Asian Art. We focused on the tall-towered *vimana* at the center of the compound. I speculated that its sculptures of Shiva embodied ideals of kingship. Dennis engaged the inscription's astonishing revelation that a king had taken initiation into a Tantric sect. David T. Sanford and Michael Rabe were among the most energetic colleagues to respond to our papers. David cracked open for me the identity of Jalandhara as the defeated figure at the center of the north wall.

Dennis would live just long enough to complete his study of the Vaikuntha Perumal. I then pursued the Kailasanatha project without him. Generous fellowships from the American Association of University Women and the National Endowment for the Humanities gave me three semesters of leave from teaching in 2001–2 that let me immerse myself in literature on goddess worship in South Asia. I began to see that goddess imagery played a larger role at the Kailasanatha than most scholarship on that monument had led me to expect.

Major grants from the Colgate University Research Council permitted me to return to the site in 1999 and 2010. South Asia scholar Kimberly Masteller; her husband, Donovan Dodrill; and my parents, Lorraine and Chandran Kaimal, joined me at the site in 1999 for delightful conversation, study, and photography. Kim brought her expertise on goddess temples. Donovan's sharp eyes caught the small sculptures of Shiva as a meditating ascetic on the tiny towers over cells 15–29 of Rajasimha's *prakara*.

That tour got me thinking about that *prakara* as a kind of goddess temple in its own right, a hypothesis I shared at the 2001 conference of the American Academy of Religion and then in its journal. Leslie C. Orr organized both projects, bringing me together with Corinne Dempsey, Whitney Kelting, and Richard Cohen in challenging the alleged marginality of goddesses in South Asian practice. I was able to continue workshopping that thesis and other thoughts about the monument with scholars and wider audiences thanks to speaking invitations from Rebecca Brown at St. Mary's College of Maryland, 1999; Rob Linrothe at Skidmore College; Vivien Fryd at Vanderbilt University; Michael Cothren at Swarthmore College; Margaret Supplee Smith at Wake Forest University; Susan Mann, Deborah Harkness, and Karen Halttunen at the University of California, Davis; Adam Hardy at De Montfort University, Leicester, England; Rick Asher at the University of Minnesota; Donald Wood at the Birmingham Museum of Art, Alabama; Indira Peterson for a symposium at the Museum of Fine Arts, Houston; Janice Leoshko at the University of Texas, Austin; Charlotte Schmid at the École française d'Extrême-Orient (EFEO) and Emmanuel Francis at the Centre d'étude de l'Inde et de l'Asie du Sud; Nicolas Dejenne at the Université Sorbonne Nouvelle–Paris 3; and Elizabeth Cecil at Brown University. At each place, lively questions from colleagues and audiences flushed out my weaker assumptions and pressed me to interrogate the monument more closely.

By 2009, I had a clear vision of the published record and the many parts of the monument, but I did not yet have a compelling story to tell. I had pieces, but they did not add new insights about the whole. That changed when I had the great fortune to spend 2010–11 at the Institute for Advanced Study (IAS) at Princeton University as the Louise and John Steffens Founders' Circle and the Starr Foundation East Asian Studies Endowment Fund Member. The time to think, read, and write was wonderful, but more precious were the guidance, the hard questions, and the fascinating conversations I had with the faculty and other members. I must extend particular thanks to Yve-Alain Bois, Caroline Walker Bynum, Nicola Di Cosmo, and Irving and Marilyn Lavin on the faculty; Marian Zelazny on the IAS staff; and fellow IAS members Norman Kutcher, Daniela Caglioti, Katrin Kogman-Appel, Menachem Kojman, Mehmet-Ali Ataç, Toni Bierl, Eleonore Le Jalle, Richard Taws, and Himanshu Prabha Ray. Mehmet-Ali transformed my understanding of how art can represent time and convinced me that reducing the past to the political does an injustice. Toni encouraged me to pursue evidence of complementarities in place of binaries by sharing his own parallel discoveries in ancient Greek materials. Himanshu urged me to consider the building's marginal sculptures as spaces in which individual artisans had room to improvise on underlying themes. At the Lavins' suggestion, their friend Frank Gehry stopped by my office to look at my photos and observe that the Kailasanatha, like his creations, was a building that could produce the illusion of movement.

Other scholars in the area who visited the institute fed my work as well. Isabelle Clark-Decès of Princeton University shared with me her profound and nuanced understandings of Tamil culture. Her untimely death has been a great loss to our field as well as to me. Erik Thuno of Rutgers University helped me understand reception theory and its principle that meaning emerges through people's interactions with objects rather than being fixed or inherent in objects. Deborah Hutton of the College of New Jersey sharpened my perceptions of the leonine forms that fill the monument, reminding me that their regular geometries and fantastic horns signal some symbolic purpose that naturalistic lions might not. Julie Romain, visiting from the Los Angeles County Museum of Art, helped me track down the inscription left at the Kailasanatha by the Chalukya king Vikramaditya II. Julie's early passing, too, leaves a sad void.

The year at the institute also gave me the time to explore the important scholarship of the French team of Charlotte Schmid, Emmanuel (Manu) Francis, and Valérie Gillet, which Leslie C. Orr of Concordia University, my precious friend and mentor for most of my academic life in all aspects of Tamil Nadu's history, had been urging on me for some time. She was right as usual. Their careful and imaginative work enabled the breakthrough I had been hoping for. That work studies the Pallavas and their monuments with unprecedented depth and scientific rigor. With a skilled support team from the EFEO in Pondicherry, headed in the field by the brilliant research assistant N. Ramaswamy (Babu to his friends), these scholars had revisited the sites, combed the surrounding landscapes, recopied inscriptions from their original surfaces, photographed everything methodically, attended closely to the materiality of all their evidence, and assembled an extensive corpus that informs their multiple publications.

Inspired to encounter work that spoke to my own explorations so forcefully and with such fresh insights, I began an enthusiastic correspondence with Charlotte that led to close collaboration and friendship with her, Manu, and Valérie. They included me in their "Archaeology of Bhakti" workshops and fieldwork tours of Tamil Nadu in 2011, 2013, and 2015. Together we crisscrossed the Kailasanatha compound, puzzling out figures and patterns. Manu worked all the way around Rajasimha's *vimana* with me, mapping the exact letters at which the inscription turned each corner of this many-faceted building. Valérie traced for me the awkward joins between Mahendra's *prakara* and Rajasimha's *prakara* on one side and on the other side to the shrines along the eastern façade of the temple complex. Charlotte walked me through the closure of the west entry to the *prakara* and her new readings of Skanda's iconographic signs. What they taught me enabled me to write this book. Their publications and insights pepper the endnotes of the book. Their generosity continued through the last phases of writing. Manu freely shared many of the book's photos. Charlotte thought through the cover photo and shared her shots for it. They and Valérie are truly collaborators, coauthors even. I thank them with all my heart and apologize if I have not sufficiently credited them for every insight they shared with me. It has become impossible to keep track.

By bringing me to their workshops, they included me in a community of scholars with whom it has been a joy to make new discoveries in the field. These include Dominic Goodall and Eva Wilden of the EFEO, Yuko Yokochi, Vasudha Narayanan, Richard H. Davis, Tracy Coleman, Richard Mann, Akira Shimada, Ute Hüsken, Caleb Simmons, Nicolas Cane, Tiziana Leucci, John Guy, Nicolas Dejenne, Emma Stein, Maishy Charan, Shubha Shanthamurthy, Uthaya Veluppillai, Elizabeth Cecil, Divya Kumar, Suganya Anandakichenin, and, yet again, my dear Leslie C. Orr. Prerana Patel, the EFEO assistant director who can manage anything without even looking anxious, handled my travel to and from all three of the workshops without one hitch. Emma Stein and Richard Mann came with me to walk through, observe, and discuss the Kailasanatha yet again in 2015. In Paris, Anne-Julie Etter, a student of Manu's at the Centre d'études de l'Inde et de l'Asie du Sud, shared with me her archival research on early modern Kanchi.

In the United States and England, too, colleagues have made this project better with their insights and suggestions. I give my profound thanks to Janice Leoshko and Richard H. Davis for being intellectual guiding lights throughout my career and also for their brilliant and close readings of this manuscript for the University of Washington Press. Both did me the honor of pressing me on weak points and suggesting substantial revisions, all of which made this a much better contribution to our field. Adam Hardy demonstrated extraordinary patience in explaining to me repeatedly his understanding of what temples and technical manuals about temple building do and do not have to do with each other. Architect Philip Harding shared with me the photos he took of the Kailasanatha as it was being renovated in 2001–2. Sanskritist Christopher Wallis volunteered references to confirm that Rajasimha had indeed taken Tantric initiation. Gudrun Bühnemann of the University of Wisconsin–Madison directed me to writing on the concept of a female lingam. Cristelle Baskins of Tufts University got me thinking in new ways about the narrative implications in figural postures in art, sharing with me David Summers's work on Italian Renaissance painting. Catherine Becker, Pia Brancaccio, Crispin Branfoot, and Shaman Hatley, superb scholars and kind friends all, kept me inspired by their findings and in line when my models got wonky. Crispin has been a constant and helpful nudge, goading me to send this book out into the world. Dr. Malini Roy, head of visual arts in the Asia and Africa collections, made my archival work at the British Library a breeze.

The new story I could tell about the Kailasanatha as a coordinated system of meaning then began to fall into place. Regan Huff, a senior acquisitions editor at the University of Washington Press, did me the enormous favor of looking over many pieces I had drafted and helping to "wrestle the alligator" (in her words) into a linear sequence. Much of that unfolded at Colgate University, where stimulating colleagues and brilliant staff have nurtured my scholarship for many years. The Colgate University Research Council provided multiple grants for me to travel, Interim Dean/Provost Constance Harsh gave me the Batza Family Chair in Art and Art History with its attendant research funds, and Dean/Provost Tracey Hucks and Associate Dean Kenneth Belanger granted me a subvention to help with the costs of publishing this book. My posse of South Asianist colleagues (Navine Murshid, Nimanthi Rajasingham, Nagesh Rao, Ani Maitra, Aftab Jassal, and Joel Bordeaux) read drafts and spent hours helping me clarify my ideas. Aftab in particular pressed me on the categories I was assigning to spatial patterns in the monument, reminding me of the relevance of Tamil notions of *akam* (interiority, love) and *puram* (exteriority, war). Georgia Frank, Elizabeth Marlowe, Eliza Kent, and Anthony Aveni provided supportive and wonderfully challenging feedback at several points.

Students and staff, too, have been indispensable to this project. The Arts and Humanities Division of Colgate University underwrote summer apprenticeships for four students to work with me on this book. Hannah Bjornson spent the summer of 2013 in the library and online, digging up conservation records, mining the British Library's online archives, finding sources on the chemistry of architectural preservation, pursuing newspaper notices, and generally tearing up the world archive to learn what changes the Kailasanatha had undergone in the centuries after its initial construction. Her work filled in key gaps in my knowledge and opened up problems I had not known to consider. The following summer, Shan Wu bravely tackled with elegance and success the challenge of translating my visual data and spatial patterns into diagrams that integrated the sculptures and words on Rajasimha's *vimana*. Daniel Berry in 2015 expanded on her work in ingenious ways, capturing on single pages the patterns that wove among dozens of sculptures spread across multiple sections of the monument. In 2016, Angel Trazo continued Daniel's work and also found brilliant strategies for diagraming patterns that implied movement or collapsed together architectural and sculptural metaphors. Jenny Steele performed quick and careful detective work for me back on campus as I edited the manuscript during a leave in England.

Mark R. Williams, an accomplished graphic artist as well as the Art and Art History Department's art studio technician, took all of their work, asked more questions, worked closely with the University of Washington Press, and transformed my students' courageous innovations into the professional and gorgeous diagrams that now grace this volume. The visual resources curator for the university, Lesley Chapman, has guided me with patience and hilarious wit through every twist in the terrifying maze of image collection and management. Assisting me with particularly gnarly scanning tasks has been the wise and wildly overqualified Michelle VanAuken, who now serves as the administrative assistant for Colgate's University Museums. At Colgate's Case-Geyer Library, interlibrary loan detectives extraordinaire Ann Ackerson and Lisa King dug up resources for me that any research library would have struggled to find. Erika Mueller, Bonnie Kupris, and Rob Capuano have made that library a productive and tranquil retreat where I could sink deep into my work, welcoming me day after day into those spaces they protect with quiet vigilance. Aleta Mayne, Mark Walden, and Daniel DeVries in communications took an early interest in this project and translated my ideas into accessible and exciting prose for the readership of the *Colgate Magazine*.

Working with the University of Washington Press has been a sheer joy, from my first conversation with Regan Huff; through months of brainstorming with Caitlin Tyler-Richards and Hanni Jalil—Mellon fellows, assistant editors, and patient saints— how to translate diagrams that captured my intimate familiarity with the monument into diagrams that could express that thinking clearly to others; to these final phases of production. The press's executive editor, Lorri Hagman, who has shepherded my manuscript since 2016, has been the kindest and most supportive editor anyone could hope to have, as well as a wonderfully sharp reader. Beth Fuget, in grants and digital projects, did her magic and secured a Millard Meiss publication grant for the project, for which I am also deeply grateful to the College Art Association. The brilliant Jane Lichty copyedited the manuscript with the kindest razor, building sensible bridges for readers to follow my thinking, unearthing crucial errors that few specialists in the field might recognize, and in so many ways rescuing it and me from many embarrassments. Any errors that remain in this book are surely my own. All translations in the book are also mine, unless credited otherwise.

For sharing with me photographs that are fundamental data for the arguments of this book, I am deeply beholden to Manu Francis. Nearly half of the photos in this book, and nearly all of the ones that attain professional standards, are his. With a free hand and unquestioning trust, he shared them with me by the hundreds as soon as I began working with his team. To Vandana Sinha and Sushil Sharma at the Center for Art and Archaeology, AIIS, I am also grateful for so quickly and generously sharing with me an archival image that broke open my understanding of a damaged relief. I thank Chris Rawlings, the licensing assistant, and especially Jonathon Vines, image and brand licensing manager at the British Library for his exceptional patience in finding a channel through which to share with me the archival photo that is figure 4.1 in this book.

To my family, most of all, I am eternally and gratefully in debt. My parents, Lorraine and Chandran, have for my whole life lovingly assured me of their faith in my intellect and judgment. They have made my research possible by accompanying me into the field in 1999–2000 and by moving to Hamilton in 1992 to help raise their grandchildren. At dinner most evenings, they ask with bated breath about the latest chapters in my career and they offer excellent advice. Lorraine has edited this manuscript. My brother, Narayan, and my sister, Maya, have been dear friends all along, shoring me up with their affection and humoring me even when I regress into their bossy big sister. Sophie and Phoebe, my precious daughters, are my daily strength and deepest pride. Their faith in my abilities gave me the strength to push forward even in the grimmest moments of this process. They admire me more than I deserve and I admire them with all my heart. And to Andy, my life partner and boon companion, I owe everything. Thank you for spending the first year of our marriage hauling camera equipment and me across India, for thinking with me through every idea I have put to paper, for taking pleasure in my strength and being kind about my weaknesses. This book, like all my accomplishments, owes everything to your love.

OPENING KAILASANATHA

INTRODUCTION

THE KAILASANATHA TEMPLE COMPLEX IS A CLUSTER OF STONE BUILDINGS constructed at the turn of the eighth century CE under the patronage of men and women of the Pallava dynasty in their capital, Kanchipuram ("the city of Kanchi"), a city full of temples in southeastern India (fig. 1.1).[1] Since the monument's birth, phases of neglect and renovation have left it as little altered as something so old might be and still survive.[2] Its sculptures preserve early iconographic forms. Its walls bear inscriptions in archaic alphabets. No one has encircled its eighth-century buildings within the multiple, concentric compound walls (*prakaras*) or monumental gateways (*gopurams*) that did grow in later centuries around other temples in the Tamil region such as Madurai, Chidambaram, and Tirukkalikkundram, or within Kanchi itself at the Ekambaranatha temple.

The Kailasanatha's earliest forms are the focus of this book, for what they can reveal about thought worlds of the ancient Indic south. Those forms include many sandstone spires crowning shrines, or *vimana*s. The tallest spire is the towering *vimana* commissioned by Narasimhavarman II Rajasimha (Rājasiṃha) Pallava (fig. 1.2). Much smaller spires link up to form a four-sided *prakara* wall that encloses Rajasimha's *vimana* in a large, rectangular courtyard (fig. 1.3). A broken row of eight medium-sized *vimana*s commissioned by Pallava queens now forms a kind of façade for the compound (fig. 1.1). A pillared, open-sided hall (*mandapam*) stands between Rajasimha's *vimana* and a *vimana* sponsored by his son, Mahendravarman (figs. 1.4, 1.5). All these elements were in place before Rajasimha's death. Only the windowless, single-storied hall that joins Rajasimha's *vimana* to the open-sided *mandapam* was added later (figs. 1.6, 1.7).[3]

FIGURE I.1 The Kailasanatha temple complex seen from the east. Foremost is the line of small *linga* shrines commissioned by Pallava queens broken by the lighter walls of Mahendra's *prakara* and its low, barrel-vaulted entry. Behind rises the taller, white barrel vault of Mahendra's *vimana* and the even taller pyramidal tower over Rajasimha's *vimana*. (Photo by Emmanuel Francis)

FIGURE 1.2 The towered *vimana* built by Narasimhavarman II Pallava (Rajasimha) seen from the northeast. At left is the north wall of the much later closed *mandapam*.

4

FIGURE 1.3 The string of tiny shrines that make up the enclosure wall of Rajasimha's *prakara*. Detail view of the south side of the enclosure seen from inside the courtyard, looking east.

FIGURE 1.4 Mahendra's *vimana* seen from the northwest, flanked by the shorter shrines on the east side of Rajasimha's *prakara*.

FIGURE 1.5 The open *mandapam*, seen from the east as one enters the large courtyard.

FIGURE 1.6 The three structures at the center of the large courtyard seen from the southeast. From right: the open *mandapam*, the much later closed *mandapam*, and the tall *vimana* built by Narasimhavarman II Pallava (Rajasimha). (Photo by Emmanuel Francis)

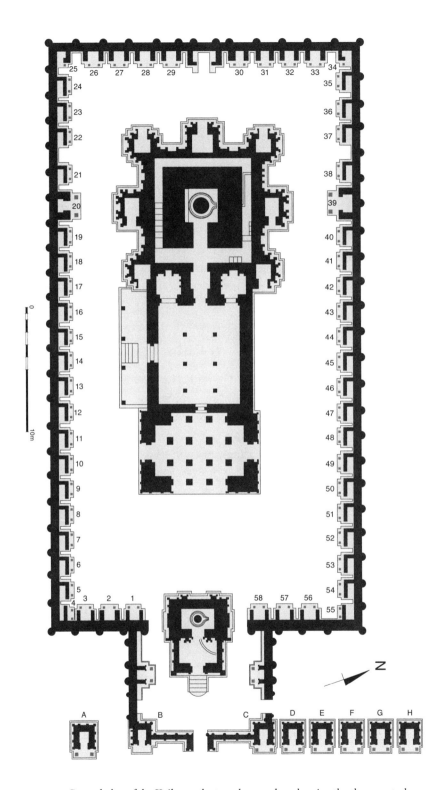

FIGURE I.7 Ground plan of the Kailasanatha temple complex, showing the three central structures in the large courtyard, the cells surrounding the large courtyard (1–58), the temples of the eastern façade (A–H), and the oblong shrine behind them. (Graphics by Mark R. Williams, after Francis, "Le discours royal")

The eighth-century parts of this temple complex fit together like the pieces of an elegant puzzle and express consistent and complex categories of thought. Sculpture, architecture, painting, and inscriptions coordinate to articulate two aspects of cyclic existence in the world (*samsara*)—one embracing nurturing, fecund energies and one celebrating triumph over threats from outside and within. This monument encourages both modes of being, holding them in dialog instead of offering them as polarities such as purity/pollution or male/female. The monument locates both modes in the Pallavas as they strive to continue their lineage and the heroic work of gods and goddesses, and to return the cosmos to a utopic time. Part of this message the monument cloaks in esoteric experience associated with Shaiva Siddhanta (Śaiva Siddhānta), a term that now refers to a set of ritual practices around conventional temple worship but that in the eighth century was part of the category of transgressive, inverting, perhaps heretical practices we now call Tantra. Close viewing of the material dimensions of the Kailasanatha temple complex offers insights that complement what surviving texts supply into what Shaiva Siddhanta ideas and practices were in the eighth century.

Many Paths

These integrating patterns can be hard to find. The monument has so many parts and so many paths around them. As people move through the eastern bank of small shrines, through the tight first courtyard, into the second courtyard with its majestic prospect of the central tower, and into the narrow chasm encircling the base of that tower, architectural and sculptural forms increasingly press in on people from both sides and loom from high above. Gods, goddesses, and their attendants, all once painted with red, green, orange, yellow, and black, fill every wall surface and crowd the cornices and moldings. Bulls as large as life crowd the courtyard floor around the central tower. Lions project from every corner, clawing the air. All of this marks a clear shift from the minimalist carving of seventh-century Pallava architecture.[4]

No matter how compelling the material in front of one, there is always something else fascinating in one's peripheral vision and behind one, pulling the gaze and the body in multiple directions at once, back and forth between *prakaras*, *vimanas*, and *mandapams*, and in and out of the cavities hollowed into each of them. When one does move, movement multiplies the already wide variety of things there are to see and paths there are to follow.

Before one chooses between those paths, one needs to find them. This, too, begins as a challenge. Perhaps disorientation was purposeful in that it could help visitors relocate their thoughts in a separate, divine space.[5] The entrance to the complex is wedged into the ragged row of small shrines that form a kind of eastern façade for the compound (fig. I.1). Over this entry sits an exceptionally small gateway (*gopuram*), its crowning barrel vault lower than the short spires on either side of it. Seen from the eastern approach, this barrel vault is also dwarfed by the spikey barrel vault immediately behind it, the roof of the Shiva shrine sponsored by Rajasimha's son, Mahendravarman III (or Mahendra). His shrine nearly fills its tiny courtyard, crowding visitors who find their way through the tiny *gopuram* and obscuring the two doorways that lead on to the next courtyard on either side of Mahendra's shrine (figs. 1.4, 1.7).

From that point onward, however, obstructions yield to a surfeit of opportunities for movement. The second courtyard instantly offers three pathways. One goes left around the open-sided pillared *mandapam* and Rajasimha's great towered *vimana* (see fig. 4.3). An equally inviting path goes to the right around those same structures (see fig. 4.4). Large and dramatically posed figures of Shiva and goddesses populate the niches of that *vimana*'s ground floor, rewarding the gaze of people who walk around it.

A third path goes straight ahead and into the open *mandapam* (fig. 1.5). A wall now divides that *mandapam* from the closed-sided *mandapam* behind it, but that wall is a recent obstacle. As late as the nineteenth century, people could walk straight through the open *mandapam* into the closed *mandapam*, and through that to the tiny, cave-like sanctum (*garbha griha*) underneath the tallest tower. In the center of that sanctum they could see a large, columnar emblem of Shiva (*Shiva-liṅga*) and, carved in the sanctum's rear wall, a relief of Shiva Somaskanda seated with the goddess and their baby son, attended by Vishnu and Brahma.[6]

The motion of the sun further multiplies the experiences people could have of this monument. Daily and seasonal light shifts keep the monument in flux, making each visit to the temple different from the previous one. Because the building's east-west axis is closely aligned with the path of the sun on the summer solstice, light brightens the north and south walls evenly at midsummer. In midwinter, when the sun tracks its closest to the south horizon, light hits south-facing walls so hard that the tan stone can be painful to look at. Raking winter light casts north-facing walls in deep shadow even at midday.

The buildings convey a profound sense of being in motion, and this contributes further to a visitor's sense of objects being in flux. Sculptures of deities, plants, and animals cover each wall, dematerializing its support function (fig. 5.1, plate 16). Dwarves form a running band of constant activity around the central tower's lowest basement molding, animating this tower just at the point where it should rest on firm ground (see fig. 5.1). Even columns and pilasters, the rhetorical weight-bearers of the architectural skeleton, balance on the curved bodies of lions, "liquefying the structure" of the building.[7] The sculptural figures' gestures of contraction, release, and containment can "make the monument breathe" (plates 1–17).[8]

The Kailasanatha temple complex eludes easy mastery. Even at the abstract remove of diagrams on paper, many are necessary in this book to show how the temple's pieces fit together. Complexity was essential to what the temple needed to be, as it was to European cathedrals. Every visit could inspire new insights, new prayers.[9] In this monument too, meaning did not hold still. It unfolded, expanded, and grew new layers.

Audience

These multiplicities can baffle visitors, but surely some eighth-century audiences could perceive these many signs, paths, parts, and ideas resolving into unifying patterns. Multiplicity did not have to generate chaos.

The temple relies on visitors and their experiences to make sense. It yields up its organizing principles to visitors who move through it multiple times, walking along various paths and gathering different impressions each time. There is nowhere to stand to see the entire monument at once. A visitor has to fit those impressions together to make the temple into a meaningful whole.[10]

These multiplicities would have resolved into coherent meaning for at least three kinds of audiences: people exposed to the diverse religious traditions already in place in eighth-century Kanchi; the Pallavas themselves; and the people who designed other temples in that city over the following decades. The sculptural program of the Kailasanatha temple complex opened up the monument to audiences of multiple faith preferences, and from the start. Shiva is the chief deity of the monument, but sculptures embed the signs of the Buddha, Jinas, Surya, Krishna Govardhana, or Vishnu Trivikrama into Shiva's own body. Other sculptures of Vishnu, Brahma, Skanda, and many goddesses appear as Shiva's courtiers, assistants, or intimate family. These appropriations can perhaps be read as signs of competition *and* homage that subordinate these other deities to Shiva and affiliate them with Shiva, thereby forging a visual language for that god who was in fundamental ways a new deity.[11] To achieve that, these iconographic signs had to work for diverse audiences in their own idioms. The monument could receive audiences who knew those multiple traditions, all of which continued to flourish in Kanchi during the eighth century.[12] People of many faiths sought connections to the same sacred ground here as at many sites in South Asia. The place itself was sacred, more than any particular building in it or even any particular faith.[13]

Members of the Pallava family were the most likely audience to have had the opportunity to experience the Kailasanatha many times in many seasons. The Pallavas were directly involved with the Kailasanatha. Their inscriptions at the monument show that they sponsored its construction and identified closely with its buildings and the deities within. No trace survives to suggest that during the lifetimes of these patrons, any other donors left inscriptions there. Their palace may have been rather near.[14] R. Nagaswamy, an expert on Tamil inscriptions, art, and history, argues that Rajasimha built the temple complex as his personal chapel.[15] I, too, think this likely, though I would add that women of his family and his son have left records that identify them just as closely with the temple complex.

The Pallavas may well have had the erudition to trace the iconographic and theological webs this book traces to provide a unified reading of the temple complex. The inscriptions declaring their patronage at this monument were in grand, courtly, formal poetry and elegant script. The poems pun, reference each other, and share subtle allusions. The Pallavas liked their media layered, elliptical, and challenging. Besides the clever poets who wrote these inscriptions, the Pallava court may have patronized other literary masters too, and one Pallava king wrote or encouraged the writing of a play full of Sanskrit puns.[16]

In the history of South Asian architecture, moreover, the Pallavas held a special place as patrons of significant cultural innovation. Descended apparently from a royal group in Andhra, just north of the Tamil-speaking region, the Pallavas built an identity as "northerners" in the southern end of the Indic subcontinent by deploying relatively northern symbols. Tamil was already an elegant, literary language, but Pallava poets wrote in the pan-Indic language of Sanskrit. Their deities fused the inviolate Durga of Sanskrit hymns with the beautiful Kotravai of ancient Tamil war poems, and the wild Shiva of Sanskrit myths with the young Murugan of Tamil songs. The practice of local rulers expressing their presence and their continuity with the divine by building in the enduring medium of stone sacred structures to house the divine and human interactions with that divine—an active practice in the center and north of the subcontinent a few centuries earlier—began in the Tamil region with the Pallavas. The Kailasanatha was the star of the first generation of their temples that were constructed of separate pieces of stone rather than hewn from living rock. Pallavas appear to have favored stone temples as sites for expressing their cosmopolitan identity and their highest aspirations.

The expansions Mahendravarman III and his artists contributed to the Kailasanatha temple complex, moreover, show a clear understanding of the thematic principles underpinning the buildings already on that site. Mahendravarman's building creates an unusual double entry into the large courtyard beyond, preserving the meticulous bilateral symmetry of structures and pathways (fig. 1.4). Through architecture, sculpture, and inscription, his barrel-vaulted Shiva shrine picks up the theme of cyclic existence through the same metaphor that recurs throughout the earlier buildings, a metaphor likening Pallava fathers and sons to Shiva and his son. A generation continues but also replaces the one before it. Life ends but death gives way to new life.

To embed such elaborate patterns and subtle concepts into this temple complex, the people who designed it must themselves have been deeply learned in sacred lore, theology, iconography, and architectural practice. They knew many stories about many deities; they were empowered to express hierarchies and interrelationships among those deities; they determined which visual signs would communicate this information to their audiences; and they knew how to organize space and mass to move that audience to these signs along the desired pathways.

Possibly those were religious specialists distinct from the people who actually cut the stone, but if so, the two groups collaborated at a very high level.[17] Fine details of sculptural execution dovetail with the grand messages across the monument, and with the elevated literary qualities of the poems cut in gorgeous letters on these stone walls. However many other people they worked with, those who cut the stone were skilled artisans in maximum control of available technologies to translate subtle philosophical

11

agendas into visually effective form. They exercised artistic agency, and that agency refined the built form.[18]

The people who designed the next few generations of temples in Kanchi also had access to the organizing principles apparent in the Kailasanatha complex. Their forms scrupulously repeat the iconography, orientations, and even the sculptural compositions of the Kailasanatha.[19]

And yet none of those other structures includes the full complement of sculptures found at the Kailasanatha. Each repeats only a subset of those compositions. The Kailasanatha looks to have served in its own time as a touchstone to be cited but never rivaled, the architectural center of the dynasty emanating outward, its refracted spots of light always paler than the jewel that was their source.[20]

The Vaikuntha Perumal (Vaikuṇṭha Perumāḷ), sponsored some fifty years after the Kailasanatha by Nandivarman II (Pallavamalla), a claimant to Pallava lineage from a distant region, also projects a deep understanding of the Kailasanatha's fundamental principles because it responds to them so directly, though with alternative, competing formulations. The later temple sits across the city center from the Kailasanatha and faces back toward the Kailasanatha, across the urban fabric of the Pallava capital. The Vaikuntha Perumal has its own tall, pyramidal spire. Around that is a *prakara* thick with sculptural narratives on its inner face about kingly virtues and the continuity of the lineage. In other words, sculptures on the Vaikuntha Perumal translate the Kailasanatha's Shaiva elements into Vaishnava counterparts. This happens in divine iconography too. For example, Shiva catching the River Ganga becomes Krishna lifting Mount Govardhana, two stories in which the deity reaches high with one arm and braces against a great force (plate 17). The later temple also retains the same sequence of moods. Clockwise circumambulation leads first past scenes of peace and knowledge but ends with action.[21] The Kailasanatha temple complex was the model to emulate to establish legitimacy as a Pallava successor.[22]

Seeing like a Pallava?

But we in the twenty-first century are such a different audience. Any thread of insight into the meaning of the Kailasanatha that Pallavas held on to broke long before our time. Why imagine we have any access to this monument's fundamental truths? I have shared something of the Pallavas' experience in being able to visit the monument many times, though years have gone by between visits because I live so far away. Biases of the present moment shroud my thinking, such as the cool analytical gaze of art history.[23]

To counter that cool gaze, I aim to give full weight to the emotions a site of worship can call forth, regarding faith as informative rather than distracting.[24] In ways like this, I aspire toward the possibility of inhabiting very particular ways of seeing that a culture can give its participants.[25] I ask this minimally altered monument to take me inside eighth-century ways of knowing, to let me see as the Pallavas saw, and to listen in on their communications with the Kailasanatha. I realize the fantasy of my request. What I grasp will be partial and contingent, filtered by the peculiar kinds of analysis in which I have been trained and by assumptions I do not realize I make. The gaps may be vast between what I bring to the monument and what eighth-century designers and visitors would have carried effortlessly into their experiences of this temple complex.

And yet I persist in believing that some information can reach across centuries and teach me things the monument's makers intended. In this search, I have drawn heavily on secondary sources produced over the past century. Quite a few mention this temple specifically because it has served as a canonical example of early southern temple architecture in art history surveys, a Florentine Duomo of Indian art history as it were.[26]

These sources propose outlines for the Pallava dynasty's history and building projects, mining ancient inscriptions to yield royal chronologies, dates for these kings and their predecessors, and suggestions of an impending dynastic crisis during the monument's completion. They yield pictures of an innovative and resourceful family group with origins in Andhra. The Pallavas were the first in the region to patronize stone temples, at first rock-cut and later constructed of separate blocks of stone.

Scholars generally agree that Rajasimha Pallava reigned for about twenty-five years at some point between 690 and 728 CE and that during those years he sponsored construction of the tallest *vimana* (fig. I.2) and the long *prakara* wall enclosing it (fig. I.3); that his son Mahendravarman III built the oblong *vimana* (fig. I.4) and its small *prakara*; and that at least one of the Pallava queens patronized construction of the row of *vimana*s at the eastern edge of the complex (fig. I.1).[27]

Studies more closely focused on the Kailasanatha trace some of the patterns that organize its sculptures. Some note how extensive and important the representations of goddesses were on the monument.[28] Several note and offer interpretations for a pattern distinguishing north-facing from south-facing imagery.[29] Royal discourse was surely implicated in the pattern, some realized, and that discourse constructed complementarity between categories that might seem contradictory—warriors and ascetics, battle and lineage, austerity and prosperity.[30]

Theoretical writings on the possibilities of metaphor in South Asian architecture suggest ways the Kailasanatha's built forms could reinforce the mountain metaphor so prominent in the monument's sculptural program and inscriptions.[31] The vivid mountain-like qualities of Rajasimha's towered *vimana* and its surrounding structures give special force to the claim in the inscription that this temple offers Shiva a home to rival his home on Mount Kailasa (appendix 2, vv. 10 and 11). This comparison between Shiva's Himalayan home and this Pallava-made mountain in the heart of the Pallava capital could translate onto an architectural scale the metaphor sounded in three of the temple's inscriptions (appendices 2, 3, 4) and in the temple's many sculptures of Somaskanda: Shiva's family and the Pallava royal family were alike in many ways, and their homes could be too.[32]

Architectural historian Adam Hardy's brilliant reading of the building-shaped components (aedicules) on temple towers and walls as visualizing processes of growth, splitting, and multiplication reinforces the possibility of reading in architectural form the cosmogonic process over geological time and the mighty presence of a deity emanating outward through the earth and cosmos.[33] That is, the buildings can teach philosophical lessons about the nature of existence. On a more literal level, the resonances between these aedicules and an ascetic's mountain hut could invite viewers to see the story of Shiva teaching ascetics (plate 4) extending up through the entire tower.[34] So, too, the capacity for the temple's many pillars to read as a forest of petrified trees could encourage people to read the entire monument as the Pine Forest into which Shiva wanders seductively, charming the wives of the sages who live there (plate 7).[35] The temple constructs heaven on earth, as Phyllis Granoff has argued, and a particularly rustic kind of heaven suited Shiva.[36]

A Feminist Reading of a Monument That Was Not Feminist

Feminist theory of the twentieth century can reveal some of this monument's underlying intellectual categories, though the monument was not feminist and though one might imagine that contemporary methods might only introduce anachronisms to that analysis. I once did regard the monument as feminist. I perceived its imagery as balancing male and female, and thus as a welcome antidote to historical erasures of women and the female divine.[37] But that view stays more deeply embedded within binary thinking about gender than I realized at the time and than I want to stay now. I now see the temple's sculptures declaring this to be Shiva's temple. I had been distracted from that by the surprise of encountering so many more female figures, and in more prominent locations, on the monument than most scholarship on the temple had led me to expect.

There are many goddess images in this monument. They face in all directions from every surface of all the structures in the compound. Durga and Lakshmi frame the paired entrances between the small and large courtyards (see figs. 2.18, 2.19). Shiva often appears with a female nearby to reinforce his efforts, though Durga only appears with males to battle them.[38] Goddesses figure foremost among a host of deities that this temple program appropriates around Shiva like a royal court.

Presumably, goddesses mattered in eighth-century Kanchi: that is why pulling goddesses so visibly into Shiva's orbit was worth doing. No matter how much they mattered, however, this proves nothing about the rights of living women at that time, even if its categories help me think outside patriarchy now. Goddess imagery most likely served to empower Pallava kings by manifesting their success in war and in perpetuating the royal lineage. Goddess figures serve as metaphors for these Pallava kings at least as often as for their queens. The foundation inscriptions compare Pallava queens with goddesses to praise the women's beauty and charm and to note their connections as mothers, wives, or daughters, to men of accomplishment.[39] Representation did not have to mean autonomy or equality; it may well have signaled the opposite.

Focus on Material Form

The primary resource for this study is material form, a focus that distinguishes this study from most earlier publications on the Kailasanatha. Each meaning proposed has its source in the temple's material form.[40] Eighth-century artists cut meaningful patterns into stone with precision and emphasis. Sustained gazing reveals the coherence of those patterns among the monument's many elements.

By presenting such an exuberant visual feast, the monument signals that it deserves that gaze. Its form insists on being seen, insists that looking matters, insists that visuality will be purposeful.[41] It merits study that is purposefully and extremely myopic,[42] an iterative and prolonged looking that reveals more than first glances can apprehend. This is about staring at lines, shapes, posture, gesture, horizontal and vertical alignments, and compositions in two and three dimensions. This is about attending to scale, balance, energy, spaces and absences, plays of light and shade; suspending expectations as much as possible; letting the monument surprise us and teach us how to see it.

This process indulges in the fantasy that I could ever see as any artists see,[43] and even what those who made this monument saw. I am working in the reverse direction the artists did, beginning with the elaborately formed temple and imagining backward toward thinking that preceded form.

I have come to see patterns organizing this monument after visiting it repeatedly since 1984. I have worked to reimagine what haptic and aural experiences the monument bears traces of. Being at the site, attending to sound, sight, and touch, I have begun to imagine how the monument lived. To do so, I needed to be there engaging its materiality, on rainy days and bright ones, at various hours of the day, in the December chill of the tower's north shadow, feeling blasts of heat bouncing off the south-facing walls, wedging into tight crevices, and taking in long vistas down the great courtyard or up the towering spire.

Image and Text

Attending to the materiality of the inscriptions carved into the monument's stones has been revealing.[44] Some of these inscriptions were chopped up and jammed into ceilings while others still flow continuously along surfaces where they are easy to see. Some inscriptions lead right around shrines, traces of the movement people had to follow to read them or hear them recited. Such recitations would have echoed off the stone walls all around them.

Rather than taking these or other verbal documents as somehow more authoritative than material evidence, I regard both kinds of evidence as informative and contingent. In some cases they reinforce each other and in other cases they fill in each other's silences. Verbal sources can be crucial for narrowing down what figural sculptures might have signified to their audiences. Some connections among the narrative reliefs on Rajasimha's *vimana* are clearer for people who comprehend the inscription running beneath them. Yet even that inscription, contemporary with and adjacent to those sculptures, does not answer the questions visual analysis can address. Why turn Shiva's spine that way? Do figural compositions follow consistent patterns? Why deploy that version of an iconographic form? The physicality and spatial disposition of that inscription, too, can reveal the text's role in cuing visitors to walk in surprising directions. Visual material can supply information that written sources did not survive to record or never recorded in the first place.[45]

The verbal documents about art and art making called *shastras* and *agamas* inform only some dimensions of this study of the Kailasanatha. It is possible that particular architectural treatises (*vastushastra*) did dictate specific elements of this temple complex.[46] Written architectural treatises do survive from before the eighth century, and they reveal that they are compilations of yet older knowledge.[47] But none of these show evidence of being specifically about this monument or of its moment.[48] Modern scholars have found explicit correlations with specific *shastras* more common in monuments built after the eleventh century.[49] It seems more likely that for the designers of the Kailasanatha, *shastras* meant broad kinds of wisdom or "fields of knowledge" in which they improvised in disciplined and learned ways.[50] Such knowledge embodied practices of artisans before them, derived from experience in wood and brick as well as stone. Designers surely applied all such written and embodied knowledge flexibly to meet the particular needs of this city, this site, these patrons and the ideas they needed the monument to carry.[51]

Such flexibility is apparent in other monuments, even when the correlations between written *shastras* and built forms are at their closest, as Adam Hardy has demonstrated in his study of Bhojpur, which preserves texts, buildings, and architectural drawings all from a project supported by one eleventh-century king, Bhoja. The texts offer quite abstract principles that awaited artisans to translate them into drawings before anyone could design actual buildings from them. Moreover, the texts were not simply the authorities for construction to follow. Wisdom flowed in both directions, with drawings or actual buildings inspiring principles in treatises. Architectural treatises behaved as an early form of art history, intellectualizations offering to make order out of visual material that already existed, once the designers were no longer there to speak for it.[52] The verbal and the material were not equivalencies for each other.

Logocentrism in scholarly discourse can obscure material cues that *shastras* do not explain. I am seeking those cues by reexamining material form.[53] A temple is not a book. Monuments cannot generalize beyond themselves; *shastras* cannot capture the dynamism of monuments or their multidimensionality.[54] People build temples to do things that books cannot do. Temples communicate in three dimensions, generating somatic experience, shaping space for bodies to move through, and requiring movement of anyone who would know them. This temple performs all these tasks at a grand scale.

Movement produces a steadily shifting array of sights to consume. Some of these are inscribed words, but other material forms compel more attention.

If these treatises were not exercising rigid control over artists' design choices, they were even less likely to have filtered how audiences read sculptures. The air of authority with which some now deploy *shastra*s may have had no force for earlier audiences. *Shastra*s may not help us much to understand how those audiences received those forms. However much was written down or memorized, the kind of knowledge those sources contain does not encompass all that gave the monument meaning. The monument's earliest viewers would have known those figures from other dimensions of their lives. They did not need to see through the lens of *shastra*s as we might. We can use *shastra*s to fill in the holes in our knowledge centuries later, the mismatches between what we know and what the designers could reasonably have expected of their audience.

In this spirit, there is merit in pausing before clapping labels on sculptures assigned to them by *shastra*s, *agama*s, and narrative *purana* and *mahatmya* texts. Let the objects of study become strange before we assume what meanings they might have carried for their makers or early viewers. Textual knowledge can get in the way of seeing what is actually there. Can we be sure Shiva is riding to destroy the three cities of his enemies if no cities appear in the relief? Might the relief stress the general idea of his riding into battle even more than that particular battle? If the wild goddess is not near him when he dances with one leg lifted straight up, can we be sure this is the dance competition in which he defeats her by taking a pose too rude for her to match? Could this be a different dance, a different story? Could his dramatically visualized power, and not her defeat, be the key point of the story? Or could that point be his resemblance to Vishnu as Trivikrama, establishing dominion over the three worlds? Absences like these may be useful in themselves, clues to shades of meaning, cultural shifts, different content. The builders of this monument may have let those absences resonate and used *shastra*s loosely.

Practicing that hesitation can let visual and haptic sensations reveal categories we do not expect to find, categories of thought unlike those of our own present cultures. Light shifts and asymmetries can show time in the monument on daily, yearly, and cosmic scales. Light can emphasize the counterposed meanings of north- and south-facing sculptures, and those meanings can erode gender binaries. Moving counterclockwise around Rajasimha's *vimana* can show a correspondence between words and images that is neither captioning nor illustration.

My method for reaching these findings has involved mapping compositions, shapes, subject matter, iconographies, and inscriptions onto ground plans. To identify those subjects, iconographies, and inscriptions, I have drawn on secondary scholarship and also my direct experience of the objects. Then I waited for the pieces to fit themselves together, for patterns to emerge that incorporate a significant percentage of the monument's parts. After years of looking and learning, I saw clearer patterns, static ones undergirding the placement of sculpture (chapters 2 and 3), and patterns involving architecture and inscriptions that the visitor's movement brings into being (chapters 4 and 5). These patterns are the "hard data" I have to offer. From that data, I speculate about what those patterns could have meant. Secondary sources again play a huge role here, framing the political, religious, and philosophical possibilities specific to that culture at that moment in that place.

The temple's pieces have snapped together in my understanding like the shards in a kaleidoscope, forming a series of patterns that make sense together and to me. Even if I can never be sure they were true, I take joy in sharing them and in the confidence that they reveal echoes from the past that might be useful to our present. I acknowledge and embrace these contingencies. I offer these readings of the Kailasanatha to encourage further looking and conversation about this and temple complexes across South Asia, and not as exclusive interpretations to shut down conversation about the monument. I offer this book as an encouragement to others to experience the temple for themselves, not as a substitute for that experience. Nor is this book an encyclopedic chronicle of every sculpture on this monument's many surfaces. There is no need for that because the temple itself already provides that complete set.

1

ORDER AND IMPROVISATION

The Elements of the Pallavas' Kailasanatha Temple Complex

THE MANY EIGHTH-CENTURY ELEMENTS OF THE KAILASANATHA TEMPLE complex coordinate closely with each other. Their inscriptions, sculptural programs, and architectural forms echo and build upon each other, creating a visual coherence and a coherent set of meanings as well. The buildings cluster systematically around the great tower near the center of their compound, rippling out from that structural climax in various symmetries. The sculptural program presents an ordered pantheon centered on Shiva, with all other deities subordinated to or absorbed into him.

The impression of order and domination these forms create was carefully fabricated. A close look at sculptural signs suggests that Shiva's domination of other deities was rather new and that the visual strategies for showing this were rather old. The architecture's details reveal that the complex was not built in an orderly sequence from the center outward, as its emanating shapes imply. Expansion was neither linear nor concentric, but rather it recentered the complex, worked back from the edges to quickly replace recent structures with new ones, reframing the monument even as it was being born.[1]

There may never have been a moment at which this temple complex was supposed to be "finished," in a twenty-first-century sense of that word. More likely, each patron expected there to be future patrons. Like most South Asian temples, this one was surely initiated with the knowledge that temples rely on the love of the faithful to stay alive as temples.[2] New construction is one way to enact that love. Rajasimha and his immediate family enacted that love by turns, modifying or expanding on each other's contributions even as they developed a consistent set of ideas.

Rajasimha's *Vimana*

The scale of Rajasimha's *vimana* marks it as the heart of the temple complex (see fig. 1.2). An enormous pyramidal superstructure rests on a many-faceted cube, which in turn rests on a tall stack of heavy basement moldings. The complexity of that cube derives from the inclusion of nine subshrines, each a small version of the great *vimana* itself, in its outer shell (see fig. 1.7). The largest sculptures in the temple complex smile down from surfaces of the faceted cube, establishing the iconographic themes to which sculptures on other buildings respond. An inscription encircling that cube describes the building as having been built by Narasimhavarman II Rajasimha Pallava, the earliest historical person to be cited at the monument as a patron (appendix 2). Little wonder, then, that most people read Rajasimha's *vimana* as the original structure of this temple compound, though this assertive rhetoric of centrality could also make sense for a building that is telling a new story about the site, forging a new center on a spot that once meant something different.

The architectural rhetoric of the rest of the temple complex further marks the great tower as the heart of the compound, the apparent source of the other buildings there, in the visual language of the *dravida* (southern; literally "Tamil") architectural mode that governs the design of this monument. All of those other buildings are shorter than this fifty-foot-tall tower, and they spread out around it, along a spine of more modestly elevated structures on the compound's east-west axis and with a quieter emphasis along the axis that cuts north-south through the *vimana*'s core. Those buildings can thereby read as lesser or younger emanations, expanding downward and outward or contracting upward and inward from the peak of the massive *vimana*. Contributing to that impression of emanation is the square ground plan of Rajasimha's *vimana*, in contrast with the rectangular plans of the surrounding structures, like shards of a perfect square breaking up around it.

The interior of the cubic first story is nearly filled with masonry, which supports the vast tower above. Cut from the center of that first story is a small, windowless chamber (*garbha griha*) opening to the east. This houses a prismatic *linga* (a columnar sign of Shiva) some seven to eight feet high made of a black basalt quite distinct from the tan sandstone and gray granite that make up the rest of the monument.[3] Carved in the west wall behind that *linga*, high enough to be visible above the *linga*, is a relief portraying Shiva with his wife and son (Shiva Somaskanda). Though figural sculpture is rare in the central sancta of Hindu temples, this grouping was common in Pallava temples, and particularly those associated with Rajasimha and his son Mahendravarman III (or Mahendra). This one has squatter figures and is higher on the wall than Somaskanda reliefs in other Pallava temples, indicating it may be later than the rest of the *vimana*—perhaps one of the renovations made under Mahendra.[4] Some of the people who now manage the site encourage visitors to walk and crawl along the passageway that cuts through the massive wall around this *linga* shrine, but the extreme narrowness of that passage suggests that circumambulation there is a recent introduction.[5]

Sculptural ornament covers the exterior of the first story on Rajasimha's *vimana*. This features large figures that have a compressed appearance, as if a pane of glass boxed their great forms into narrow doorways leading out from the heart of the shrine (plates 1–17). The walls around those door-like niches surge with carvings of natural and fantastic creatures, plants, and divinities. The fundamental contours of these sculptures are original to the eighth century. All are of a piece with the walls around them, carved out of the very same stones, a technique that yields in the ninth and tenth centuries to one that inserted figures carved from separate pieces of stone into waiting temples niches. Sculptures on this temple's walls could not have been moved or significantly reshaped without chopping up buildings. The traces of such traumas would be easy to see. Spots that were renovated show what changes to this wall look like, such as the gouged area beneath the sculpture of Shiva Tripurantaka where the spout draining lustration fluids from the inner chamber was altered (plate 15).

The large sculptures evoke Shiva and other deities. This variety of subjects is common on temples to Hindu deities, which regularly present a broad pantheon ranged in tiers like the hierarchies of an orderly royal court.[6] The crowd makes the event. The universal assembly acknowledges the importance of the main actor as well as that of the assembly. The sculptural program of the Kailasanatha does this too, subordinating various deities to Shiva but also drawing on the authority of their forms to give Shiva an august form.

The divine court that attends on the quite kingly Shiva at this monument features Vishnu and Brahma prominently. The two are twinned frequently throughout the monument, perhaps as a kind of shorthand for the assembled pantheon. They stand behind Shiva's shoulders like trusted generals or fraternal rivals for royal succession, while he sits on his throne. Brahma stands to Shiva's right, Vishnu to Shiva's left, and both are smaller in scale than Shiva (plates 18, 19). They stand, he sits. Two of the nine shrines embedded in the outer skin of Rajasimha's *vimana* contain a relief depiction of this triad (see fig. 3.2a and b). Narrative subordinates Vishnu and Brahma too. Shiva as Lingodbhava makes fools of them both by exceeding their capacity to understand his greatness (plate 6). Brahma plays the charioteer to Shiva's archer riding into battle (plate 15). These sculptures parallel the spirit of one-upsmanship that suffuses the mythologies in the roughly contemporary Sanskrit texts called *purana*s.

Skanda and the gentle goddess Uma occupy positions of special subordination and special honor as Shiva's son and wife, sharing his throne, at the heart of the monument and inside most of the shrines embedded in this *vimana*'s outer surface. Other aspects of the divine feminine encase and protect Shiva. Lakshmi and goddesses of battle appear a further step removed from him, in separate, flanking niches, attendants in an outer chamber, as it were (plates 3, 15).

Distinctive signs of other deities translate onto Shiva's body, so that he absorbs them and they infuse him, in figures of Shiva dancing with extended legs (Urdhvatandava) (plate 11), riding a war chariot (Tripurantaka) (plate 15), and catching the River Ganga in his hair (Gangadhara) (plate 17). The three manifest in especially large reliefs and lined up in a row on the west wall of Rajasimha's *vimana* (plates 10, 11, 12). The straight leg he lifts in the air closely assimilates him to Vishnu Trivikrama, who takes giant steps to claim the earth and the sky as his kingdom. Compare the relief of Trivikrama carved on the outer wall of cell 12 of the large *prakara* (see fig. 2.12).[7]

Shiva riding a chariot into battle is surely a close citation of the already ancient imagery for the sun god Surya (Sūrya), which, like that of Apollo and Mithra, showed the sun in a chariot drawn by horses across the arc of the sky.[8] The likeness is particularly strong inside the embedded shrine on the northwest corner of Rajasimha's *vimana*, where Shiva rides his horse-drawn chariot straight toward the viewer in a bilaterally symmetrical composition (plate 12). This figure is even riding to the west, as the sun does each day. He also wears the sun god's distinctive high boots. This is not a common image type at the early Tamil monuments, though the idea of Shiva as the sun god was strong in the *Agni Purana*, a document of the ninth century.[9]

The monument's sculptures of Shiva catching Ganga in his hair (plates 10 and 17) could recall the large, seventh-century figure in nearby Mamallapuram of Krishna lifting Mount Govardhana.[10] To protect his people from devastating floods, Krishna reaches a long left arm up and to his left, bracing against the mountain's weight by shifting his weight onto the opposite hip. His opposite hand hangs down near that hip. A woman is close by, gazing up from under the mighty arm. Further north, along the same rocky hillside, is the enormous relief that can read as the story of Shiva catching Ganga, though Shiva does not hold out a lock of his hair in that relief.[11] Two other reliefs from that century, however, one in Trichy (Tiruccirāppaḷḷi) and one in Mamallapuram, do show Shiva making that gesture,[12] so viewers could have known by then to associate the outstretched arm with Shiva's story as well as Krishna's. Presumably, these people also understood that the shared form could imply a shared promise of heroic protection from kingly gods and godly kings. Designers of the Kailasanatha could likely count on those associations a century later.

The absorbed deity's presence continues to hover within view like the extra dimension of a print by M. C. Escher. The visual signs of Vishnu, Surya, and Krishna remain too strong for the appropriation to read as surreptitious theft. Nor do notes of subordination ring loudly in these translations. Undertones resonate of something more like homage or a display of kinship between Shiva and those he absorbs. The Shaiva versions of these forms do ramp up the dynamism, however, rendering the shared gestures a few degrees more muscular or triumphant or spectacular in his vigorous body.

This process of overt appropriation extends to religious traditions that modern culture defines as distinct from Hinduism. Shiva Dakshinamurti teaching in the forest is strikingly close to older renderings of the Buddha preaching his first sermon (plate 4).

Here, too, a tree trunk rises behind the teacher's spine, a crown of branches extends to frame him, he takes up a yoga posture, and one hand makes a gesture of teaching and communication as human followers and wild animals gather around him, among them a pair of crouchant deer beneath his seat.[13]

Walking figures of Shiva reveal strong affinities to a long sculptural tradition of portraying the Buddha, Jaina teachers, and their followers as wandering mendicants.[14] One figure on this *vimana* walks directly toward the viewer with a soft, unassertive gait, the pelvis tucked slightly under, the rear leg dragging slightly (fig. 1.1). He is completely alone. A figure of Shiva Bhikshatana charming the wives in the Pine Forest shows Shiva in profile and enhances his identity as a wanderer by giving him thick sandals and a bundle of possessions on a stick over his shoulder (plate 7). And he is nude, whereas the frontal figure

FIGURE 1.1 Shiva as a wandering mendicant. This figure is carved on the north wall of Rajasimha's *vimana*, facing west from the back of the shrine that protrudes from the center of that wall. (Photo by Emmanuel Francis)

wears a loin cloth. His nudity could further evoke the intense degree of renunciation practiced by "sky-clad" (*digambara*) Jaina ascetics. The Bhikshatana reliefs add women to the image, however, and renunciation shades into seduction. The faithful Buddhist's longing for the absent teacher who was himself without desire becomes the aching desire, or *viraha* (*vīraha*), the women of the Pine Forest feel for the beautiful beggar.[15]

The motif of Vishnu and Brahma standing on either side of a larger, seated figure of Shiva also draws on Buddhist and Jaina precedents. Seated Buddhas and Jinas were frequently represented in unequal triads too. A pair of smaller bodhisattvas or Jinas flanked those seated teachers. Sitting and standing reinforce hierarchical scale to amplify the importance of the central figure. The attendants can also suggest a larger pantheon radiating outward from that central figure, like a shorthand version of a mandala.

This shared fondness for the hierarchical triad and the wandering, nude mendicant surely reflects the adjacency of multiple religious traditions in eighth-century Kanchi. Buddhism and Jainism both flourished openly in that region in the eighth century and for centuries before that. Anyone entering the Kailasanatha when it was new would have walked past Buddhist stupas and Jina statues. Whatever modern distinctions people draw between Buddhist, Jaina, and Hindu traditions were apparently absent or permeable or useful to transgress when iconographers designed the Kailasanatha.

The Open *Mandapam*

The open *mandapam* is the single-storied, flat-roofed hall that is the first building people now see when they enter the large courtyard (see fig. 1.5).[16] Entrances pierce this building's east, north, and south walls (see fig. 1.7). One pierced the west wall too, before the closed *mandapam* existed. Wider than the north and south walls, the east and west walls frame entryways wide enough to accommodate a pair of columns. Inside the hall, eight more columns form an open grid (fig. 1.2). No walls break up the interior space. The structure was open to flows of people, air, and light in four directions.

This building can seem younger than Rajasimha's *vimana* because it is smaller than that tower, apparently an emanation from that tower, and creates a low pathway leading to the dead-end finality of the *vimana*'s inner chamber (see fig. 1.6). But it is likely that the open *mandapam* is the oldest structure surviving in the Kailasanatha temple complex.[17] Single-storied, rock-cut halls of the early seventh century had pillars like the ones inside this open *mandapam*—blocky, monolithic shafts square in section for the top third and bottom third, chamfered into an octagonal section for the central third.[18] Few of these early cave temples leave the shaft square in section from top to bottom like the austere pillars in the entryways of this open *mandapam* (see fig. 1.5), and most of those are unfinished.[19] That austerity could indicate an especially early date for the open *mandapam*. The capitals on these pillars, however, are more complicated than the blunt brackets of the early seventh century and not as refined as the octagonal and almost floral capitals of cave temples attributed to the middle of the seventh century.[20]

handwritten note in margin: soft cushion capitals

FIGURE 1.2 Granite pillars inside the open *mandapam*. Their austere form suggests they are older than the rest of the temple complex. The inscriptions cut into them are from the tenth to fourteenth centuries. (Photo by Emmanuel Francis)

These in the open *mandapam* have square cushions that seem to float between a series of widening courses below and a softly molded bracket above (many now restored in a tan stone). All of these are in turn simpler and blockier than the pillars and pilasters on the other structures in the Kailasanatha complex, which are fluted and rest on the backs of rampant or sejant stone lions (see fig. 1.3). By these criteria, the open *mandapam* could predate Rajasimha's *vimana* by nearly a century.

This *mandapam*'s lowest layer also hints at an early date. Its floor is much closer to the courtyard level than the floors of the compound's other buildings are (see figs. 1.4, 1.5, 1.6). Its stack of basement moldings, though comprising fundamentally the same shapes as that on other buildings, is significantly shallower and smaller. A greater proportion of that stack seems to be obscured under the courtyard's paving stones. This *mandapam*'s moldings, moreover, bear no foundational inscription marking the building's patron or construction. The inscription on the open *mandapam*'s granite molding was added in the tenth or eleventh century and says nothing about who sponsored construction.[21] Structures built by Rajasimha and his family bear inscriptions on their granite moldings declaring their patronage.

Sculptural style cannot contradict these other hints of early construction. The figures on the open *mandapam* are buried under especially thick layers of plaster that give them clumsy contours and stiff expressions. They still look like the rest of the monument's sculptures did before their twentieth-century cleanings. The plaster layers on the open *mandapam*, however, have not budged in any of that century's site renovations. It is tempting to deduce that there is no lovely sandstone layer underneath to reveal by removing the plaster from the outer walls of this *mandapam,* or that the underlayers represent different iconographic identities that are no longer appropriate to the program Rajasimha's *vimana* lays down.

The sculptural iconography on this *mandapam* may not specify a dedication to Shiva. The male door guardians at the outer ends of the façade show his signs. Shiva's tall pile of matted locks crown the figure at the left, and a cobra rears beside the lowered knee of the figure at the right, but these details may be no deeper than the top layers of plaster (see fig. 1.5). The other reliefs on the building are Durga and Jyeshtha on the north wall, Lakshmi and perhaps Saraswati on the south wall (fig. 1.3a and b). All would be appropriate to a shrine dedicated to goddesses. The goddess sculptures could also suit a temple dedicated to Vishnu. Lakshmi and the goddess beside her could evoke his wives, Shri and Bhu. Durga appears on Shiva temples but also temples to Vishnu, such as the Varaha and Adivaraha (Ātivarāha) temples in Mamallapuram.

The open *mandapam* could have been built before Rajasimha's *vimana* and could have stood in front an earlier shrine that Rajasimha's *vimana* then replaced, a shrine built perhaps of brick like the Skanda temple in Saluvankuppam (Cāḷuvaṉ Kuppam).[22] Rajasimha could have appropriated this site, kept the *mandapam*, and replaced its shrine just as he appropriated and rededicated to Shiva the older shrines dedicated to Vishnu in Mamallapuram.[23]

Rajasimha's *Prakara*

Rajasimha's large *prakara* is a hypaethral structure that circumscribes a rectangular courtyard around his *vimana* (see figs. 1.3, 1.7). Fifty-eight tiny cells line its inner surfaces. It is the most elaborate version of such a structure to have survived at any of the temples attributed to the Pallavas.

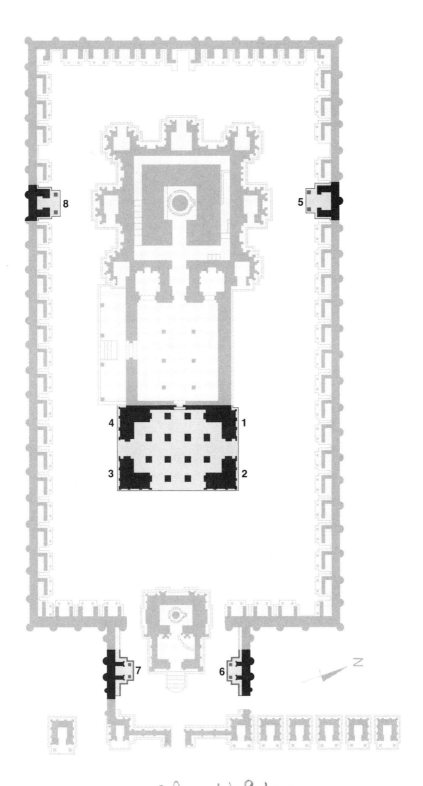

To Rajasimha's Prakara

FIGURE 1.3A Ground plan showing location of figures 1.3B and C

FIGURE 1.3B Placement of goddess figures on the open *mandapam*.
(Graphics by Mark R. Williams)

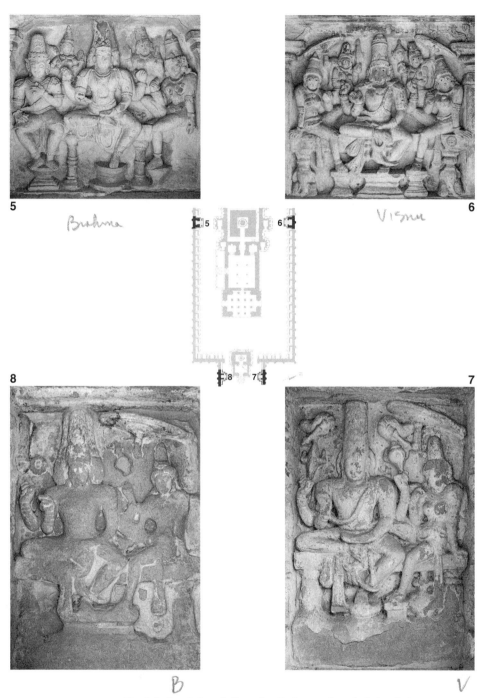

FIGURE 1.3C North-facing shrines dedicated to Brahma and south-facing shrines dedicated to Vishnu on the *prakara*s around the large and small courtyards. Each pair of these shrines flanks a *linga* shrine to Shiva. (Graphics by Mark R. Williams)

Its embrace includes the open *mandapam* too, creating a geometric balance between that structure and Rajasimha's *vimana*, and thus potentially inventing a relationship between two structures built at different times. The courtyard is twice as deep as it is wide. In plan, then, it covers the area of two adjacent squares. Rajasimha's *vimana* stands at the center of one of these squares, the western one. The open *mandapam* dominates the eastern square, set not quite at its center but slightly back toward the *vimana*. This opens a reception space at the courtyard's eastern end, offering people who stand there a full view of the open *mandapam* and Rajasimha's *vimana* in all their majesty, aligned together on the central east-west axis of this elegant courtyard.

Rajasimha's *prakara* is a string of fifty-eight small, linked cells, most of which are miniature versions of Rajasimha's *vimana*. They, too, are cubic forms, resting on the same combination of basement molding shapes and supporting their own pyramidal superstructures, each capped by an octagonal crown. Surrounding and echoing the great tower, these tiny reflections can suggest the tower's form multiplying and radiating down to the earth and then to the north, south, east, and west, deploying the metaphorical language of cosmic expansion.

Rajasimha's large *prakara* was surely built after his *vimana*. From an engineering perspective, assembling materials for the *vimana* would have been easier to do before that *prakara* cut off access to it. The style of its sculptures is a touch more fluid and dynamic than those of Rajasimha's *vimana* (compare fig. 2.12, nos. 22 and 24, to plates 13 and 17). But this *prakara* is probably not much younger than that *vimana*. The two stand in such close dialog, echoing back and forth off each other through shared architectural form, sculptural iconography, and inscribed verses.[24]

The basement moldings of these small shrines carry an inscription in the same archaic script as the one on Rajasimha's *vimana*, praising the same king (see fig. 4.6). The content of the *prakara* inscription is a long list of honorific names (*birudas*) for him (appendix 1). This list could have been a straightforward way of announcing the king and making him present in this space he had made possible. It could also have served as a reassuring conclusion to the more elliptical, poetic narrative about that king inscribed on his *vimana* (appendix 2). After many puzzling allusions, a long string of names for the king could sound one after another, clanging a recitation ceremony to its close.

The spatial organization of Rajasimha's large *prakara* suggests a map of the cosmos that ranks deities by their proximity to the centered deity, as painted mandalas do. In its more remote corners, this *prakara* houses a wide pantheon including older Vedic deities such as Indra, Agni, and the seven mother goddesses (*sapta matrika*).[25] Vishnu and Brahma get their own shrines on this *prakara*, expansions into architectural form of the sculptural forms they take in niches embedded in the outside walls of the *vimana*, but are perpetually subordinated to Shiva. At both scales, Vishnu manifests to Shiva's left, Brahma to Shiva's right. With Shiva in his two east-facing *vimana*s, this places Vishnu to his north and Brahma to his south (fig. 1.3c). Both gods gaze directly upon Shiva's *vimana*, while Shiva turns his gaze away from them and toward the east. Sculptures inside these shrines to Vishnu and Brahma make their occupants look like Shiva's clones, as they, too, sit enthroned with one leg pendant and a wife beside them.

Access to the large courtyard inside this *prakara* was once bilateral. Mahendra's shrine has since replaced whatever structure initially framed the *prakara*'s eastern entry, but before that was built, something at the east end of the large courtyard surely lined up with the east-facing doorway of Rajasimha's *vimana*. The large *prakara* originally had an entrance through the center of its western wall too. This carried a low, barrel-vaulted *gopuram* tower, a small version of the form typical of later South Indian *gopurams* (fig. 1.4).[26] This *gopuram* shows every sign of being contemporary with the eighth-century *prakara* it pierces. Cornices, corbels, and polygonal pilasters consistent with the rest of the monument's Pallava-period work transfer the weight of this superstructure down through the basement molding. Chubby dwarves (*ganas*) seated on crouching elephants support the pilasters, a touch that emphasizes the entry by breaking the rhythm of rearing lions along the rest of the *prakara* exterior. People could readily have found this portal from its courtyard face too. Snake deities (*nagas*) support the pillars, a shift from the leonine supports under the rest of this *prakara*'s pillars (fig. 1.5). The sharp rise of the barrel-vaulted superstructure from the roofline of the *prakara*'s other spires is also visible from the courtyard. The bricks that now fill the western *gopuram* were probably inserted when Mahendra expanded the entry at the opposite end of the courtyard with his new *vimana* and its small *prakara*.[27] Foreclosing bilateral access required visitors to experience his additions.

The *prakara* repeats all of the sculptural subjects and compositions that appear on Rajasimha's *vimana*.[28] The Somaskanda sculptural composition featured inside Rajasimha's *vimana* recurs in each of the east-facing cells that line this *prakara*'s west side and each of the west-facing cells that line its east side (see figs. 3.4, 3.5). The cells of its north and south sides swivel to face east instead of opening directly onto the courtyard. Some of these, too, contain Somaskanda groups in painting or sculpture on their innermost walls (plate 19). With their doorways facing to the east, these shrines along the *prakara*'s north and south sides present a solid wall to the courtyard, an opportunity sculptors exploited for elaborate figural compositions that unfold toward the courtyard visitors occupy (see fig. 1.3). These figural groups repeat at a smaller scale and at ground level all the grand compositions that look down from the outer walls of Rajasimha's *vimana*. And because this *prakara* offers so many niches on its long walls, the sculpted tableaux spin out multiple variations on the *vimana*'s compositions and themes.

The long strings of sculpted tableaux along the inner surfaces of Rajasimha's *prakara* clarify the iconographic appropriations that construct Shiva's identity at this monument. For example, visitors walking clockwise encounter Vishnu Trivikrama before Shiva Urdhvatandava (see fig. 2.12, nos. 12 and 25). They see the older form before they see it translated onto Shiva's body. A cluster of reliefs on this *prakara* exchange Shiva's features with Skanda's and Murugan's and cast him as Skanda's father.[29] Skanda's infant form in the far right side of figure 2.12, no. 11, is a mash-up of Shiva and his dwarves: Skanda

FIGURE 1.4 (*left*) The low *gopuram*, now sealed, that once led into the large courtyard
through the western side of Rajasimha's *prakara*. West view of the *gopuram*,
from outside Rajasimha's *prakara*.

FIGURE 1.5 (*right*) East view of the now-sealed *gopuram* in the west side of Rajasimha's *prakara*,
seen from inside the large courtyard. *Naga*s (snake deities) carry the central pillars.

carries Shiva's bow and arrows rather than Skanda's spear and he has a small, plump
body. The tableau of Skanda's marriage in figure 2.12, no. 44, uses the postures found in
other monuments to show Shiva leading his bride by her right hand to the god on his
left who will officiate.[30] But the groom sports Skanda's conical hairdo and the double
threads crossing his chest, and Brahma officiates here, as he does for Skanda's wedding
in the *Mahabharata*. Skanda is a "Shiva-to-be," the "son is another self for the father."[31]

Sculptures on Rajasimha's *prakara* also strengthen an identity—or effect a transformation—between the ascetic wanderer heroized in Buddhist and Jaina traditions and
the seductive Shiva Bhikshatana. Sculptures of the two are next to each other on the
north wall (see fig. 2.12, nos. 52 and 53), permitting visitors to read them as the same

wandering character in sequential moments of a single story. Adjacency also highlights the several features they have in common—the conical headpiece resting on a halo of bouffant matted locks and the striding posture with left leg straight and right leg bent, right toe dragging. Visitors seeing them in clockwise order will first encounter the frontal version, the form familiar from older religious practices and also a direct address to viewers. Next they will confront the profile view, the posture onto which newer stories were being grafted. Also, as Bhikshatana's body turns toward the visitors' right, it continues in the same direction those visitors are already heading. The god has met up visitors in their space and joined them on their journey.

Note that Bhikshatana's figure faces the opposite direction on Rajasimha's *vimana* (plate 7). There he walks toward the visitors' left. Both figures of Bhikshatana, however, move in a clockwise direction. Maintaining his clockwise flow seems to have mattered enough to flip the composition. They appear on opposite sides of visitors who move in that direction too, first on their right from the *vimana* and then on their left from the *prakara*. He has joined them on their journey more than once.

The Eastern Façade

What now serves as the monument's eastern façade is a bilaterally asymmetric row of small shrines (see fig. 1.1). All open to the east, turning their backs to the rest of the temple complex. Each one shares all its essential features except its size with Rajasimha's tall *vimana*. All carry pyramidal, *dravida*-style roofs. In the center of each shrine is a black basalt, faceted *linga*, or an empty platform to support such a *linga*. Each shrine houses on its rear interior wall a relief presenting Shiva Somaskanda, Shiva with his wife and son (see fig. 3.3). These sculptures of Somaskanda appear to be contemporary with the construction of these little shrines. They are more graceful in their proportions and more comfortably integrated with the *linga* sculpture in front of them than the Somaskanda panel is in Rajasimha's *vimana*.

The asymmetry of this row in the otherwise symmetrical temple complex suggests it is a remnant of something longer. The shrines may have extended all the way around another courtyard to their east.[32] Several at the center of the row were probably removed to build Mahendra's shrine. Temples A and B to the south of the main entrance were surely joined by at least four others like them to mirror the six temples to the north (see fig. 3.3).[33] The space between temples A and B is precisely wide enough to fit another temple of the same size. Temples that now seem to be missing could have fallen down over the centuries, as ashlar masonry will do in a land of earthquakes and heavy rains, or they were deliberately disassembled, as temple A would be in 2000, and for some reason never reassembled by the various groups that would restore the monument periodically. Archaeological authorities regularly carry out the complete disassembly and reassembly (anastylosis) of stone monuments like this one as part of maintaining and renewing them.[34]

Temples C, E, and G carry foundation inscriptions (appendix 4). For at least some of the nineteenth century, these were illegible because someone built brick walls to join these temples to each other in a solid row.[35] Like Rajasimha's inscription, they are cut as a single line of text running along the granite basement molding, starting on the eastern wall and running counterclockwise across one or three walls (as indicated for temples C, E, and G in fig. 4.5). They are in the same archaic script as the inscription around Rajasimha's *vimana*.[36] They resemble Rajasimha's inscription in content too. They follow similar conventions. The one on temple G identifies and praises the person who had the temple built, a Rangapataka. The inscription on temple E praises a queen as surpassing Lakshmi. The single word inscribed on temple C, "Shrinityaviniteshvara-griham [Śrīnityavinīteśvaragṛham]," names the temple by combining a name for Shiva (Ishvara/Īśvara) with a woman's honorific (Shri) and proper name (Nityavinita).

It is possible these three inscriptions refer to the same queen, but they more likely index a group of women in the Pallava household. Rangapataka might have been a queen of Rajasimha, the queen who surpassed Lakshmi may be Rajasimha's mother, and Nitya-vinita could be yet another person.[37] Collectivity seems evident in this row of temples' nearly identical architecture and Somaskanda reliefs as well as the shared motifs on their exteriors (for more on which, see chapter 3). Their orderly placement also suggests collectivity. They mark the first, third, and fifth shrines to the right of the entrance to the temple complex. The second, fourth, and sixth temples in that row carry no inscription. Alternation can be inclusive, a technique for embracing multiples with a few. It can also imply regularity and connectedness.

The qualities these inscriptions share with those on Rajasimha's buildings suggest that this row of shrines was built close to them in time. Like Rajasimha's *prakara*, these structures closely echo, but in miniature, the architectural and sculptural elements, too, of Rajasimha's huge, central *vimana*. Most likely they went up soon after Rajasimha's *vimana* and shortly before or after his *prakara*. In any case, they went up before Mahen-dra's *vimana* and *prakara*, as the fabric of those structures reveals.

The *Vimana* and *Prakara* of Mahendravarman III

Rajasimha's large *prakara* breaks at the center of its eastern side to admit another *vimana* (see fig. 1.4), a Shiva temple identified by the inscription that girdles its basement as having been built by Rajasimha's son, Mahendra (appendix 3). Mahendra's *vimana* is much shorter than his father's *vimana* and roofed by a barrel vault instead of a square-based, pyramidal tower. That vault and its rectangular ground plan, an example of the oblong, barrel-vaulted *shala* architectural type, are the common forms for temple gateways (*gopuram*) but unusual for a *vimana*. This shrine is moreover placed where other temple complexes would place a *gopuram*—at the midpoint of a *prakara* wall and on axis with a square-planned *vimana* (Rajasimha's *vimana* in this case).[38] In form and location, Mahendra's shrine reads as a hybrid between a *vimana* and a *gopuram*, a graceful architectural solution for a structure serving as a shrine in its own right that also respect-fully subordinates itself to the shrine built by the patron's father.

A small *prakara* encloses Mahendra's *vimana* in its own courtyard. Sculptures on this *prakara* and Mahendra's *vimana* repeat the topics and compositions that appear on Raja-simha's buildings. This *prakara*, just like the large *prakara*, plays out the unequal triad of Shiva, Vishnu, and Brahma in architectural form by embedding shrines for Vishnu and Brahma in the *prakara*'s north and south walls, respectively (fig. 1.3a and c). They align with the front wall of Mahendra's *vimana* to Shiva.

The walls of this *prakara* seem contemporary with Mahendra's *vimana*. They are certainly younger than the two architectural masses they link together, Rajasimha's large *prakara* and the shrines of the monument's eastern façade. They abut quite suddenly the outer surfaces of Rajasimha's *prakara*, the north and south walls of the smaller *prakara*, and at asymmetric spots, leaving the large *prakara* to overhang the juncture more deeply on the north than on the south side (see fig. 1.7). Compare the smooth and symmetric resolution of right angles at the northwest and southwest corners of Rajasimha's large *prakara*, where the joining walls were built at the same time. At the opposite end of Mahendra's *prakara*, the points of collision are even less resolved. The newer walls run directly into figures of Shiva on the finished exteriors of temples on the eastern façade (fig. 1.6).[39] Similar collisions occur at the sides of temples B and C where the third side of Mahendra's *prakara* elbows into the center of the eastern façade.

Sculptural style on Mahendra's *vimana* shows later features too. The role of Shiva Gajasamharamurti (who kills the elephant) is growing; and Shiva's dance is fading in significance (fig. 2.11b).[40]

That the son's *prakara* was built after his father's is hardly a surprise, but for Mahen-dra's *prakara* to be younger than the temples of the eastern façade contradicts the visual and spatial rhetoric of the temple complex as forms emanating and multiplying outward from Rajasimha's huge tower at its core to many smaller structures like these spreading outward and downward across the ground. Instead of expanding the monument's foot-print further to the east, beyond the queens' preexisting row of temples, the designers of Mahendra's *vimana* chose to wedge it between older structures, which surely entailed removing whatever structures previously wove the older buildings into relationship with each other.

The *shala*-roofed *gopuram* over the eastern entry to Mahendra's small courtyard is remarkably small. It is the low, mud-colored oblong just to the left of the white tower of Mahendra's *vimana* in figure I.1. The doorway below it is the only aperture in that façade to break the basement moldings. The massive *gopuram*s of later temples dwarf it certainly, but even the *gopuram* at the west end of Rajasimha's *prakara* is a full story taller (fig. 1.4). Mahendra's *gopuram* reverses the general trend that the later a *gopuram* is built, the taller it will be. Its diminutive size does, however, appropriately set a visitor's expectations for the very small courtyard and *vimana* immediately within. This *gopuram* also coordinates well with the unusually squat tower over Mahendra's *vimana*. Seen from

FIGURE 1.6 The juncture of the eastern façade with
the east wall of Mahendra's *prakara*, at right. View is
from inside Mahendra's *prakara*. Note how abruptly
the *prakara* wall abutts the fully carved figure of *Shiva*,
at left, in a niche on temple C of the eastern façade.

outside the temple complex, it provides a proportional first step in the mounting ascent
past the barrel vault over Mahendra's *vimana* to the pyramidal climax of Rajasimha's
vimana (see fig. 1.1). The tiny *gopuram* suits the building project Mahendra sponsored,
in all its idiosyncrasy.

Mahendra's renovations reveal that the temple complex experienced substantial mod-
ification while it was still young. Mahendra seems to have predeceased his father,[41] in
which case Rajasimha was still alive and apparently raising no objections when his son
changed the monument.

Concluding Remarks

The most likely sequence in which the standing structures at the Kailasanatha temple complex arose jumps about from a subsidiary hall to the central tower, from interior spaces to the margins, and back inward again. The open *mandapam* may be the oldest structure to survive and a remnant of an earlier complex, possibly dedicated to a different deity, on that site. Rajasimha's tall *vimana* was next, followed soon by his *prakara* and the eastern façade sponsored by Pallava queens. Soon after that, and while Rajasimha still lived, his *prakara* was altered to accommodate newer buildings sponsored by his son. Mahendra's buildings wedge in between older structures sponsored by Pallava queens on the east and by his father on the west. These additions shifted the architectural energies of the monument distinctly toward the eastern approach. A western approach became no longer useful.

Sculpture presents an orderly cosmos dominated by Shiva, the king of a court peopled by Vishnu, Brahma, Skanda, Uma, and other deities in their own, distinctive bodies. Shiva's own body also absorbs the signs of Vishnu, Surya, Krishna, the Buddha, and Jinas, suggesting that their powers have become his. These principles manifest first on Rajasimha's *vimana* and then get elaborated upon in sculptures of the eastern façade, Rajasimha's *prakara*, and Mahendra's buildings.

2

LOOKING NORTH AND SOUTH

N⟨Celibacy and Intimacy, Struggle and Grace⟩
S.

A CONSISTENT PATTERN DISTINGUISHES NORTH-FACING SCULPTURES FROM south-facing ones throughout the Kailasanatha temple complex. This pattern manifests in the shapes and postures of these two groups of sculptures and in the stories they tell. Angular, celibate figures of Shiva and goddesses dominate other beings and face to the north. In gentler bodies, the same deities govern, teach, and flirt, when they face to the south. These visual and narrative dimensions coordinate. Fierce bodies, centered in their frames, enact stories of renunciation, death, and transcendence. Relaxed bodies share their frames with those they desire. South-facing figures nurture continuities across time by teaching followers or marrying.

These sculptures' visual forms are the primary evidence that documents this pattern. Ancient myths that modern scholars link to these forms reinforce the pattern, though some of those identifications are best to regard as contingent.[1] Sculptures at the Kailasanatha often differ from those at other temples in their details and compositions, perhaps because many sculptures at the Kailasanatha are the oldest surviving examples of their subject in the region. Iconographic templates were not yet set by 725, it seems.

This north/south pattern governs the sculptures on nearly every building in the Kailasanatha temple complex, including the sculptures of other deities and the shrines dedicated to them. Rajasimha's *vimana* set up this iconographic pattern. Other structures in the temple complex played variations on the pattern that *vimana* set out, revealing the pattern's core logic by condensing or expanding on it. The same pattern also manifests through the same iconographic markers on other Pallava temples until the mid-eighth century.[2]

The shapes and stories that these spatial arrangements group together hint at a world view underpinning this pattern. Aspects of that view are noteworthy for their difference from some assumptions in the world I was raised in. Rather than a simple gender binary, sculptures show celibacy having similar effects on males and females, whereas desire can polarize them into contrasting bodies and behaviors. Voluptuous goddesses model ideal action for male rulers. The same deities shift between states of celibacy and procreation, inside and outside of marriage. These are complementary states, not polarities, a subtlety that becomes clear in the monument's recesses. There ascetic and procreative energies fuse in the figures of teaching goddess-women (yoginis) and childless royal couples. The sculptural program seems to presume that complementarity will take time for visitors to comprehend. Gross binaries can be easier to see in its patterns at first. For those who stay longer and explore nooks and crannies, apparent polarities can resolve into coherent wholes.

Rajasimha's *Vimana*: Facing North, Alike and Apart

The pattern organizing north- and south-facing sculptures is easiest to see on the north wall of Rajasimha's *vimana*, particularly in winter when the tall tower veils those sculptures in shadow. The five, large sculptures on the north wall share many shapes (plates 13–17; fig. 2.1, A–E). In all of them, one figure lunges, pounces, or sits above other beings. Vertical hierarchy accompanies dominance. Silhouettes are "open," bristling with the jagged contours of weapons and pointing fingers. Intense energy charges the bodies of the victorious, forcefully extending their limbs or bending their joints at acute angles. Limbs and weapons and fingers emanate outward from the heart of each frame. They are the radials of an explosive composition. Brandishing weapons or deep in yogic trance, these lithe, taut bodies look poised for a fight or fresh from one. Deadly creatures around them are on alert. Lions snarl. Elephants crouch. Cobras rear.

Most of those figures represent Shiva and goddesses among visual signs that can evoke stories found in the Sanskrit *purana*s and in early Tamil literature. The stories scholars associate with these five reliefs tell of mighty deities physically overpowering dangerous threats. Moving clockwise around this building, and thus from west to east along this north wall, the first figure a visitor will encounter could represent Shiva Kalarimurti, the destroyer of Death or Time itself (plate 13). (Both English words for these enemies translate the Sanskrit *kāla*.) In most versions of that story, Shiva kicks Kala away to protect his young devotee Markandeya, who has invoked Shiva by embracing that god's aniconic emblem, a stone *linga*. Shiva rescues Markandeya from an early death and thus promises deathlessness to those who follow him.

Shiva's identity is legible in the matted locks of hair, the three-headed cobra by his raised foot, and the trident that cuts across the top half of the composition. The noose in his upper hand could raise the topic of death, but the miserable figure he crushes bears no unusual signs except his coarse facial features and perhaps his fangs, and Shiva

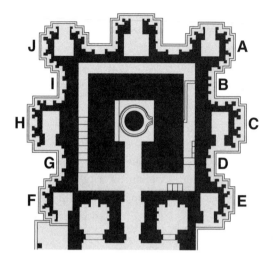

A Shiva kicks Kala
B Shiva rides a chariot into battle
C Shiva meditates above Jalandhara
D The Goddess with her lioness
E Shiva catches Ganga in his hair
F Shiva touches Uma's chin
G Shiva and Uma enthroned
H Shiva Dakshinamurti teaching
I Shiva manifests in an endless flaming pillar
J Shiva Bhikshatana charms the sages' wives

FIGURE 2.1 Sculptures facing north (A–E) and south (F–J) from
Rajasimha's *vimana*. (Graphics by Mark R. Williams)

has fangs too. Shiva looks just as likely to be leaping on him as kicking him. Neither Markandeya nor the *linga* is rendered here in stone. The sculpture shows simply that Shiva is vigorously crushing someone beneath his feet.[3]

In the deep wall recess just to the east of this scene, the tableau suggests Shiva riding into war. Many read this as his destruction of the three cities (Tripurantakamurti) of the *asuras*, denizens of the lower world (plate 15).[4] This scene, too, is short on the narrative detail that identifies other examples of this subject. Shiva holds before him a bow he could use to shoot those cities, but the three cities are not rendered in stone. He does not draw his bow or reach for arrows. Brahma, identifiable by his extra heads, could be acting as a charioteer, but he holds no reins, nor are there other signs of a chariot such as wheels or horses.[5] Shiva rests his foot on the ledge before him, which does show that he is not walking. The ledge could be a chariot's rim. What this sculpture does emphasize is Shiva's bow, his spray of powerful arms, and his mighty lunge toward the viewer's right. A trio of round-bellied dwarves (*gana*s) below him head in that direction too, waving arms and weapons in the air.

In the relief at the center of the north wall, the lower form is legible as the *asura* king Jalandhara because of the circular *chakra* blade in his shoulder, which will soon cut him in half (plate 14). A mace leans useless behind his hip. The platform Shiva sits on balances on that lethal disc as if driving it deeper into Jalandhara. Shiva, who has thrown that blade, sits in yogic meditation. Perhaps he is fighting interior battles for self-control because, as one version of the Jalandhara story tells it, Shiva seeks this battle out of his desire for Jalandhara's wife.[6] In another version, Jalandhara temporarily distracts Shiva from battle with an illusion of heavenly musicians (*gandharva*s) singing and heavenly maidens (*apsaras*es) dancing. This motif appears on several other Pallava temples, though it does not match the descriptions in early iconographic texts.[7] Those call for a sword under Jalandhara's arm and for Shiva to look like he wishes to move quickly. The Pallavas had this other way of picturing this story.

Shiva's perfectly symmetrical form sets up a still point at the center of the north wall. It is Jalandhara's posture, which is nearly identical to Kala's (plate 13), that weaves this relief into the larger visual flows of the north wall. Both fallen figures crumple beneath Shiva, their heads to the right, one leg flattened beneath the torso, one leg folded into the left corner of the frame. Their tangled limbs fill the bottom third of each rectangular frame. Only the tilt of their faces and upper arms distinguish these defeated creatures from each other. Jalandhara looks up toward his destroyer and lifts his right hand to gesture at him or to support Shiva's platform.

The second recess one passes in this wall holds a glorious representation of a deity one could call Devi, the Goddess, or Durga, names for the supreme form of the female divine (plate 16). Her ten arms hold out a bristling fan of weapons around her relaxed yet confrontational body. The halo of weapons around her could signal her military expertise and the story in which the male gods generate Durga and give her their weapons to destroy the buffalo demon named Mahisha, whom they cannot control. Traces of a band across her breasts show she is equipped for battle. So do her jaunty posture and her comfort with the lioness that is her war mount. One hand dangles easily around her bow, one hip thrusts out over the straight leg she plants on the ground, one knee folds sharply as she places her foot upon the shoulder of the lioness.

That lioness turns to nuzzle that knee and lifts a leg to support her foot. Goddess and lion blend into a single contour, the line of her lifted thigh continuing directly the contour of the lion's head, the curve of her hip and sashes leading smoothly into the curve of the lioness's rump. The animal occupies nearly the same shape that Kala and Jalandhara do (plates 13 and 14), a trapezoid filling the lower third of the relief and rising on the upper right for the creature's head. Visual composition suggests something kindred among them. Content as well may connect this figure of Durga to Shiva Kalarimurti, the destroyer of Death or Time. The final hymn of the fifth- or sixth-century Sanskrit text the *Devi Mahatmya* sings of the Goddess transcending time, standing outside of it, existing always. Both deities could offer comfort to people who contemplate entering battle, a prospect often before Pallava kings.

This image of the female divine combines elements of two lion-riding goddesses adored for their youthful and inviolate beauty as well as for their embodiment of gore and glory on the battlefield: Kotravai of the early Tamil epic *Silappadigaram* and Durga of the Sanskrit *Devi Mahatmya* hymns in which she kills multiple demons.[8] The Pallavas were fond of synthesizing Tamil and Sanskritic traditions.[9] The Pallavas constructed their identity as outsiders from the north through heavy applications of Sanskrit language, deities, myths, and geographies. Making that work in the Tamil region surely also required deep connections to local stories, deities, geographies, and visual practices.

Kotravai needed to resonate in goddess images that would matter to local people, and so did a Sanskritic goddess in order to signify the Pallava patron.

The prominence of her lioness aligns this goddess with Durga.[10] But none of the male characters who might be associated with Durga appear in this relief—the buffalo demon Mahisha, whom she decapitates; the male gods who create her; or Shiva, who marries her—even though the motif of Mahisha was well known by the early eighth century, having played a prominent role in sculptures across the subcontinent, in this kingdom (figs. 2.2, 2.3), in this city, and in this very monument where his decapitated head appears beneath her foot on Rajasimha's *prakara* (fig. 2.14, C).[11]

It is possible that this relief shows a moment in the narrative before Durga meets Mahisha, or after she has killed him, or that he is virtually present, implied by all these weapons that Durga used to kill him. It is simpler to read this, and the many eighth-century Pallava representations of this goddess without Mahisha, as part of a broad iconographic shift away from the seventh-century emphasis on Durga's battle with Mahisha toward a goddess who personifies victory itself, transcending any particular instance or victim.[12]

The last north-facing image on Rajasimha's *vimana* wall clearly evokes Shiva Gangadhara catching the Ganga River. His outstretched lock of hair awaits her fall from the heavens (plate 17).[13] That lock of hair and the hand that holds it span the top edge of the relief. The splayed fingers of another hand point back toward the distended lock. The rest of the composition dramatizes the force with which the river lands and which Shiva must brace against. The right hip shoots out, the leg below it as strong and straight as a column. The other leg lunges sharply in the opposite direction, its foot planted on a ledge of rock. He could be on Shiva's Himalayan mountain home, Kailasa. A wifely form of the goddess, identified by most iconographers with the name Parvati slips in under his outstretched arm, her shoulder supporting his ribs, her hand braced on the mountain rock, her leg bent around his planted foot. Her helpful presence was common in Pallava representations of this subject, though elsewhere on the subcontinent her figure pulls away from him as if she were jealous of his contact with Ganga.[14] This relief does not depict Ganga, but she only appears in some Pallava-period representations of this subject. Perhaps people could recognize the story from Shiva's outstretched lock alone because the subject had been rendered so often.[15] Ganga does show up in other Gangadhara reliefs at the site: on Rajasimha's *prakara* and on this *vimana*'s west wall, the largest and most richly populated relief of this story at the temple complex (fig. 2.12, no. 24, and plate 10). The latter version also includes a *gana* at the lower left, a kneeling devotee supporting Shiva's raised foot, and a dog or jackal howling.[16]

The smaller goddess (frequently read as Parvati) beside Shiva gazes upward from the right, just as the Goddess's lioness does, and as Jalandhara and Brahma do (plates 14 and 15). Parvati is not being crushed, however, nor is she constrained to the lower third of the relief. The story is not about conquering her or even Ganga, whose force Shiva will subdue so that she may flow gently down to earth. Like Brahma, Parvati stands only a bit below Shiva, aiding him in his struggle.

FIGURE 2.2 Relief tableau of the goddess Durga fighting the buffalo-headed Mahisha. North wall of the Mahishasuramardini cave temple, Mamallapuram, Tamilnadu. Seventh century.

FIGURE 2.3 Relief tableau of the goddess Durga fighting the buffalo-headed Mahisha. On a boulder outside the Adiranachandeshvara temple in Saluvankuppam, a short distance north of Mamallapuram. Eighth century. (Photo by Emmanuel Francis)

These five large compositions on the north wall of Rajasimha's *vimana* have many common elements. All feature energized, angular, taut bodies centered in explosive compositions. Each is the heart of heroic action that will transcend some superhuman threat. Figures interact vertically within each frame in acts of domination. The deity rises above the vanquished (Kala and Jalandhara) or assistants (dwarves, the lioness).

Ally or enemy, most of these figures share a frame only with others of the same sex; frames keep males and females separate from each other. Kala and Jalandhara display brawny male chests as Shiva crushes them. Shiva rides into battle in the company of Brahma and male dwarves. The Goddess rests her foot on a lioness. (Male genitalia feature prominently on the rearing lions at every corner of this building, as in plate 7, so their absence on Durga's lion is noteworthy.) None of the males who kneel at her feet in other Pallava monuments intrude upon her frame here. Like the goddess of the *Devi Mahatmya* hymns, this Durga can embody inviolability, defending herself vigorously against sexual contact. As the goddess of the hymns kills several demons who threaten to "marry" her, this figure could embody the choice of the battlefield over the bedroom.[17]

The exception to this pattern is the relief of Shiva catching Ganga (plate 17). He leans against his wife to accomplish his heroic feat. The river one might imagine winding through his hair would be a goddess too. This helps the Gangadhara relief stand out among the reliefs on this wall. It does so in ways that make special claims about the Pallava kings themselves, a subject I return to in chapter 3.

Males and females who are separated from each other on this wall are also very like each other, despite their clear sex differences.[18] Male and female are essentially equal in height, and they all have multiple arms. Prominent weaponry characterizes both as warriors and war as a female as well as a male space. The Goddess, Shiva on his chariot, and Shiva catching Ganga strike nearly the same triumphant pose—the right hip projects to the side above a leg that is straight as a column (plates 15–17). The left leg turns out, rises, and bends deeply at the knee. The deities' torsos pull diagonally away from their right hip and curve up through the waist and rib cage, creating a sinuous diagonal across the center of each niche. That line continues through the shoulder and into a raised arm that bends slightly at the elbow and extends the diagonal of the torso toward the upper right corner of the niche. The head tilts back along the opposite diagonal. Arms fan out in a radiant frame around these sinuous torsos. At precisely the same angle on each figure, one arm slopes downward, the wrist cocks sharply, and the fingers rest against the outthrust hip. Some form that supports the central deity fills in the lower right quadrant of each composition. The left foot braces on that creature or prop. The tall bows of Durga and Shiva on his chariot each slice the composition just to the right of the panel's centerline. The umbrella, a common sign of royal affiliation at Pallava monuments, hovers over each figure.

When Shiva kicks Kala, his posture is a more dynamic variant of the one those three compositions share (plate 13). The right knee rises a bit higher, which tips the torso onto the opposite diagonal. The bent, raised arm reaches toward the upper left corner of the frame. His weight-bearing leg turns out more fully and bends more deeply. His trident, however, echoes the rightward diagonal vector emphasized by Shiva Tripurantaka, the Goddess, and Shiva Gangadhara. The four of them form two pairs of right-tilting compositions, one pair to the east side and one pair to the west of the bilaterally symmetric shape of Shiva over Jalandhara at the center of the wall (plate 14). What male and female deities share weaves the whole cast of that wall into a unified visual whole. Collectively, they can suggest a battle line drawn up to challenge the forces of darkness and death.

Collectively, they also aggregate a picture that looks very like the ideals Emmanuel Francis believes the Pallavas cherished for themselves. From his intensive survey of Pallava inscriptions and monuments, Francis sees Pallava rulers aspiring to be master yogis as well as masters of war, controlling the self as well as dominating the world. A particular hero of theirs was Ashvatthaman, the fiercely disciplined warrior ascetic of the *Mahabharata* epic.[19] The north wall of Rajasimha's *vimana* captures that hybrid goal on several levels. In the Jalandhara panel alone, on the wall's central and most prominent facet, Shiva is at once a supreme yogi and a victorious warrior. Other brilliant warriors flank him, including forms of Shiva and the Goddess transcending time, a cherished goal of advanced yogic practice.

Attending Goddesses on the North Wall: Seeing through Gender

Four small figures of goddesses set in the two deep recesses of the north wall reinforce the impression that females and males are more alike than different on this face of the building. One pair of these goddesses flanks the tableau of Shiva riding into battle (plate 15). The other pair flanks the Goddess standing with her lion (plate 16).

Beside the figure of Shiva leaning on his bow, the goddess "ahead" of him—and to viewers' right—charges in the same direction, holding her own bow before her at a similar angle (plate 15). She and the goddess on Shiva's other side wear the breast bands (*kuchabandha*s) of female warriors. This second goddess holds the same trident Shiva brandishes in his attack on Kala.[20] She has four arms.

These and her ballooning mane of untamed hair make it easy to mistake her for Shiva. Her seated posture could also lead contemporary viewers to misread her as male. Instead of sitting on the ground, which has long been the common practice in South Asia, she rests on a wide seat raised on legs high enough that she needs a footstool for her pendant leg. Her other leg lies folded on the seat. Both legs spread out wide across the seat. Her back is ramrod straight and she faces directly forward. Shiva takes precisely this posture on the south wall of this *vimana* when he sits enthroned (plate 3). Figures of Pallava kings take this posture in reliefs across town at the Vaikuntha Perumal temple.[21] Iconographers call it the posture of royal ease.

Sitting in the same position is the small figure of a goddess to the right of Durga (plate 16). A pair of rather formal columns supports her throne. The lion and deer near her shoulders suggest that she, too, carries elements of Kotravai, the forest-dwelling

45

warrior goddess of early Tamil literature.[22] The small goddess on the other side of Durga is Jyeshtha, whose name means "the elder one." She also sits on a colonnaded throne, her posture frontal, but with both her legs pendant. Posture here is a meaningful sign. This is an especially regal pose. It is how Pallava princes sat for the *abhisheka* lustration ceremony that turned them into kings. Figures of goddesses who sat that way could serve as metaphors for Pallava kings, embodying the qualities kings aspired to.[23] Female divine bodies could read as emblems for human male bodies, governing from thrones and charging into battles they will win.

This possibility eluded me for years, as I assumed that female figures could serve as metaphors only for women. I was equating gender with sex, tying the infinite possibilities of imagination and culture to the limits of physical bodies. But gender is flexibly applied and variously shaped by culture and individuals. It is not tied to the sex of a body, particularly in the fluid realm of visual symbol. The sex of the symbol need not be the sex of the referent.[24]

Symbols deployed across sex difference are common in South Asia. Quite often these associate kings with goddesses. Martial masculinity could be forged in a goddess temple in early modern Gujarat.[25] Odishan kings' power and the power of martial arms could be coded as female.[26] Men as well as women in Bengal and Tamil Nadu may visualize themselves as the Goddess and the Goddess as themselves.[27] The *linga*, though capable of signifying the male sexual organ, has also signified the feminine, the mother, and the female breast.[28]

The sculpture of Jyeshtha on this wall (plate 16) suggests another category of thought organizing this monument's iconographic program. Her presence indicates celibacy as a significant quality the north-facing figures on this building share. This quality could justify the similarity of male and female figures on this wall: celibacy could be understood to have similar effects on male and female bodies.[29]

Though now considered dangerous, Jyeshtha carried positive connotations during the Pallava period and into the sixteenth century. The female and the bull-headed male behind her could read as her adult children. The round belly and full breasts could recall past pregnancies and thus a history of having children. Later traditions associate her with the oldest wife in a polygamous household. Once sexually active, she has become celibate as her husband's attentions have shifted to younger wives.[30]

Jyeshtha's celibacy is not voluntary, then, nor is she in a state of virgin purity.[31] Her current state of sexual inactivity in combination with her previous fecundity is the source of her power. She sits on a throne with legs pendant like a prince about to be made king or a deity receiving worship. Her back erect, she faces confidently forward, her children in attendance as Vishnu and Brahma attend Shiva.

Her thick body and slack legs differentiate her from every other goddess on this building. Her companions on this wall, among them Durga, who inspired suicidal levels of desire, are more youthful. Jyeshtha has only two arms. Most of them have at least four. She has nothing to do with war or demons either.

Her exceptionality clarifies a deeper commonality. What she does share with all of her neighbors on this north wall is a state of separation from procreative activity. War is significant to the category, but it is not the category itself. War reads here as an arena of ascetic renunciation. Warriors of both sexes on this wall are isolated from those of another sex when they prepare for or engage in conflict. Those conquests are not only on the battlefield. Shiva transcends time and death when he kicks Kala. After dispatching Jalandhara, Shiva withdraws within to control his own mind and body. Encompassing these stories and bodies is a fearsome kind of power, power born of discipline and isolation, power that cauterizes and ends things.

Rajasimha's *Vimana*: Facing South Together and in Difference

On the south wall of Rajasimha's *vimana*, power is again on view but in a personality distinct from the violent, ascetic muscularity of the north wall.[32] Most figures on the south strike "closed" postures, meaning that limbs drift toward the body's center instead of splaying outward (plates 2–4 and 6–7; fig. 2.1, F–J). Silhouettes are curved rather than jagged. Contours wrap inward. Limbs are relaxed, even languid. Prominent joints are loose, bending at moderate angles. Elbows drop below shoulders; knees drop below hips.

The subjects in the wall's five major tableaux emphasize some combination of stability, teaching, continuity, warmth, and desire. Shiva manifests in five states (in clockwise order): charming his wife; enthroned with her; sitting underneath a banyan tree lecturing and performing yoga; manifesting within a flaming pillar or *linga*; and as the seductive mendicant (plates 2–4 and 6–7). He again dominates others, but here he does that through charm, wisdom, and light.

Two tableaux bracket the ends of this wall and in those positions enclose the entire wall visually and thematically (plates 2 and 7). Both present erotically charged interactions between males and females, a marked departure from the segregation of sexes on the north wall. Whereas a single figure dominates the center of the large compositions on the north wall and turns toward the viewer, these reliefs present male and female figures on either side of the composition's centerline turning to interact with each other through glance or gesture or touch across the bit of space open between them. Bodies pull toward each other from the left and right.

These two reliefs are put together in common ways. In both, Shiva's head and torso fill the upper right quadrant. Face and shoulders turn in three-quarter profile, hips are in full profile, and a left arm reaches across his chest. Adoring females train their gazes upon him from slightly below. Body contours soften, spines relax, and bodies glide into sympathetic alignments. Limbs angle toward the space between Shiva and these females.

At the east end of the wall, Shiva puts a hand under the chin of a female figure, probably his wife, the goddess called Parvati or Uma (plate 2).[33] Their eyes meet. She looks like others throughout the monument who appear at Shiva's side when he is at rest, which is to say she is lovely and calm and has only two arms and no other distinctive iconographic markers. This relief still carries disfiguringly thick layers of lime, cloaking any details of iconography the stone layer might hold, but the placement of major limbs is probably unaltered.[34] His outstretched arm, her face, her arm, and his leg alternate in layers of touch and shared shapes. Note the harmonious lines of her hand as it crosses her waist, palm down, and his as it crosses his waist, palm up. His upper arm aligns with her lower arm. Her hand and his lower arm parallel each other.

At the west end of the wall, Shiva Bhikshatana, naked and walking in the sandals of a traveler, tempts the wives of the sages who live in the Pine Forest (plate 7). Two women kneel in his path, while a cuckolded sage shakes his useless fist in the upper distance. Shiva smiles over his voluptuous backside and out of the frame toward the viewer as he twists his unclothed loins toward the enraptured wives of the sages. Neither woman actually touches the walking god, but touch seems imminent, prefigured by a virtual interlace of their limbs. His left knee bends toward the women. He lowers an open hand just above the further woman, and she raises an open hand in a mirroring gesture. The closer woman tilts her forward thigh at the same angle as his shin; her knee touches the ground immediately in front of his toe. A slip of cloth dangling from his hips falls lightly along his thigh, past his shin onto her further knee. Their faces turn to look out at the viewer instead of looking at each other. Are they pretending they do not feel the warmth of each other's bodies, or are they drawing the viewer into that warmth?

At both ends of this wall, then, Shiva and goddesses and women take "closed" postures when they face south, their limbs languid, their contours soft. Males and females trade knee positions when they proffer or receive sexual invitations. When Shiva reaches out to his beloved, her knees bend toward each other and his spread apart, and when the wife of a sage offers herself to him, her knees part.

This kind of intimacy occurs with inequality between the sexes.[35] Gentling here is not about equality. Female sexuality is not a sign for female empowerment as it has been at times during the modern era.[36] Shiva dominates the women he seduces. He is substantially larger than they are. They sit or stand on a surface that is lower than his, though they are not so far below him as the beings he conquers on the north wall. Interaction takes place along horizontal or diagonal vectors, not vertical ones. He has four arms, they have only two. Their spines curve when his is straight. He may be frontal, but they turn toward him. He may carry iconographic markers, such as the staff of the wanderer, but they have none. He acts, they react.

The same dynamics operate in the other large tableau on this wall that brings together male and female (plate 3). Iconographers identify this subject as Shiva Umasahita ("Shiva with his wife, Uma"), a primarily descriptive title rather than one that indexes a narrative.[37] This relief is set into the first recess a visitor would pass when walking clockwise around the *vimana*, right after the tableau of Shiva lifting the chin of his beloved. The recessed panel seems to repeat the same figures on a grander scale, but some of that gentle intimacy persists. Touch connects Shiva to his companions, and their bodies have some languor about them. His knee rests between Uma's knees. One of her knees leans against his shin. She may brush his elbow with her shoulder and hand. Both of them touch their feet to a helpful dwarf who sits on the ground, resting his face on one hand and gazing up at them. He parks a casual arm on a shelf and lazes against it.

Compositionally, too, this relief follows principles visible in this wall's two other scenes of male/female interaction. At the center of the panel are small open spaces across which Shiva and Uma touch. She faces at a three-quarter angle, splitting her address between him and her viewers. Shiva's body is frontal, but he sits to one side of the centerline. He is substantially taller and broader than she is, and his seat is higher than hers. He has six arms. She has two.

Shiva's posture, though, is frontal and his back erect. Some of his elbows drop below his shoulders, but others rise above. With one leg pendant and one leg folded along his wide bench, he is taking the posture of royal ease that minor goddesses take on the north wall. An element of public address mixes with the scene's air of quiet intimacy. This husband is also a king with responsibilities beyond his beloved.

The relief's setting reinforces the idea of kings and marriage. Shiva and his wife occupy the center of a regal triad. The goddesses flanking them are perfectly frontal, their spines erect and elbows near their sides. To the left is Lakshmi, her throne a lotus flower and her footstool a lotus pad. The two abraded items in her hands were probably lotuses too.[38] She takes up the especially royal pose of two legs pendant, the posture of coronation (*abhisheka*). Two elephants empty pots of water over her head, bathing her but also enacting the exact ritual that made men into kings.

The goddess to the right of Shiva and Uma is probably Saraswati, though erosion has deprived her of any signs in her hands (fig. 2.5). She sits with one leg pendant in the posture of royal ease. The two damaged figures carved above her niche in a swirl of foam may be Saraswati in her form as a river, her fishtail embracing her husband, the multiheaded Brahma. (A similar group appears above Lakshmi, too, however, and she is not identified with a particular river.) She seems at any rate to signify Brahma's wife, thus perpetuating through wifely representatives the male triad so frequently represented on this monument of Shiva flanked by Vishnu and Brahma (see fig. 3.2a and b). Lakshmi is often cast as a wife of Vishnu, and Saraswati the wife of Brahma.[39]

This south-facing space in which Shiva engages with women is also a space made calm by kings on their thrones asserting order, stability, and hierarchy. Bilateral symmetry organizes the ensemble in this recess as well as each goddess and her environment. As goddesses and as Shiva, kings fill this niche. The projecting wall at the left side of this niche shows a densely packed line of men on a long throne, representing perhaps a line of royal ancestors looking down over that reassuring prospect (fig. 2.4).

The two other large reliefs on the south wall take up stories of teaching, communication, and grace, carrying the themes of continuity and interactivity beyond the realm of the sexual. The figure at the very center of this *vimana* wall evokes Shiva as Dakshinamurti, a teacher in the forest (plate 4).[40] A common motif on the south wall of temples in the Tamil region, this example explicitly cites the visual language of teaching that had

FIGURE 2.4 (*above*) A frieze of male figures, wearing tall crowns and seated on thrones. The frieze runs above the doorway to the cella at the center of the south wall of Rajasimha's *vimana* and faces toward the large relief of Shiva enthroned with Uma by his side. (Photo by Emmanuel Francis)

FIGURE 2.5 (*right*) A goddess, perhaps Saraswati, to the right of Shiva and Uma enthroned (Shiva Umasahita) on the south wall of Rajasimha's *vimana*. Compare plate 9. Note, too, the erosion of the sandstone surface.

flourished already for centuries in Buddhist contexts.[41] Like a Shakyamuni Buddha, Shiva sits at the foot of a great tree and two deer kneel below him facing each other. He practices yoga, though Shiva uses a strap (*yogabandha*) around one knee. Around him are signs of the wilderness—undomesticated animals (lions) in cave-like niches and lotuses growing in clusters. Human followers attend him too, a sagely bearded man with matted hair locks at the lower left and a kingly, clean-shaven, broad-chested man with a crown and flowing hair at the lower right. Two more men sit beside them. All show their status as followers by sitting on the ground. Their teacher sits above them, his superior status signaled by his elevated, even throne-like, seat. He makes the *chin mudra* loose fist of teaching and communication. His followers seem to signal they are listening. They mirror his hand gesture but turn the palm to face out.

Shiva Dakshinamurti is a new Buddha, but he also introduces signs the Buddha does not display—the luxuriant hair, large earrings, fangs, and the rearing cobra that shares his bench. One hand holds a rosary. The flaming torch in Shiva's upper left hand may signal the ritual for new initiates into a guru's spiritual lineage. Gurus in the Shaiva Siddhanta community used a flaming torch to purify initiates by burning their fingers.[42] Such lineages in particular and teaching in general are commitments to the continuity across time of generations following each other on this earth. These could be spiritual counterparts of royal lineages, other declarations of sustained engagement with existence on this earth into the past and into the future.

The shapes of this Shiva Dakshinamurti might seem to break the visual patterns of sculptures on the south wall of Rajasimha's *vimana*. From head to hip he is close to the centerline of his relief panel. He faces outward rather than touching other figures. One knee rises well above his hips.

And yet he is much less rigid than the strictly symmetrical figure of his yogic counterpart on the north wall where he sits above the dying Jalandhara (plate 14). Dakshinamurti's head tilts and turns to his right as his hips and legs swing around to his left. The yoga strap holds only one leg. The other rests on his seat and then dangles loosely to the ground. (This lower foot is strangely truncated, a sign perhaps of recutting in a shallow stone matrix.) He is communicative too. His yogic practice involves interacting with others through teaching. Those he might be teaching are diagonally below him, not vertically, and they sit upright, attentive and alert.

On the north wall, Jalandhara falls over and life leaks out of him. Directly above him, Shiva's yogic figure retreats into the absolute isolation of deep meditation. Even any intimacy of violence that joined them in battle has passed. A small platform isolates Shiva despite the demon's reaching hand, and the sharp line of the yoga strap reinforces the platform's horizontal splitting of the niche. There, Shiva's body is perfectly frontal.

As these yogic forms of Shiva are on opposite walls, no one can see them at the same moment. Only people who walk repeatedly around this *vimana* could put together the imagery that makes these reliefs counterpoints within the theme of yoga. But as visitors who connect these two sculptures could note, the theme of yoga marks an axis that slices north-south through the very center of the *vimana* (fig. 2.1, C and H). Yoga connects the continuities that face south and the isolations that face north.[43] Yoga also stands out. It occupies also the most prominent facet of each wall, projecting into the circumambulatory path.

Teaching is also fundamental to the other large relief on this south-facing wall that does not include female figures, and so is fire (plate 6).[44] Whereas Dakshinamurti brandishes a flaming torch, Shiva Lingodbhava ("born from the *linga*") manifests *as* fire. In this relief, which fills the second recess of the south wall, Shiva Lingodbhava manifests in an endless *linga* of fire to school Vishnu and Brahma in his magnitude. He appears through a diamond-shaped opening, resplendent with many weapons in his eight arms, the crescent moon in his hair, and a three-headed cobra above his shoulder. The cylindrical mass around him curves at the upper corners like tops of *linga*s do inside the *vimana*s of this temple complex.[45]

Directly beneath him are the eroded traces of Varaha, the boar form of Vishnu, diving in vain to find the *linga*'s origins. Brahma takes the form of a bird at the upper left, flying up to find the *linga*'s summit. At the lower left and right, he and Vishnu reappear without any animal traits to acknowledge that the *linga* and therefore Shiva are unending.[46] Each salutes him with an open palm raised to the head. Again, the monument presents these three deities as an unequal triad dominated by Shiva.

Fire can manifest as blinding light in this recess when the low sun beats against this wall in midwinter and makes this sculpture of Lingodbhava glow with that borrowed light. Angled light sharpens the contrasts between the *vimana*'s north- and south-facing figures, cloaking ascetics, warriors, and demons in deep, cool shadows while it drenches couples and teachers in warmth.

The centralized and bilaterally symmetrical composition of this relief and the frontal figure of Shiva are elements that admittedly also characterize reliefs on this building's north face. So is Shiva's visual isolation within the *linga* and his vertical domination over the burrowing Vishnu he is educating. But the composition of this Lingodbhava relief is most like that of the Dakshinamurti tableau, where those Shiva teaches form two stacks of figures on either side of him (plate 4). Those students receive his grace along diagonal vectors rather than vertical ones. Two columns of figures similarly flank Lingodbhava (plate 6). At the bottom of each, and thus diagonally below Lingodbhava himself, stands a fully human form of Brahma on the left and Vishnu on the right. They raise a palm to their brow as they gaze up at Shiva, acknowledging his superiority. And Shiva will not even crush that mistaken boar directly below him. He may humiliate them, but he leaves them intact, just as Bhikshatana humiliates the sages with cuckoldry and as Dakshinamurti's students learn Shiva's wisdom and survive. In these south-facing stories, he confers knowledge through grace rather than destruction.[47]

Other Surfaces of Rajasimha's *Vimana*

Rajasimha's *vimana* is a multifaceted building with offsets and recesses complicating every wall. Producing these facets are nine small towered rooms shaped like small temples embedded in the skin of the building at ground level (see figs. 1.2, 1.7). Valérie Gillet calls these rooms "cellas," which I will do, too, as a way of distinguishing them from the many other temple-shaped elements that this temple complex comprises. Four of them completely fill the east wall on either side of this *vimana*'s entrance. An oblong cella marks the center of each of the other three walls, and a square one marks each corner. They are only partially embedded in the surface of the main shrine, so they project outward from the building's core, exposing parts of their outer shells. Some of these are narrow surfaces that face to the north or south from the east and west sides of the *vimana*. Likewise, narrow walls face east and west from the north and south.

Even in these twists and turns of the exterior surface and the cella interiors, gentle, rounded, nurturing figures face to the south and more jagged, energetic, solitary figures face to the north. From inside cellas at the center of the north and south walls, Uma faces south with her chubby son in her lap. A goddess in nearly the same languid posture as she takes to watch Shiva dance faces the same direction in the cellas of the east wall. Each of these four goddesses has only two arms and sits with her legs pressed together, twisting away from frontality. Beside each is a much larger figure of Shiva on the adjacent, east-facing wall. A wife sits beside her husband. A male child nestles in his mother's lap. They are a family group of intimately connected males and females, sitting down together.

Ganesha faces south from the outer surface of the cella at the center of the west wall (fig. 2.6). His posture is frontal, and he sits in the center of his niche, but his volumes

FIGURE 2.6 Ganesha, an embodiment of auspiciousness, facing south from the outer surface of the shrine embedded at the center of the west wall, Rajasimha's *vimana*.

53

are rotund and his posture relaxed. Stories associate him with food, plenty, protection, and auspicious beginnings.

The goddess who faces Ganesha, and thus faces north, from the side of the southern-most cella of the west wall is a spikey array of multiple arms, splayed fingers, fluttering drapery, and weapons (fig. 2.7). Only a multiheaded cobra keeps her company. Dancing at the center of this radial composition, she looks so much like Shiva that early sources identify her as him.[48] Only the conic hips and a thin breast band suggest the figure is female. Perhaps viewers are meant to understand her to be in the company of Shiva on the adjacent wall (plate 9), but that seems more likely the role of the languid goddess interposed between them (visible in the left margin of fig. 2.7).

FIGURE 2.7 A fierce goddess dancing with weapons. This figure faces north from the outer surface of the shrine embedded at the south end of the west wall, Rajasimha's *vimana*.

On the north side of the cella at the center of this wall, Shiva plays music on a *vina* (fig. 2.8). Above his shoulder, a cobra fans out its hood, poised to strike. Like other north-facing figures, he shares the frame only with a male dwarf who sits directly beneath him, verticality emphasizing his subordination. Female figures on the wall are in separate frames.[49]

The figures discussed above demonstrate that this north-south pattern persists among sculptures that face the same direction from different surfaces of Rajasimha's *vimana*. The wildly dancing goddess, for example, is closer to the south side of the *vimana* than the north, but her shapes, energy, and solitude align her with figures that face north as she does. Directionality rather than location is the factor around which this pattern

FIGURE 2.8 Shiva plays music on a single-gourded *vina*. This figure faces north from the outer surface of the shrine embedded at the center of the west wall, Rajasimha's *vimana*.

aligns. The consistency of this principle emerges with increasing clarity on the other buildings in the temple complex.

The pattern also trickles into this *vimana*'s marginal spaces, where artisans might have had the chance to improvise a bit.[50] This suggests either that the people who chiseled stone details were in close communication with the masterminds of the program or that they were the same people. Consider the dwarves (*ganas*), Shiva's attendants, in the lower margins of the grand tableaux. They run toward battle below Shiva on the north wall, bristling with weapons, their fingers spread (plate 15).[51] On the south wall, they sit cross-legged beneath large sculptures of the divine couple (plates 2, 3). Their limbs relax and their bodies make soft silhouettes. Beneath the standing couple, a *gana* seems to slide a cushion below Shiva's dangling foot. The *gana* below the seated couple acts as that cushion, carrying Shiva's foot as he rests his cheek on one hand and looks at the deities in tranquil admiration. The *gana*'s other hand flops loosely from the wrist. Some early texts on iconography (*shastra*) do advise that *ganas* reflect Shiva's qualities, and in some cases those qualities have some association with spatial orientation.[52]

The Eastern Façade

Among the sculptures on the small temples of the eastern façade, the general patterns of north- and south-facing imagery repeat. Most of the north-facing walls show Shiva in his war chariot (fig. 2.9a, no. 1), destroying the elephant demon (no. 2), or seated in meditation over a crumpled enemy (no. 3). Most of the south-facing walls show him as the teacher seated beneath a tree (fig. 2.10). Another has him manifesting in the fiery *linga*, another subject suitable for a south-facing wall.

Some irregularities also appear. I suspect these are products of incorrect reassembly after anastylosis before the twenty-first century. (Temple A was left blank on all sides after being taken apart and reassembled in 2000.) In their current locations, they resist the internal logic set up by similar figures at this monument. Elsewhere on the monument, the saluting forms of Brahma and Vishnu address Shiva as he stands in the pillar of fire or *linga* (Lingodbhava) (plate 6), but on the south side of temples E and F they flank seated forms of Shiva, leaving Lingodbhava alone and unrecognized on temple D (fig. 2.10). The reason for his manifestation has disappeared. The group of three appears together as they should be on temple F, but uncharacteristically facing north (fig. 2.9b, no. II). The wandering ascetic on the north face of shrine H (fig. 2.9b, no. I) faces west or south elsewhere in the monument (see figs. 1.1; 2.13e, no. 52). Another apparent mismatch appears on the north side of temple D where a goddess watches Shiva destroy the elephant demon (fig. 2.9a, no. 2). Elsewhere in the temple complex, other goddesses take up this posture to watch Shiva dance.[53]

FIGURE 2.9A Figures of Shiva as an ascetic and destroying foes (1–3) on the north-facing walls of the eastern façade of the Kailasanatha temple complex. These figures follow the orientation that similar figures follow in other parts of the monument. (Graphics by Mark R. Williams)

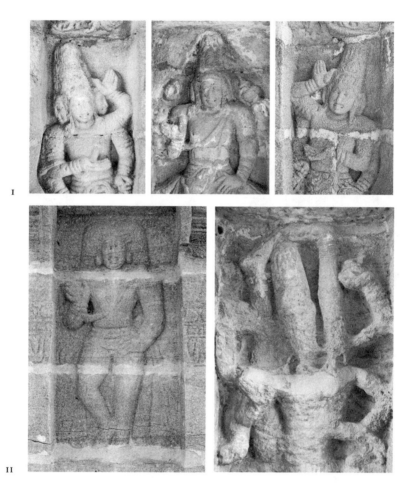

I

II

III

FIGURE 2.9B Figures of Shiva Lingodbhava manifesting in a pillar of fire (I) and dancing (II) on the north-facing walls of the eastern façade of the Kailasanatha temple complex. These figures do not face the same direction as similar figures in other parts of the monument. (Graphics by Mark R. Williams)

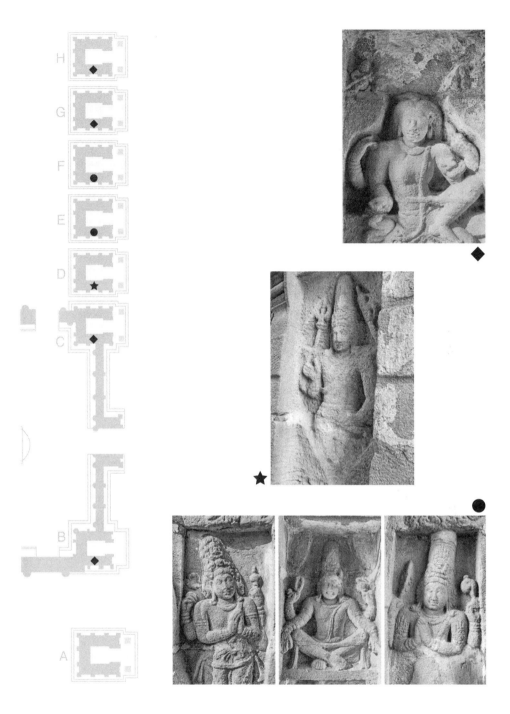

FIGURE 2.10 Figures on the south-facing walls of the eastern façade of the Kailasanatha temple complex. Shiva Dakshinamurti teaching (marked with a diamond) and Lingodbhava manifesting in a pillar of fire (marked with a star) face south, as do similar figures in the rest of the monument. Shiva as an ascetic (marked with a circle) faces north in other parts of the monument. (Graphics by Mark R. Williams)

Mahendra's *Vimana* and *Prakara*

This pattern that aligns celibate, violent, charged bodies to face north and gentle, fecund, relaxed bodies to face south continues on all the eighth-century structures in the Kailasanatha temple complex. It manifests through many of the same subjects and compositions that appear on Rajasimha's *vimana*, and at the same orientations, sometimes on a different scale. Other sculptures intensify and clarify the pattern by introducing new stories and compositions that follow the same principles. Altogether, the number of figures involved in this pattern is prodigious. The few exceptions that do exist are part of another pattern, the multidirectional orientation of themes that had special royal resonance for the Pallavas (see chapter 3).

Mahendra's barrel-vaulted *linga* shrine and the small *prakara* around it repeat some sculptural compositions from Rajasimha's *vimana*, and they introduce several sculptural variations. Shiva meditating over a recumbent Jalandhara again faces north, but here Jalandhara is much longer and Brahma and Vishnu intrude into the frame with Shiva (fig. 2.11a and b, no. 2). The many-armed goddess who rides a lioness recurs once in a familiar form and once in a new form, with twelve arms rather than ten and seated on the lioness's back instead of resting her foot on its shoulder (fig. 2.11a and d, nos. 10 and 12). Shiva destroys the elephant demon, stretching its skin over his head, in a large relief here, whereas on Rajasimha's *vimana* this scene is a tiny panel above the large tableau of Shiva catching Ganga (fig. 2.11a and b, no. 3; plate 17). All of these face north as they did on Rajasimha's *vimana*. Figures of Dakshinamurti, Lakshmi, Ganesha, and Shiva enthroned with his wife face south on these buildings too (fig. 2.11a–c). Dakshinamurti and Ganesha are rendered at the large scale they were on Rajasimha's *vimana*, but Shiva and Uma get only a small panel here, and Lakshmi gets two much larger representations (figs. 2.11a and b, no. 4; 2.11c, no. 7; 2.11b, no. 1; 2.11c, nos. 5 and 8).

Brahma and Vishnu become more important here than they were on Rajasimha's *vimana*, where they merely stood in attendance on Shiva. Mahendra's small *prakara* awards them each a separate shrine. Brahma the multiheaded ascetic with matted locks piled high on each head faces north (fig. 2.11d, no. 11). Vishnu faces south (fig. 2.11c, no. 6).

The Open *Mandapam*

The open *mandapam* just inside Rajasimha's *prakara* also seems to follow this pattern, though its thick layers of old and new stucco make it impossible to know what these figures looked like in the eighth century. The cast of characters is much reduced from that of Rajasimha's *vimana*, and those are rendered at a larger scale than anywhere else in the compound. The lion-riding Goddess fills half the north wall. Jyeshtha fills the other half, rising to the lion-rider's equal in scale, whereas on the *vimana* Jyeshtha is only Durga's much smaller attendant (see fig. 1.3a and b, nos. 2, 3; plate 16). The open *mandapam*'s south wall carries the same pair of goddesses portrayed as small attendants

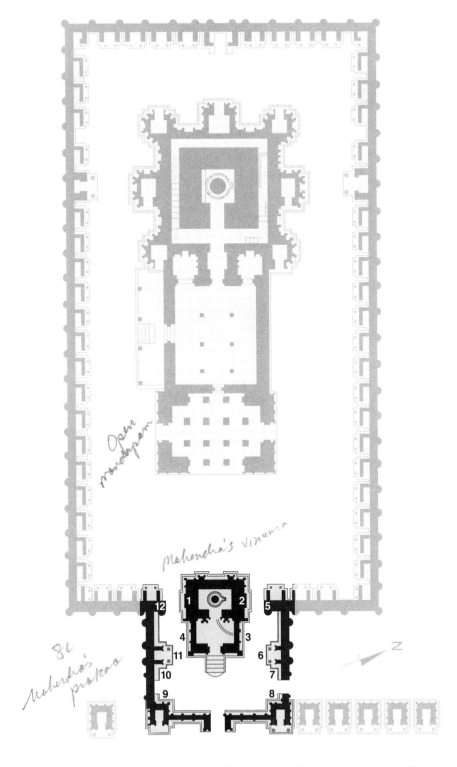

FIGURE 2.11A Ground plan showing location of figures 2.11B–D. (Graphics by Mark R. Williams)

FIGURE 2.11B Placement of sculptures on the *vimana* sponsored by
Mahendravarman III. (Graphics by Mark R. Williams)

FIGURE 2.11C Placement of sculptures on the north wall of the small *prakara* sponsored by Mahendravarman III. (Graphics by Mark R. Williams)

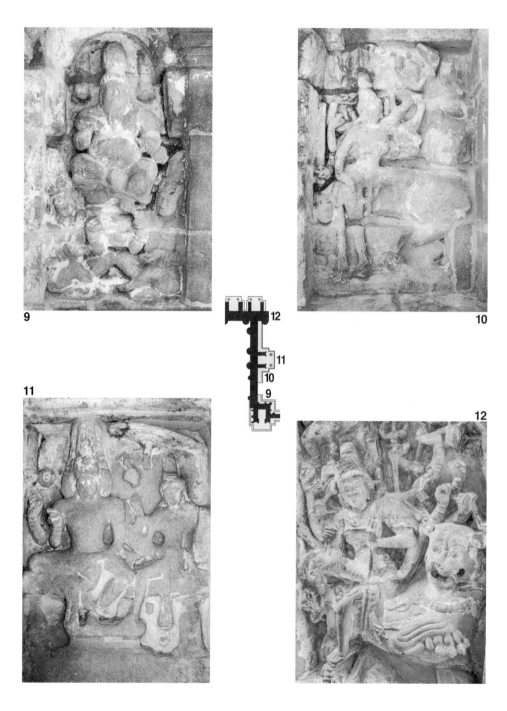

FIGURE 2.11D Placement of sculptures on the south wall of the small *prakara*
sponsored by Mahendravarman III. (Graphics by Mark R. Williams)

to Shiva and Uma on the south side of Rajasimha's *vimana* (see fig. 1.3a and b, nos. 1, 4; plate 3), but they are enormous and their positions are reversed. Lakshmi with her two lotuses and a pair of elephants above her, trunks raised, is to the right of the south entry to the open *mandapam* (see fig. 1.3b, no. 4). The other goddess, perhaps Saraswati, is to the left of that entry (see fig. 1.3b, no. 1). If this building is later than Rajasimha's *vimana*, its sculptural program adheres to the *vimana*'s pattern in a distilled form that emphasizes goddesses. If this building precedes Rajasimha's *vimana*, these reliefs could have been restuccoed to suit the principles of this north/south pattern established by Rajasimha's *vimana*. It is also possible these figures were not changed much and that they anchor the pattern to a time before Rajasimha's *vimana*.

Rajasimha's *Prakara*

Rajasimha's *prakara* makes the north-south pattern especially clear by expanding it to more than fifty sculptures that introduce variations and expansions on the central theme. These reliefs are located along the inner face of the *prakara* on what are exterior walls of the tiny, east-facing, temple-shaped cells that line the *prakara*'s north and south walls (see figs. 1.3, 2.12a). These cells are packed so tightly together, front to back, that their identity as separate structures may not be obvious from the courtyard. The reliefs fill each wall to bursting, implying a stream of activity flowing east and west behind the pairs of pillars that bracket each sculptural scene. The complexity these surfaces present to the courtyard can encourage visitors to move in for a better look.

Gillet identifies the subjects of the reliefs on the south wall as follows (fig. 2.12).[54] (The number corresponds to the aedicule or cell they adorn. Aedicules are numbered in clockwise sequence from the southern entrance into this *prakara*.)

4. Ganesha
5. Goddess with a lion
6. Skanda
7. Goddess seated under a tree
8. Tripurantakamurti (Shiva destroying the three cities)
9. Vishnu sitting astride Garuda
10. Narasimha
11. Skanda and Indra battle
12. Trivikrama
13. Churning the ocean
14. The "archer type" of Dancing Shiva
15. Shiva cutting off Brahma's head
16. Shiva and Arjuna fighting
17. Jalandharasamharamurti (Shiva destroying Jalandhara)
18. Shiva protecting the *naga*s from Garuda

19. Andhakasamharamurti (Shiva destroying Andhaka)?
20. Brahma seated with his spouse (see fig. 1.3c, no. 5)
21. Tripurantakamurti (Shiva destroying the three cities)
22. Kalarimurti (Shiva defeating Kala)
23. Gajasamharamurti (Shiva destroying the elephant demon)
24. Gangadhara (Shiva catching Ganga)
25. The "leg lifted to vertical type" of Dancing Shiva

On the north wall, in frame after frame, Shiva shares his throne with his relaxed wife, his gentled body in some combination of the regal and teaching postures he strikes on the south side of Rajasimha's *vimana* (plates 3, 4), calmly gracing and receiving supplications from Arjuna, students, Ravana, and Rati (fig. 2.13, nos. 36, 37, 40–42, 47, 54). Gillet identifies the subjects of the reliefs on this wall as follows:

34. empty
35. Chandesha (Caṇḍeśa) cutting off his father's leg
36. The granting of the invincible weapon (*pashupatastra/pāśupatāstra*)
37. The god at the banyan tree (also known as Dakshinamurti)
38. The "two bent legs type" of Dancing Shiva
39. Vishnu seated between two wives (see fig. 1.3c, no. 5)
40. Ravana playing music on the tendons of his own arm
41. Ravana as devotee of Shiva
42. Ravana lifting Mount Kailasa
43. Vishnu adoring the *linga*
44. Marriage of Skanda and Devasenā
45. Shiva and Parvati seated
46. The "foot to knee type" of Dancing Shiva
47. Destruction of Kama and the supplication of Rati
48. Shiva as a musician
49. Lingodbhava (Shiva manifesting in the infinite *linga*)
50. Gangadhara (Shiva catching Ganga)
51. Somaskanda (Shiva with Uma and Skanda)
52. Shiva wandering
53. Shiva begging
54. Ravana conquered by Valin, the monkey king, adoring the *linga*
55. Chandesha

This *prakara* repeats, sometimes more than once, most of the tableaux on Rajasimha's *vimana* and the open *mandapam* and still has space left over for other figures that strike similar poses and tell more stories about conquest or grace and asceticism or conjugality. The Goddess with her lioness, Shiva on his war chariot, Shiva over Jalandhara, and Shiva kicking Death face north on this large *prakara* (fig. 2.12, nos. 5, 8, 17, 22), their shapes as

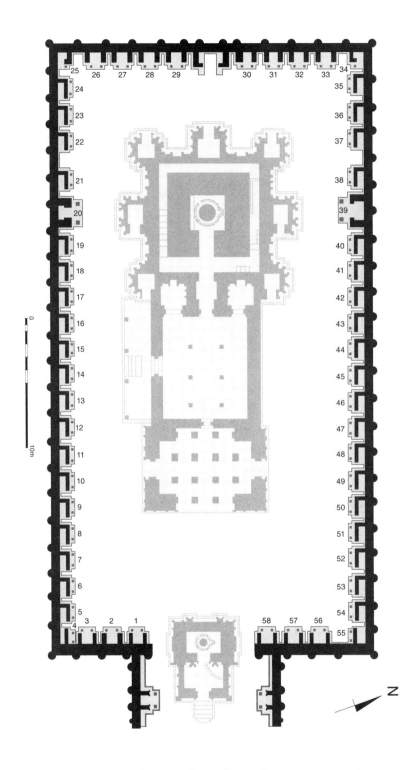

FIGURE 2.12 Ground plan numbering the 58 cells of Rajasimha's *prakara*.
(Graphics by Mark R. Williams)

67

FIGURE 2.12A Sculptures facing north in the easternmost cells (1–4) of the south wall.

FIGURE 2.12B Sculptures facing north in cells 9–12 of the south wall.

13

14

15

16

FIGURE 2.12C Sculptures facing north in cells 13–16 of the south wall.

FIGURE 2.12D Sculptures facing north in cells 17–21 of the south wall.

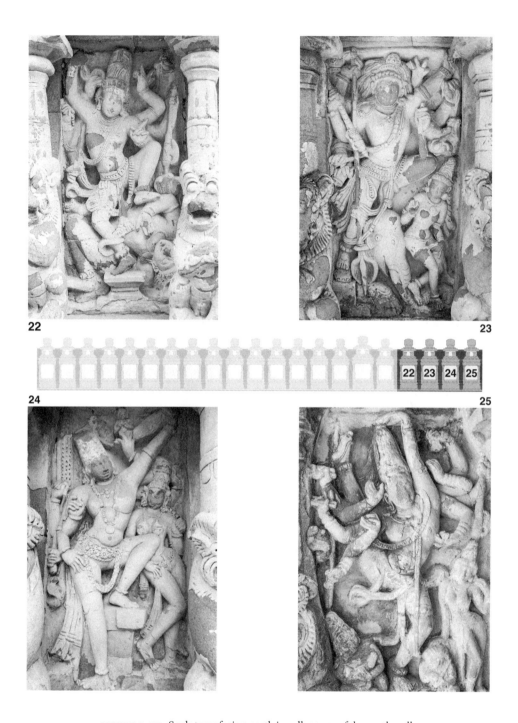

FIGURE 2.12E Sculptures facing north in cells 22–25 of the south wall.

FIGURE 2.13 Gentle and teaching figures that face south and onto the large courtyard from the north wall of Rajasimha's *prakara*. (A) Sculptures facing south in cells 35–38 of the north wall. (Graphics by Mark R. Williams)

40

41

42

43

FIGURE 2.13B Sculptures facing south in cells 40–43 of the north wall.

FIGURE 2.13C Sculptures facing south in cells 44–47 of the north wall.

48

49

50

51

48 49 50 51

FIGURE 2.13D Sculptures facing south in cells 48–51 of the north wall.

FIGURE 2.13E Sculptures facing south in cells 52–55 of the north wall.

well as their northward orientation echoing sculptures of the same subjects on Rajasimha's *vimana* (plates 13–16) and the open *mandapam* (see fig. 1.3b, no. 3). So, too, Shiva faces south on Rajasimha's *prakara* as he does on Rajasimha's *vimana* when he teaches under the banyan tree, sits enthroned with his wife, and wanders as a mendicant (fig. 2.13, nos. 37, 45, 53; compare plates 3, 4, 7). On Rajasimha's *prakara*, this last aspect of Shiva reduplicates on adjacent cells, first in a frontal view, then in profile (fig. 2.13, nos. 52, 53).

Some reliefs on this *prakara* look so much like their neighbors that they can seem to be reduplications, but they more likely emphasize the shared natures of separate stories. For example, twice Shiva rides toward viewers' right into battle on a chariot, a slightly smaller deity standing just ahead of him (fig. 2.12, nos. 8 and 18). Again and again on the north-facing surfaces of this *prakara*, dynamic figures of Shiva cut strong diagonals with his angular, tense body as he transcends threats—*asuras*, Brahma, Arjuna, Garuda, Andhaka, Death, an elephant demon—in a world pretty free of females (fig. 2.12, nos. 13, 15, 16, 18, 19, 21–23).

Other reliefs loop new subject matter into the same categories. Four of the lunging figures facing north portray not Shiva but Indra attacking the newborn infant Skanda (fig. 2.12, no. 11) or Vishnu swooping down on Garuda, or killing Hiranyakashipu, or taking his three steps as Trivikrama (fig. 2.12, nos. 9, 10, 12). Facing south, one relief takes fecund interaction to its most fruitful outcome, showing Shiva and Parvati with their son Skanda nestled between them (fig. 2.13, no. 51). Another relief on the same wall shows Skanda's wedding (fig. 2.13, no. 44).

More sculptures following the north-south pattern fill the wider recesses between the forty-four reliefs listed above. Goddesses shown at a small scale on Rajasimha's *vimana* become larger figures on the *prakara*, with a recess or wall to themselves. Lakshmi fills a wall outside the cell beside Vishnu's shrine on the south-facing side of the large *prakara* (fig. 2.15, A; compare plate 3).[55] Inside Vishnu's shrine, he sits between two goddesses, one of whom could be Lakshmi again (see fig. 1.3c, no. 6). The other might be Bhu, the Earth. On the opposite wall, close to Brahma's shrine, Jyeshtha and the enthroned goddess with long matted locks face north as they do on Rajasimha's *vimana* (fig. 2.14, D and A; compare plates 16 and 15). In between those goddesses, two more recesses expand the pantheon of fierce goddesses. In one, Durga sits with her foot on the buffalo demon's decapitated head (fig. 2.14, C).

In the other, a vibrant group of the seven mother goddesses (*sapta matrika*) share a wide throne and tilt restlessly at different angles (fig. 2.14, B). A regal umbrella hovers over each of them. From left to right they represent Brahmi (Brahmī) with three heads; Maheshvari (Maheśvarī) with matted locks; Kaumari (Kaumārī) with a sword perhaps; Vaishnavi (Vaiṣṇāvī) with the disc (*chakra*) and conch; Varahi (Varāhī) with a sow's face; Indrani (Indrāṇī) or Aindri (Aindrī) with a lightning bolt (*vajra*); and Chamunda (Cāmuṇḍā) with a trident and cup made from a skull. Chamunda's untied hair billows around her head. She appears again in the next recess by herself with more arms and more weapons, enthroned and frontal (fig. 2.14, A). All of these *matrika*s are

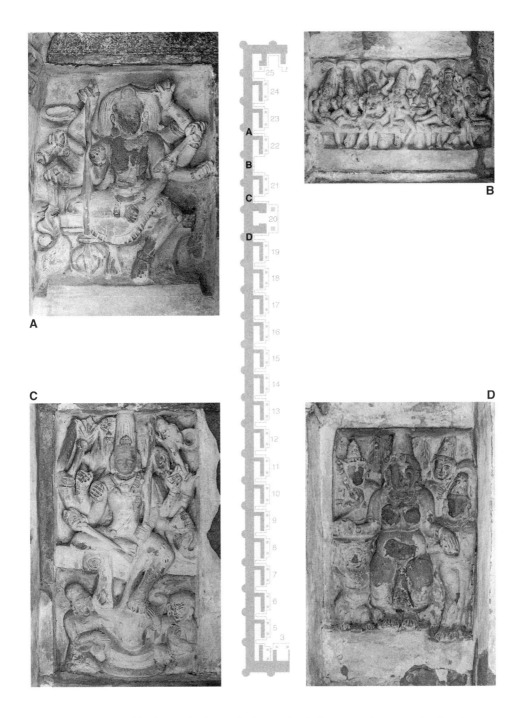

FIGURE 2.14 This cluster of goddess reliefs occupies the long recess just west of Brahma's
shrine (20) on the south wall of Rajasimha's *prakara*, between cells 19 and 23.
Jyeshtha enthroned (D); Durga enthroned with one foot resting on the decapitated
head of a buffalo (C); the seven mother goddesses (*sapta matrika*) (B); and
the seventh *matrika* on her own, bearing her skull cup and trident (A).

A

B

FIGURE 2.15 Lakshmi enthroned on a lotus (A) and a subtly variegated band of ten male figures, perhaps planetary deities (B). These reliefs occupy the long recess just west of Vishnu's shrine (39) on the north wall of Rajasimha's *prakara*, between cells 36 and 38.

more explicitly celibate and martial than earlier *matrika* figures in northern India, who act out the idea of maternity by holding babies.[56] The male deities Ganesha and Skanda (or Shiva's fierce Bhairava form) sit to the *matrikas*' proper right but are on a separate, perpendicular wall. They are no larger than the *matrikas*.[57]

An equally wide recess on the opposite side of the courtyard holds ten male figures disposed much like these *matrika*s, as a subtly variegated band packed together tightly on a long bench (fig. 2.15, B). R. Nagaswamy suggests they are the planetary deities, which would suit nicely the strong light—real and represented through imagery like Lingodbhava—that characterizes the monument's south-facing surfaces.[58] They sit on a lion throne, one leg pendant in a kingly way.

Another way this *prakara* expands on the themes of Rajasimha's *vimana* is to translate the sculptural triad of Vishnu-Shiva-Brahma onto an architectural scale. The *prakara*'s largest shrines are for Vishnu and Brahma (see fig. 1.3c, nos. 5 and 6). These are directly in line with the *linga* at the center of Rajasimha's *vimana* and with the cellas at the center of the *vimana*'s north and south walls, cellas that themselves hold sculptures of that triad (see fig. 3.2a and b). The shrine of Brahma, the ascetic with matted locks, faces north; the husbandly Vishnu faces south. Inside, a wide carved panel shows these deities looking very much like Shiva does in the *linga* shrine, enthroned with a wife (or two, in Vishnu's case) and attendants. Buildings reinforce the message this triad can express in sculpture, that Shiva subordinates and receives homage from these two gods.

This *prakara* makes explicit the importance of spatial orientation to the coherence of the north-south pattern. When motifs from the *vimana* recur on the *prakara*, they manifest on the opposite side of the compound but facing in the same direction. The Goddess, Shiva on his war chariot, Shiva over Jalandhara, and Shiva kicking Death face north from the north wall of the *vimana* (fig. 2.1) and north from the south wall of the *prakara* (fig. 2.12, nos. 5, 8, 17, 22). Shiva teaches under the banyan tree, sits enthroned with his wife, and wanders as a mendicant facing south from the south wall of the *vimana* (fig. 2.1) and south from the north wall of the *prakara* (fig. 2.13, nos. 37, 45, 53). This inversion reflects the fact that these sculptures on the *prakara*s line the *inner* surfaces of those structures, whereas these sculptures on *vimana*s fill their *outer* surfaces. (The *prakara*s' outer surfaces carry only rearing lions and, on the west, a pair of dwarf door guardians. See figs. 1.4 and 4.2) There is no subregion of the temple complex where either kind of imagery clusters. Both are spread throughout the compound, on every building of the eighth century. North and south are relative concepts, defined by the position of visitors as they encounter these sculptures.

Complementarity

These strong and consistent distinctions between north-facing forms and south-facing forms might seem to present opposite polarities, but the material evidence casts them more precisely as complementarities. Bridges across their differences draw them into dialog, sometimes minimizing difference, sometimes implying interchangeability, and sometimes weaving them together into the same image. These bridges become apparent to visitors over time. They manifest as seasons change, or they are tucked into architectural recesses, or they are apparent in fine details, or they operate between surfaces a visitor cannot see at the same time. Only people who spend extra time at the monument are likely to perceive that these two groups of form are two sides of the same coin.

The broad contrasts between north- and south-facing imagery are comparatively easy to see because they characterize so many sculptures and because those sculptures are on the most prominent facets of buildings and on the first surfaces visitors see when they enter the temple complex. Extreme lighting contrasts, for instance, intensify when midwinter approaches, but they fade as summer returns. Much more light falls on the north-facing walls in summer, when the sun tracks high along the compound's east-west axis, than in December, when it rakes diagonally from the south. The even light of midsummer enhances the similarities among north- and south-facing figures—their grace, voluptuous or yogic; the universality of Shiva's control; the equivalent magnitudes of regenerative and transcendent power. Shiva has fangs and wears skulls when he faces south or north.

Visitors can unlock the complementarity and connectedness between north- and south-facing sculptures by moving through the narrow valley between Rajasimha's *vimana* and *prakara* (see figs. 4.3, 4.4). The two groups of symbols face each other across that corridor, though they turn their backs on each other from opposite sides of the *vimana*. They again face each other between Mahendra's *vimana* and *prakara*, and in the narrow spaces between the small temples on the compound's eastern façade (figs. 2.9, 2.10). In these interstices, contrasting forms gaze at each other and visitors see them at the same time, to their left and right. Commonalities and interactions between the two types of images can charge the space people walk through, unfolding across and through them.

Visitors circumambulating Rajasimha's *vimana* will find that their orientation to these two image types flips after they round the western wall. They have begun their circumambulation by walking west through the south half of the large courtyard where images of prosperity and nurture appear on their right. As those visitors return toward the east along the north half of the courtyard, images of prosperity and nurture appear on their left. Sculptures maintain their consistent north/south orientations, but they have switched places relative to moving visitors. This can destabilize initial impressions of a simple binary opposition and could even imply that these two sculptural groups are interchangeable.

The recesses of this *vimana* reveal other commonalities between north- and south-facing sculptures. Compare the north-facing figure of the Goddess of the battlefield and the south-facing figures of Shiva and his wife sitting beside each other (plates 3, 16). They occupy recesses in the eastern half of the building, meaning that though they face in opposite directions, they are also joined at the back. Without the technology of photography, visitors cannot see them at the same time. Only memory and repeated visits can enable visitors to realize how much they resemble each other. And they resemble each other very much.

A triptych fills the back surface of each of these recesses, a tall, busy rectangular panel flanked by a pair of smaller panels that contain one female figure each. All four females face directly outward from the wall and sit straight-backed on a wide bench, a symmetrical pair of creatures or fly whisks in the corners above them. In each triptych, the goddess on the right hangs one leg pendant to rest on a stool and folds the other horizontally on her sitting platform. Each has four arms, of which the back pair curves outward like the petals of an open flower. The left forward hand rests in the lap, palm up. Each raises her right forward hand in front of the shoulder, palm forward.

The small goddesses on the left side of each triptych both sit with two arms held close to their sides, hands at their shoulders, palms facing outward. Both rest their feet upon the petals of an open lotus. As Lakshmi, the south-facing one carries connotations of prosperity, wealth, food, and wifely support for her husband, Vishnu. As Jyeshtha, the north-facing figure is no longer fecund or subordinate to a husband, though she once was. Another name for Jyeshtha is Alakshmi (A-Lakshmi).[59] (*A-* is a negating prefix in Indic languages.) Names associated with these two figures thus pair them and distinguish them at the same time, just as their common shapes and counterposed locations on this building invite viewers to consider what binds them together as much as what opposes them.

The larger figures they frame also share qualities. The charged body of Durga and the soft one of Uma have the same voluptuous curves and long limbs that twist and bend with supple grace. They wear the same conic crown and disc-shaped earrings.

Another type of female figure at this monument combines austere and nurturing elements within a single body. This is a two-armed female sitting beneath a tree, her legs pendant and crossed at the ankles (figs. 2.16, 2.17). Blocky, irregular forms beneath her suggest rocks and perhaps mountains. A small herd of elephants, water buffalo, rams, or antelope—wild animals, that is—wanders in one corner of each landscape. Near each female figure is an ascetic male, a male warrior, or both. The ascetics face forward, hair piled high on the head, palms pressed together in front of the chest in *anjali mudra*, a yoga strap supporting their folded legs. The male warriors face the female figure and wave a shield or hand over their crowned head. Their legs are concealed behind a low barrier, perhaps a war chariot, but thick layers of plaster obscure these details. They are clean-shaven men with hair flowing past their broad shoulders.

There are seventeen of these figures, set into fifteen of the narrow spaces between the cells on the north and south sides of Rajasimha's *prakara*, spaces so inconspicuous that people caught up by the exciting sculptures on the outside of these cells might not even notice them. Seven figures face north (fig. 2.16), ten face south (fig. 2.17).

These women in the wilderness are hybrids of Uma and Shiva Dakshinamurti in form, and thus potentially in meaning.[60] Like the figure of Uma seated beside Shiva

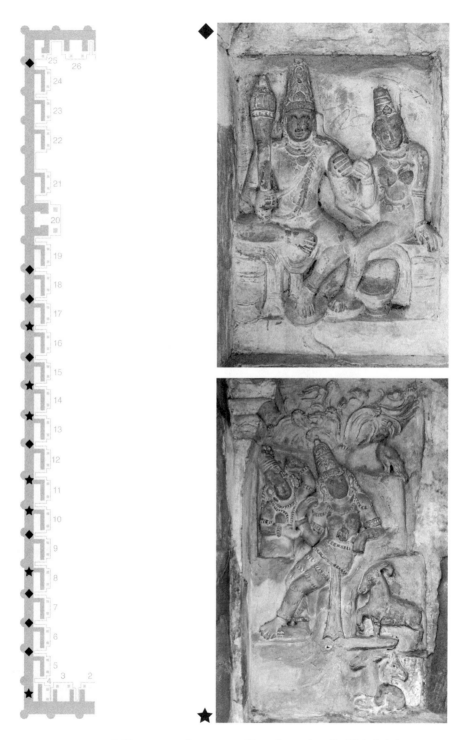

FIGURE 2.16 The two most frequent motifs on the south wall of Rajasimha's *prakara*: yoginis teaching men in the wilderness (marked by stars) and childless couples enthroned (marked by diamonds). (Graphics by Mark R. Williams)

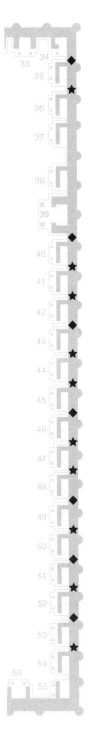

FIGURE 2.17 The two most frequent motifs on the north wall of Rajasimha's *prakara*: yoginis teaching men in the wilderness (marked by stars) and childless couples enthroned (marked by diamonds). (Graphics by Mark R. Williams)

on Rajasimha's *vimana* (plate 3), their bodies are gentle. They let both legs hang at a relaxed angle and may cross one shin over the other, as Uma does. One palm rests on the seat, the elbow hyperextended and pressing against the ribs. Waists are slender, unlike Jyeshtha's. Breasts are full and unbound, unlike the warrior goddesses who face north.

But Shiva is not with these women in the wilderness. Males share their frames, but they do not snuggle. These males have only two arms. They resemble the ascetic and regal men gathered around Shiva Dakshinamurti in the forest, to learn from the teaching god (plate 4). The relaxed women in these mountain scenes bring to mind Dakshinamurti himself, the ascetic who sustains a form of continuity by passing knowledge to new generations of followers. Like him, these women sit in a wilderness with wild animals, rocky outcroppings, and a tree that rises behind their back and branches over their head. Their right hand, like his, seems to gesture in the fist-like *chin mudra*, which can signify lecturing. Their postures have similarities too. Hips and legs turn to the side, while shoulders and chests face forward. The pelvis tucks. One leg drops at an angle not quite perpendicular to the ground.

Orientation and visual signs place these women of the wilderness at a confluence of south-facing interactivity and north-facing solitude, the palace and the wilderness, the divine and the royal. Many of them face north, many face south. They encompass the two categories within a single body, which can express the complementarity of those categories. They are wifely Umas without Shiva, interacting with other males but not touching them. They act like the ascetic Dakshinamurti, in renunciation and in engagement. They, too, could be handing down wisdom to ascetics and kings. With only two arms, they are distinct from the sculptures of yogini goddesses who would become the focus of temple worship a few centuries later. Perhaps they evoke the living, female teachers, yoginis whose lives and practices expressed continuities and transformations between humanity and divinity.[61] Their signs make it possible to read them as teachers, spiritual guides, Umas for Pallava kings who sought spiritual perfection as ascetics and earthly domain as warriors.

Female figures very like these women in the wilderness recur in this same kind of architectural space and in these same postures, but with kingly husbands. In sixteen other recesses of this *prakara*'s north and south walls, the male figure sits in the posture of royal ease, one leg dropped down. The female drops one leg or two. With only two arms apiece and this courtly setting of wide thrones and tall crowns, both members of each couple seem distinctly human and royal.[62]

They otherwise bear a strong resemblance to both Shiva and Uma in the large relief on the south-facing wall of Rajasimha's *vimana* (plate 3) and in multiple variations on that composition that recur along the south-facing wall of Rajasimha's *prakara* (fig. 2.13, nos. 36, 40–43, 45, 47, 51). He is frontal. She turns her relaxed body slightly toward or away from him, but they touch somehow.

These couples in the *prakara*'s narrow recesses face south and north, just as the women in the wilderness do. The couples appear in rough alternation with the women in the wilderness (figs. 2.16, 2.17), a spatial device that can imply similarities and inter-changeabilities. Their meanings seem somehow linked, despite their exclusions or repo-sitionings of the male figure.

As hybrids of two other motifs—women in the wilderness and Shiva enthroned with Uma—these couples link south-facing interactivity with north-facing asceticism, the palace with the wilderness, the divine with the royal. Rajasimha's *prakara* repeatedly intersperses them with women in the wilderness, in recesses, and Shiva/Uma couples on the projecting walls in between, making those linkages available to visitors who can wander in and out among this structure's richly sculpted layers. These crowned couples face east and west too. They have wider resonances that play off other imagery facing east and west, the subject of chapter 3.

Finding Names for Categories That Mattered

This material evidence sends strong signals. Motifs repeat many times and in consistent spatial arrangements on every surface that faces north or south. This indicates the pat-tern is deliberate and had meaning for its designers. The subjects and affects of those motifs fall consistently into two categories, as table 2.1 summarizes. Those categories do seem to offer some access to the thought world of the Pallava court.

Naming them with modern words is, however, a challenge. Locating nurture, pro-creation, teaching, and continuity on the *vimana*'s south wall and conquest and celi-bacy on its north might seem to invert ancient Tamil and Vedic associations with those directions. Those associations hold north to be the abode of the auspicious and south the abode of the lord of Death.[63] But this need not contradict the patterns at the Kaila-sanatha as long as we understand categorization functioning around orientation rather than around location within the micro-geography of the temple complex. Rajasimha's *prakara* already demonstrates that orientation and not location governs the placement of figures: south-*facing* surfaces in every quadrant of the complex share imagery. So, too, for north-facing surfaces. Their orientation to the visitor determines their category. By that principle, a sculpture located on the south face of the *vimana* may be understood to reside in the auspicious north because it *faces* to the south. Orientation places that relief in the north *relative to the viewer*. Put another way, sculptures with their backs to the north reside in the north. Deities emanate outward and in the opposite direction from the places where they reside. North is the direction these auspicious deities are *from*. Directionality expresses the figure's cosmic location in relationship to the seer. Deities who dwell in the north must face south to see the viewer. Those in the north radiate their auspicious energies southward toward the viewer. Those in the realm of death, to the viewer's south, face north as they struggle against dark forces.

Modern students of the Kailasanatha assigned some useful names to other pieces of this pattern derived from the tone of its sculptures. Michael Lockwood and his colleagues identified Shiva's forms on the north side of Rajasimha's *prakara* as terror inspiring and

TABLE 2.1. Qualities that align north- and south-facing sculptures
at the Kailasanatha into two consistent categories

Concept	Sculptures facing north	Sculptures facing south
Bodies	Angular, fierce	Relaxed, rounded
Figural positions	Centered compositions	Adjacent pairs
	Hierarchy, dominance	Lateral glances and touches
Sexes	Sexes separate and equivalent	Sexes connected and different
Forms of interaction	Celibacy, asceticism	Intimacy, desire
	Conflict, violence	Granting grace
	Battlefield triumph	Peaceful governance
Yoga	Conquest, restraint, severing	Teaching, continuity
Phase of *samsara*	Death, transcendence	Beginnings, continuities
Climate	Austerity, renunciation	Prosperity, warmth

on the south side as bestowing grace.[64] The team of Emanuel Francis, Valérie Gillet, and Charlotte Schmid agreed that figures facing south were "appeasing," "beneficial," and grace dispensing. They saw the pattern distinguishing between married and unmarried forms of deities, they associated the pattern with orientation rather than location, and they saw complementarity rather than contrast between the two groups. They gave a more heroic reading of the armed, active figures facing north as Shiva "incarnated to save a world in peril."[65]

This team mapped these categories onto Pallava constructions of kingship. Gillet read the north-facing category as war, victory, and royalty and the south-facing category as beneficence, with an emphasis on the gift through which gods and kings exercised and shared power.[66] Francis and Schmid perceived in both directions an articulation of royal discourse within which royal and divine forces of wisdom, knowledge, peace, and the spirit of bhakti face south, while figures facing north are dynamic and "underline actions of a god who guarantees the equilibrium of the worlds, conquering with his *shakti* [energizing female partner or self] the demons who threaten that equilibrium, protector of his devotees, master of the Ganga."[67] The hybrid identity Francis perceived Pallavas as cultivating aimed to resolve tensions between two fundamental aspects of kingship, the spiritual search and the work of reigning and war. As Brahmin warriors and ascetic kings, they traced their lineage not from the sun or the moon but from Brahma.[68] Schmid has built a strong case for reading the same hybridity in goddess imagery. She shows that the goddess of prosperity, Lakshmi, and the goddess of battlefields, Durga, were the same goddess for the Pallavas and that both were emblematic of the king. Rather than assigning the two goddesses distinctive attributes, she finds, their sculptures at Mahabalipuram mixed the attributes thoroughly between them, forging a kind of continuous network, or *reseau*, of imagery that wove the goddesses into one. That suggested the Pallavas perceived war and prosperity, violence and nurture to be interdependent and perhaps even indistinguishable. The kingdom's prosperity relied on the booty of war.[69]

Édith Parlier-Renault, too, perceived complementarity between the two groups, and she noticed the groups were organized by their orientation, and on all the structures in the compound.[70] She suggested the sculptural program could express the spatial metaphor of *akam*/*puram* of early Tamil poetry, the inner world of thought, feelings, and subjectivity and the outer world of royal, public performance, and the realm.[71] Tamil literature treats *akam* and *puram* as complementary categories. Love becomes a battleground; bloodshed has its own erotics.[72] The Kailasanatha does employ space to express its principles and to transmit them to visitors. The battlefield is a grand public arena. The same spaces witness the interior world of Shiva and Uma's tender eroticism.

The concepts of *mangalam* and *amangalam* also offer a logic that could make sense of much of the north-south pattern of sculpture on the Kailasanatha. Observed in Tamil poetry and Oriya devotional songs and practices, *mangalam* and *amangalam* identify two distinct personalities of power, neither of which is circumscribed by gender but both of which affect gendered bodies.[73] These categories also offer a logic for why sculptures about topics that can seem so different—married love, cuckoldry, renunciation, government, teaching—could make sense together on south-facing walls.

Mangalam and *amangalam* are often translated from the Tamil as "auspiciousness" and "inauspiciousness," though the terms are unsatisfying for the judgmental valences they carry in English. They characterize two pathways or modes of being, one that perpetuates and one that transcends life in this world and the cosmic cycle of birth and rebirth (*samsara*). *Mangalam* things can include fecundity, nurture, water, procreation, marriage, prosperity, and kings on their thrones. *Amangalam* things can include infertility, asceticism, renunciation, transcendence, and celibacy, both female and male. Neither mode is simply negative or positive, making this system of thought fundamentally different from the binary of purity and pollution, a hierarchical, privative paradigm for understanding existence, comprising hard-edged categories and extremes of opposition.[74] *Mangalam* and *amangalam* are complements. Neither is more valuable than the other. Both are necessary, and they are inextricably linked to each other. In the earliest Tamil literature, *mangalam* and *amangalam* suggest a practical form of wisdom for an agrarian world where the cyclicality of life and death are manifest realities, and where fertility has immediate impacts on daily existence.[75] Perceiving *amangalam* and *mangalam* and their interconnections could help people to encounter the challenges of existence and to dream of transcending them.

At the Kailasanatha, north-facing imagery groups together celibacy, self-control, destroying enemies, and transcending death and time. It presents them as conditions where male-female difference is irrelevant. Both kinds of bodies are hard, solitary, and often hidden in shadows. The kind of power displayed here ends lives. South-facing imagery is about power too, but of the kind that keeps things going. These figures enact continuity, communication, sexual difference, seduction outside and inside marriage, and kings on thrones. Bodies can be soft. Fecund, procreative, *mangalam* energies could gentle male and female bodies alike just as ascetic, celibate, *amangalam* energies could galvanize males and females into angular postures. All are bathed in light during midsummer, the *mangalam* time of year, making complementarities between the two categories easiest to see.[76]

The *amangalam* category can explain why the matron Jyeshtha belongs in the company of deities engaged in mortal combat. All are exercising the kind of power celibacy enables. The *mangalam* category could rationalize the pairing on the south wall of Shiva and his beloved with his seduction of other men's wives (plates 2 and 7), though these subjects may be opposites according to modern rules that order social interaction in South Asia. But both of these stories are auspicious because of their focus on procreative sexual energies. Even sexual infidelity can be "auspicious."

The *mangalam* category also offers a rationale for setting between those brackets the tableaux of Shiva acting like a king on his throne, like the Buddha teaching his pupils in the forest, and as an endless *linga* that other gods cannot fathom. All three feature governing or teaching or both, which are, like procreation, modes for maintaining the world and perpetuating lineages. Kingdoms can prosper when kings are firmly on their thrones. Royal power must include the *mangalam* to guarantee kingdoms as places of regeneration, renewal, and prosperity.

The monument's twinning of Lakshmi and Jyeshtha on Rajasimha's *vimana*, where they sit in identical postures in the left corners of back-to-back recesses, could embody *mangalam* and *amangalam* in goddesses and highlight their complementarity. Lakshmi is the *mangalam* principle itself. Her other name is Shri, a synonym for *mangalam*.[77] Her husband is Vishnu, a deity associated with preserving kingdoms, followers, and life, and whose shrines on both this monument's *prakara*s also face south. On the south wall of this *vimana*, Lakshmi is surrounded by signs of water, the essence of auspiciousness. She holds two lotuses, flowers that grow in water and that embody the *mangalam* too. Her throne is a giant lotus resting on a lotus pad. Elephants pour pots of water over her as priests would do to a new king when anointing him. Regal-looking figures of Shiva and Uma sit enthroned beside her. Imagery of prosperity, blessing, protection, water, and kings on thrones converges around her on this wall.[78]

Jyeshtha's other name is Alakshmi, meaning *amangalam*. Twinning Lakshmi with Jyeshtha calls out the *mangalam* more explicitly than the pairing of Lakshmi and Durga did at monuments of the previous generation.[79] Durga can be about many things including war, or triumph, or rejecting gender binaries, whereas Jyeshtha is quite specifically Lakshmi's *amangalam* counterpart.

The Kailasanatha does also pair Lakshmi and Durga. This occurs at the twin entrances from Mahendra's courtyard into Rajasimha's courtyard (figs. 2.18, 2.19). This pairing, too, could evoke *mangalam* and *amangalam* categories, though perhaps less directly. Schmid has demonstrated that Pallava-period representations of Lakshmi and Durga articulate the dependence of the kingdom's prosperity upon the austerities of battlefield victory. "Prosperity" and "austerity" can translate the terms *mangalam* and *amangalam* well. Pallava culture understood that the goddess of austerity who rides the lion and the goddess of prosperity who is lustrated by elephants were one goddess, in other words. That unity expressed the understanding that prosperity relied on war, the auspicious on the inauspicious, which Pallava kings would have known well.[80]

Mangalam, amangalam, and their interconnectedness also capture old Tamil ideas about kingly power. Tamil scholar George L. Hart finds that the king in ancient Tamil poetry "does not seem to be in either an auspicious or an inauspicious state; rather, both conditions apply to him at once. Accordingly, the same poem shows him killing indiscriminately on the battlefield and then being generous, merciful, and careful of his kingdom's welfare. . . . He is the main figure who makes possible the creation of an ordered condition of the world, and he does this by tapping the disorder, chaos, and death endemic to it. . . . Because of the king, the rains come, enemies are kept at bay, and the fields are fertile."[81] The poems liken war to harvest. War could be auspicious and inauspicious,[82] and the ancient Tamil king needed to manage both.

FIGURE 2.18 The goddess Durga on her lion. This relief is carved in the southern passageway between the small courtyard and the large courtyard, seen from the large courtyard (the west).

FIGURE 2.19 Lakshmi being bathed by elephants. This relief is carved in the northern passageway between the small courtyard and the large courtyard, seen from the small courtyard (the east).

Right at the Kailasanatha, the inscription on Rajasimha's *vimana* praises Pallava kings for commanding what correspond to the *mangalam* and *amangalam* spheres, "secretly seducing women skilled in the arts" (appendix 2, v. 6) at one moment and at another being direct descendants of the ascetics par excellence, Drona and Ashvatthaman of the *Mahabharata* epic (appendix 2, v. 3). These two heroes moreover harbored within themselves the *amangalam* and *mangalam* in their ascetic excellence and in having been born into the *kshatriya* caste of kings and warriors.

Sculptures all over the temple complex glorify both modes and separate them into two distinct groups that stand back-to-back on *vimana*s and *mandapam*s and also face each other across the pathways that visitors must walk. Both protect and both are heroic. On one side is the skillful lover, reigning and dispensing grace from his seat of authority, Lakshmi by his side. On the other is the fearless ascetic dealing out death, his triumph assured.[83]

The sculptures that suggest complementarity by integrating the components of north- and south-facing figures—the crowned man and woman sharing a throne and the female teachers in the wilderness—also carry strong royal overtones. They have crowns and thrones, for starters. With the teachers in the wilderness are warriors in chariots and ascetics practicing yoga. Perhaps these female figures inspired meditation on those goals. The monument directs whatever these two motifs have to say toward people who could visit often and look in nooks and crannies.

The royal family, in other words, may have been its ideal audience. To its most frequent visitors, this monument could teach the complementarity of *mangalam* and *amangalam* forms of power. By presenting imagery of prosperity and imagery of austerity as two clear groups and also holding them in dialog with each other, the Kailasanatha presented a vision that could be useful and appealing to the monument's royal patrons. Each set of actions comprised ideal behavior for Pallava kings.

3

LOOKING EAST AND WEST, WITH AND WITHOUT SONS

Deities, Royalty, Family, and Lineage

THE MOTIF THAT APPEARS FAR MORE OFTEN THAN ANY OTHER IN THE
Kailasanatha temple complex is of a plump baby boy sitting between Shiva and Uma on
a wide bench (plate 18). Modern iconographers call this set of signs Shiva Somaskanda,
meaning Shiva with Uma and their son Skanda (*sa Uma Skanda*). Rajasimha's *vimana*
bears the site's oldest Somaskanda reliefs. The motif then multiplied in quantity and
scale with each layer of construction the Pallavas added to the temple complex, until
Somaskanda reliefs came to dominate the east-west axis of the expanding monument.

The motif was clearly fundamental to the temple's meaning, surely because of the
close identification, at this site and others, between Rajasimha's family and Shiva's family.[1] This monument's sculptures and inscriptions liken deities and royalty to each other
so often that flow between them emerges as a major theme of the site.[2] Interestingly,
these inscriptions compare reigning kings to Skanda, not to Shiva. It is the reigning king's
father whom they compare to Shiva, and their mothers to Uma.[3]

Concern for the continuity of the lineage is another dominant theme of the site,
and for good reason. With Rajasimha, or perhaps with a king Parameshvara reigning
briefly right after him, the line of kings that claimed direct descent from the Pallava
king Simhavishnuvarman (Siṃhaviṣṇuvarman) II ended.[4] Throughout the Kailasanatha,
Somaskanda groups sit in alternation with couples who look very like them except that
they are smaller, they have no baby, and the crowned male has two arms to Shiva's four.
These are the childless, royal, human couples mentioned in chapter 2. The insistent alternation between these couples and Somaskanda groups maps the idea of continuity and

transformation between fathers and sons, and between divinity and royalty. Inscriptions on four of the compound's *vimana*s reinforce the idea that the son continues his father's legacy. The last Pallava son named in these inscriptions weaves his ancestors together in his prayer. Architecture he sponsors conveys the same ideas through spatial devices.

Childless couples are among only five motifs at this monument that face north and south as well as east or west (see figs. 2.16, 2.17, 3.4, 3.5). All five motifs carried particularly regal valences for the Pallavas. The multidirectionality of these motifs may be another visual marker of royal significance, a reference to the *digvijaya*, the ruler who commands all directions.

Somaskandas Proliferate as the Temple Complex Expands

Shiva Somaskanda imagery lies at the heart of the Kailasanatha temple complex, spatially and figuratively. Inside each of the compound's ten surviving *linga* shrines is a relief of Shiva Somaskanda. This is a common arrangement in Pallava temples, though many Hindu temples have no figural sculptures inside their central sancta (*garbha griha*s).

Somaskandas manifest at this monument in all media—as paintings, poetic inscriptions, and architecture as well as sculpture. Twenty-nine sculptures and three frescoes survive. Consistent spatial patterns organize them. All but one of them face east or west. From Rajasimha's *vimana*, the compound's core, sculptures of Somaskanda spread east and west to blanket the short ends of Rajasimha's large courtyard, and beyond that to seed Mahendra's *vimana* and the small *linga* shrines of the compound's eastern façade.

All the eighth-century buildings in this complex bear Somaskanda images except the open *mandapam*. This could be more evidence that the open *mandapam* predates all the other structures surviving at this site, and thus predates the patrons who took a great interest in this motif.

The motif arrives on this site marked with royal implications. Two of them on Rajasimha's *vimana* bracket the west wall as small reliefs over the openings of attached shrines (plate 18; figs. 3.1, 3.15). Beneath the relief to the north end of that wall runs the section of the inscription that likens Rajasimha to Skanda (appendix 2, v. 5). Very large Somaskanda reliefs fill the shrines attached at the center of this *vimana*'s north wall and south wall. Shiva fills the back wall, facing east (fig. 3.2a and b). To his left, Uma and Skanda extend the group onto the south-facing wall. The fifth Somaskanda relief in this building is at the focal point of the entire temple complex, inside the central shrine itself, in the back wall looking east over the *linga*. Mahendra may also have been responsible for adding this relief to his father's *vimana*.

The motif appeared in each of the small temples of the eastern façade of the temple complex (fig. 3.3).[5] In most of them, particularly elegant versions of the type still fill the wall behind each *linga*. All face east, at the eastern edge of what remains of this temple complex. They are the first sculptures to greet anyone who would enter the monument now.

FIGURE 3.1 The shrine embedded at the north end of the west wall of Rajasimha's *vimana*. This is the only side of the building where the basement molding carries regal lions and elephants instead of rows of dancing dwarves. At this corner of the building, the inscription in the granite course declares the arrival of the patron in the Pallava lineage. Inside the shrine, Shiva Tripurantaka drives his chariot. Above the doorway sits Shiva Somaskanda attended by Vishnu and Brahma.

A   B

FIGURE 3.2 A Shiva Somaskanda group spreads across the back and right walls of the shrines embedded at the center of the south wall (A) and north wall (B) of Rajasimha's *vimana*. Vishnu and Brahma stand behind Shiva, on the right and left, respectively.

Somaskanda reliefs are most numerous on Rajasimha's *prakara*. They inhabit the eight cells along the west wall and the six cells along the east wall (see the diamond marks in figs. 3.4 and 3.5). These cells open directly onto the courtyard, so sculptures on the west wall open to the east and those on the east wall open to the west. They face each other across the great length of that courtyard. They also seal off the ends of that space with a wall of Somaskandas. People approaching either wall will see no other motif within its shrines.

Traces of the paint that once covered the entire monument show Somaskandas painted on the east-facing surfaces inside cells 23, 41, and 43 of this *prakara* (plate 19). Most of these cells have lost the frescoes that once lined their interior walls, so it is possible that many of them, too, once contained pictures of Somaskanda.[6] These cells are embedded in the south and north walls of the *prakara*, and like all the cells on those walls they open through their east sides instead of facing directly onto the courtyard.

One more Somaskanda relief on Rajasimha's *prakara* fills the surface of cell 51 and faces south onto the large courtyard (see fig. 2.13, no. 51). This is the only surviving

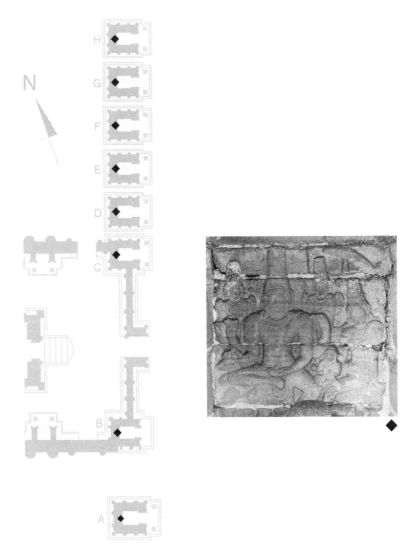

FIGURE 3.3 Shiva Somaskanda (Shiva with wife and son) reliefs (marked
by diamonds), set into each of the shrines that form the eastern façade of
the Kailasanatha temple complex. (Graphics by Mark R. Williams)

representation of Somaskanda at this temple complex to face south, but its location fits
logically into two other patterns organizing this monument's sculptures. There it joins a
cluster of reliefs and paintings facing east and south on that *prakara* that tell the story of
Skanda's life (fig. 3.6). By facing south on this side of the *prakara*, this Somaskanda also
joins a wall of reliefs in all of which Shiva sits with his wife (see fig. 2.13). In all seven of
these he sits to her right, hanging one leg pendant and folding the other across it or on
the bench. She sits close to him but a bit behind him, some part of her leaning into him.
These are their postures in this Somaskanda panel too.

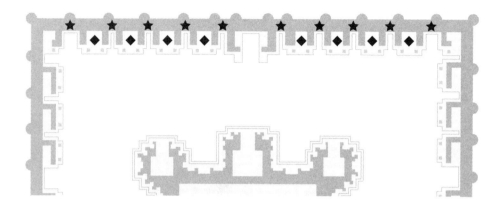

FIGURE 3.4 Sculptures on the west wall of Rajasimha's *prakara*. Relief carvings of Shiva with wife and son (Shiva Somaskanda; marked by diamonds) alternate regularly with relief carvings of a royal couple who have no baby (marked by stars). The divine couples with babies sit inside the temple-shaped cells. The royal couples without babies sit in between those cells. (Graphics by Mark R. Williams)

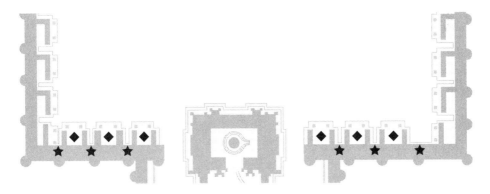

FIGURE 3.5 Sculptures on the east wall of Rajasimha's *prakara*. Relief carvings
of Shiva with wife and child (Shiva Somaskanda; marked by diamonds) alternate
regularly with relief carvings of a royal couple who have no baby (marked by stars).
The divine couples with babies sit inside the temple-shaped cells. The royal couples
without babies sit in between those cells. (Graphics by Mark R. Williams)

FIGURE 3.6 Diagram mapping the sculpted and painted imagery on Rajasimha's *prakara* that tells the story of Skanda. His parents sit enthroned with him as a baby (top; marked by diamonds) and without him (middle; marked by a star). Skanda as an adult marries (bottom; marked by a circle). (Graphics by Mark R. Williams)

The smaller *vimana* built by Rajasimha's son Mahendravarman III houses its own Somaskanda relief in its inner shrine.[7]

The Somaskanda groups that face east or west can receive people moving along the main axes set up by the compound's only entrances, which originally cut through the east and west *prakara* walls. People are already oriented toward multiple Somaskanda images as they enter these courtyards. Whether visitors approached from the east or the west, this motif waited to receive them inside various temple-shaped spaces, often behind a *linga*, framed as objects of worship.

Alternating with Royal Couples

Most Somaskanda groups at this monument occur in spatial alternation with regal, childless, human couples who otherwise look quite like them. The key differences between these royal and divine pairs are the presence or absence of the child and the number of arms on the adult male.

These juxtapositions occur in greatest concentration on the east and west ends of Rajasimha's *prakara*. A royal couple sits in each of the recesses flanking the temple-shaped niches that contain the Somaskanda groups (figs. 3.4, 3.5). In other words, between every childless couple that sits outside a small temple in these walls sits a nearly identical divine couple with their son. The alternation is steady and insistent. It fills the lengths of these two *prakara* walls. No other motifs intercede.

Somaskanda sculptures also pair off to face their childless counterparts in a chain that runs down the spine of the temple compound's long east-west axis. The Somaskanda figures and royal couples on the west wall of Rajasimha's *prakara* face two small Somaskanda panels on the west wall of Rajasimha's *vimana* (plate 18 and fig. 3.4). Inside that *vimana*, the Somaskanda group looks east. The east wall of Rajasimha's *prakara* throws the gaze of Somaskandas and royal couples back toward the west (fig. 3.5). Somaskandas inside Mahendra's *vimana* and inside the eight temples of the eastern façade carry the gaze eastward once more (fig. 3.3).

The most dramatic point in this chain is the very grand relief of a childless couple overlooking the courtyard from the back wall of Mahendra's *vimana* (see figs. 1.5, 3.7). They face the largest open court in the temple complex, and before the closed *mandapam* intervened, they looked through the open *mandapam* to see and be seen by the Somaskanda relief in the inner sanctum of Rajasimha's *vimana*. This is the monument's grandest instance of a childless couple exchanging gazes with a Somaskanda group.

Thick plaster applied in 2000 now obscures the remnants of ancient sculpture in that grand relief, leaving room to doubt whether this was originally a Somaskanda group. But earlier photos demonstrate that Skanda's little body did not sit between this couple before the relief's lower margins eroded in the twentieth century.[8] That erosion was significant in 1984 (fig. 3.8), but the remaining layers show the woman's arm where Somaskanda reliefs show the baby's head (compare figs. 3.3 and 3.4). A thin strip of

FIGURE 3.7 The large relief on the rear, west-facing surface of Mahendravarman III's *vimana*. A king and queen sit enthroned without a child, attended by three women bearing fly whisks (*cauri*). This photo from 2010 shows the plaster coating applied in 2000.

FIGURE 3.8 A photo taken in 1984 of the large relief on the rear, west-facing surface of Mahendravarman III's *vimana*. An older layer of plaster remains only on the upper third of the relief. Below, plaster and much of the sandstone below has eroded away. Nearly all of the stone has been lost from the place between the seated figures where a baby could have sat.

stone extending from the woman's hip is also visible, which is obscured by the baby in Somaskanda reliefs. Her knee rises higher than her hip as it does in the childless relief on Rajasimha's *prakara* (see fig. 2.13, no. 51).[9] A photo from 1920–21 confirms that there was no baby in the relief at all when all the figures were then intact (fig. 3.9). The queen's folded leg is fully visible. The adult male had only two arms instead of Shiva Somaskanda's four arms, moreover, and the attendants behind him are women, not Vishnu and Brahma who attend other Somaskanda groups at this monument (compare fig. 3.8 with fig. 3.2a and b.[10]

Yet this large sculpture of a childless, royal couple is not likely to have served as anything so literal as what people today may think of as a portrait.[11] The inscription below this relief does name Mahendra as the monument's patron (appendix 3), but inscriptions at this monument did not function as anything so literal as captions. The idiosyncrasies of a historical individual's appearance could drag the image into the mundanities of a particular moment instead of letting it signify king after king in an unending lineage, a story that other elements of the temple tell emphatically.

Repetition and Variation as Continuity and Transformation

This flow of strikingly similar royal and divine tableaux can express their shared identities and a potential for transformations between them.[12] Designers may have wanted viewers to hesitate in just the way scholars do now as to whether this grand couple was royal or divine. A baby boy would have prevented any such ambiguity, sealing the relief's meaning as Shiva Somaskanda. The absence of a baby, which the visual evidence suggests here, could keep that meaning open. This childless couple could evoke royalty, encompassing the identity of Mahendra and signaling beyond him to a long lineage through the line of royal couples sitting in the small cells on either side of this *vimana*, the cells of the east wall of Rajasimha's *prakara*.

This large relief is on the opposite side of the same wall that supports a Somaskanda inside Mahendra's *linga* shrine. In the spatial language of Hindu temple architecture and sculpture, addorsing can signify that the two items joined back-to-back are aspects of the same beings or principle. Here that arrangement sets up a figural and spatial analog of the trope in inscriptions comparing the king's family to Shiva's.[13]

Side-by-side alternation between couples who do and do not have babies, which fills the east and west walls of Rajasimha's *prakara*, can also signal continuity because it keeps repeating those two kinds of couples. That arrangement lets people look back and forth between these couples more easily than addorsing does, and that reveals the details that tilt one group toward the divine, the other toward the royal. Several of those differences mark hierarchy. The king has fewer arms than Shiva. The divine family sits inside a temple; the royal family sits outside.

Hierarchy is less relevant when it comes to explaining why deities have sons and royal couples do not. Babies can interject an element of time into this visual sequence, a

FIGURE 3.9 The west face of Mahendra's *vimana* in 1920–21, when the large relief was
fully intact. No figure of a baby is present in the relief. Photo taken by the Archaeological
Survey of India during its refurbishment of the monument. (Photo © The British
Library Board, reproduced by permission of the British Library/1008/14[1470D])

circumstance for transformation across difference. Couples without children are potential parents. Babies grow up to be kings. The insistent repetition of these contrasting
adjacencies, back-to-back, face-to-face, side by side, down the east-west axis, and along
the ends of Rajasimha's *prakara*, extends that time and multiplies those transformations
into a long series. Interspersing these groups repeatedly could show continuity across
difference, a process of becoming, a spectrum joining kings and gods, babies and adults,
sons and fathers.

The binary of Somaskandas and childless royal couples melts into such a spectrum
in the cluster of sculptures and paintings telling Skanda's story on the north wall of
Rajasimha's *prakara*. These delineate multiple stages in the transformations of couples
to parents and of Skanda to Shiva, as Charlotte Schmid has figured out. Scenes of Skanda's life sit between and link together sculptures of childless couples and Somaskandas.
Somaskanda groups are sculpted on the outer face of cell 51 and painted on the interior
walls of cells 25, 41, and 43 (fig. 3.6). Childless, royal couples sit in seven of the recesses
between cells along this wall (see fig. 2.17). The two types hybridize into variants that
assimilate their differences, a relief of Shiva and Parvati without their son on cell 45 and
another sculpture of a four-armed male with a wife but no son inside cell 44. In the midst
of this cluster, outside cell 43, is a wedding ceremony. A young man leads his bride by
the hand toward Brahma, a composition used elsewhere to show Shiva's marriage to
Parvati, but here the young man wears the double threads crossed over his chest that
mark representations of Skanda. On his head is either Shiva's pile of matted locks or the
conic Pallava crown. Royal parasols hover above him and his bride. This image marries
Skanda, Shiva, and Pallava royalty as well as these male and female figures. Shaiva iconography uses Skanda's and Murugan's older signs to provide a visual iconography for
Shiva's relatively new body.[14]

This spectrum encourages readings of the continuities. Childless men in royal couples along the east and west walls of Rajasimha's *prakara* could be married kings who
were once Skanda-like babies and who are on the path to becoming fathers and thus
like Shiva. Sons are like Skandas, Skandas become Shivas, babies become kings. These
transformations recur repeatedly in an endless lineage of sons becoming kings who like
Shiva beget sons. Childless couples could suggest procreative potential as yet unrealized,
the fecund energies manifest in the monument's south-facing sculptures translating onto
the east-west axis where they sit juxtaposed with Somaskanda groups whose chubby
sons could materialize prayers for sons.

Somaskanda Imagery in the Monument's Inscriptions

The foundation inscriptions on the *linga* shrines of the Kailasanatha temple complex
add dimension to these analogies between Pallava families and Shiva's family, and to the
vision of continuities between gods, kings, and future generations. These inscriptions

build directly upon each other in conversational layers across time, from Rajasimha to Pallava queens to Mahendravarman III. Each of those layers speaks consistently from the time of the son. They consistently cast the reigning kings as Skanda-like sons, not Shiva-like fathers, even though the alternating sculptures of royal and divine couples might seem to assimilate the king to Shiva. The evidence of these inscriptions indicates that Somaskanda imagery speaks in the voice of the son. So, too, a queen's inscription compares her to Parvati and locates her Shiva-like husband in the past. Kings of the moment are Skandas. Their fathers have become Shivas. Sons transform their once Skanda-like fathers into Shivas.

One phase of this process unfolds on Rajasimha's *vimana*. Verse 5 of the inscription there states that Rajasimha is like Skanda, just as his father was like Shiva (appendix 2). The following three verses compare Rajasimha to several deities but never to Shiva. They capture a sense of Rajasimha's transforming self too, from his Skanda-like birth to a fully accomplished king. All this unfolds within the parts of verses 5–8 that fit onto the west wall beneath the two, high Somaskanda reliefs.

The foundation inscription wrapping around Mahendra's *vimana* casts him as a new Skanda and transforms his formerly Skanda-like father into a Shiva (appendix 3). Verse 2 invites Shiva and Skanda to Mahendra's temple, stating that it is near Rajasimha's temple. The inscribed prayer thus seeks physical proximity between the royal son and his father and the divine son and father inside the temple. By styling the younger man as Skanda, this text recasts his father into a counterpart for Shiva, though that father's inscription had compared *him* to Skanda. The metaphor shifted its referents from one generation to the next. Agency lay, it seems, with the generation of the Skanda-like son to declare the father to be like Shiva.

The rest of Mahendra's inscription declares in all three of its intact verses that Mahendra is the son of Shiva-like Rajasimha.[15] The fourth may have done so too, but it is partially effaced. This inscription itself even reads like a direct descendent of the inscription on Rajasimha's *vimana*. It recapitulates specific imagery and names, even though his inscription is a prayer full of wishes (May Shiva do this and that), whereas the poem on Rajasimha's *vimana* is a panegyric to the king. Both texts invoke the ancient lineage Mahendra and his father share, citing descent from the line of Bharadvaja, praising Rajasimha's father for destroying Ranarasika and Pura, and crediting Rajasimha with bringing about the return of the utopic *krita* (*kṛta*) age.[16] The poems enact continuity through the act of citation, carrying the ancient lineage from primordial time, through Rajasimha, and right up to Mahendra.

Mahendra's inscription develops the Somaskanda analogy beyond what Rajasimha's does by bringing a goddess into the equation. Skanda's mother is absent from Rajasimha's inscription, but Mahendra's extends his invitation to include her: "May Isha [Shiva] *together with Uma* graciously take for his permanent dwelling this temple of Mahendreshvara" (italics mine). Mahendra's inscription expands the verbal tally of the divine family into an equivalent of the sculptural Somaskanda group.

One of the queens' inscriptions sets up this opportunity for Mahendra (appendix 4). The text around temple E praises a queen who was as beloved by her Shiva-like husband as Parvati (another name for Uma) was by Shiva himself. The second verse names her beloved as Narasimhavarman, which was the official name of Rajasimha.

Mahendra's *vimana* inscription picks up on the very terms of reference shared between this queen's and Rajasimha's foundation inscriptions, weaving together his female and male ancestors as children weave together their parents. Each point of connection involves members of Shiva's family, the Pallava family, or both. Rajasimha's inscription paid homage to his father, Parameshvara; a queen's inscription paid homage to Rajasimha as well as Parameshvara; and Mahendra's inscription acknowledged Rajasimha, Parameshvara, and the goddess to whom the poet compared that queen. Where Rajasimha's inscription invited Shiva to come live in his temple, and a queen's inscription compared her to Shiva's wife, Mahendra's inscription invited Shiva together with his wife to come live in his temple. Mahendra's inscription also joined Rajasimha's and this queen's inscriptions in singling out Shiva's aspect as the destroyer of Pura. The queen's inscription compares her husband to Shiva's aspect as "the Death of Death (or Time)" (Kalakala), and Mahendra's inscription cites Shiva "who puts an end to Time (or Death)." That aspect of Shiva may manifest in sculptural form on Rajasimha's *vimana*, just above the passage in the inscription describing Parameshvara (plate 13). Table 3.1 summarizes these points of overlap.

The great weight these inscriptions give to concerns about the continuity of their lineage invites readers to see a prayer for sons as one element in Somaskanda visual imagery. Somaskanda sculptures could speak in the voice of parents, perhaps, even when inscriptions speak in the voice of the son. In those sculptures, Shiva faces visitors directly, as if in conversation. He receives them into the monument. Skanda and Uma usually appear in three-quarter profile or full profile that can deflect attention. They turn toward Shiva, but not as fully as visitors do. They are intermediaries, rather, directing visitors' gaze toward him, inviting them into his presence. In this way, they are more of the visitor's time or space than he is.[17]

Somaskanda on an Architectural Scale

Under the patronage of the royal son Mahendravarman III, the Somaskanda theme rose to architectural dimensions,[18] a climax to the steady increase of Somaskanda imagery over the course of the monument's development. Architecturally as sculpturally, the diminutive son sits between his august parents. The same *linga* shrines that bear inscriptions analogizing their Pallava patrons to Shiva, Skanda, and Parvati build that architectural metaphor. Rajasimha's *vimana* corresponds to Shiva, Mahendra's *vimana* corresponds to Skanda, and the string of temples along the compound's eastern façade corresponds to Uma (fig. 3.10). These are also the *linga* shrines that hold Somaskanda reliefs in their inner sancta. The theme of that divine family permeates these buildings

TABLE 3.1. Shared references among the foundation inscriptions at the Kailasanatha temple complex

Concept	Rajasimha's *vimana*	Mahendra's *vimana*	Eastern façade temples built by Pallava queens
Skanda is to Shiva as the king is to the king's father	v. 5: "begotten from Ugradanda, . . . a pious prince took birth—like Subrahmanya Kumara Guha took birth from the supreme lord Ugradanda (i.e. Shiva)"	v. 2: "May the skin-robed (Shiva), surrounded by a troop led by Skanda, be present at this dwelling . . . constructed (near) the holy Rajasimhesh-vara by . . . Mahendra, the son of king Rajasimha"	
God and king as Ugradanda/ Parameshvara	v. 5: "begotten from Ugradanda, the supreme lord"		*Vimana* E, v. 1: "Of a husband . . . she was the most profoundly beloved darling, like the daugh-ter of the King of the Mountains was to Shiva (Parameshvara)" or "the dearly beloved wife of Parameshvara"
Calling out Shiva's aspect as destroyer of Pura	v. 5: "(King) Ugradanda, the supreme lord who crushed the city of Ranarasika, . . . the supreme lord Ugradanda (i.e. Shiva) who crushed the bellicose Pura"	v. 4: "Maheshvara, . . . who . . . has made an end of (the demon) Pura"	Temple E, v. 1: "Shiva (Parameshvara), he whose bow revealed its force in murdering Pura"
Rajasimha's father destroyed Ranarasika	v. 5: "(King) Ugradanda, the supreme lord who crushed the city of Ranarasika"	v. 2: "Rajasimha, who sprang from that Lokadi-tya whose valor dried up the army of Ranarasika"	
Rajasimha destroys his enemies	v. 5: "chief of the Pal-lavas, by whose spear/ power the multitude of the enemies has been destroyed"		Temple E, v. 2: "lord Narasimhavishnu, . . . who shattered the breast of his enemies"
Affiliation with Himalayas (Shiva's home)	v. 11: "(in this house) which robs Kailasa of its charm"		Temple E, v. 1: "she was . . . like the daughter of the King of the Moun-tains . . ."
Shiva as a crest-jewel or wearing a crest-jewel	v. 12: "May Rajasimha . . . Shivaculamani [who wears Shiva as a crest-jewel] . . ."		Temple G, v. 3: "this beautiful temple for the god who wears the moon as his diadem"
Descent from the line of Bharadvaja	v. 2: "the glorious trea-sure (or source) of the Pallava lineage who was named Bharadvaja"	v. 1: "Mahendra who sprang (from) the chief of the princes of the holy Bharadvaja-gotra"	

TABLE 3.1. (*continued*)

Concept	Rajasimha's *vimana*	Mahendra's *vimana*	Eastern façade temples built by Pallava queens
Rajasimha brings the return of the Krita age	v. 7: "in the Krita (age), a bodiless voice coming from the sky had been heard by kings . . . the king Shribhara again heard that voice"	v. 3: "Rajasimha, . . . creator of another Golden Age (*krita yuga*) thanks to his sinless virtues"	
Destroying Kala (Death/Time)	Sculpture of Shiva as Kalarimurti, defeating Death/Time	v. 4: "Maheshvara, . . . who puts an end to time"	Temple E, v. 1: "of a supreme lord whose unblemished glory spread with the name of Kalakala, she was the most profoundly beloved darling"

and links them together across scales, from tall towers through their large sculptures to the small letters on their basement moldings.

Through architecture as through inscriptions, Mahendra's contributions drew older buildings into new relationships. His *vimana*, like the foundation inscription on it, emphasizes the lineage he shares with Rajasimha and weaves together the king and queens who built before him. The shape of Mahendra's *vimana* expresses through the language of South Indian temple architecture its subordination to the Shiva temple his father built. In elevation, the modest height of Mahendra's shrine defers to Rajasimha's taller tower. So does its barrel-vaulted *shala* form (see fig. 1.4) in its rectangular plan. In architecture of the Tamil region, this is the shape of a temple gateway (*gopuram*), the function of which is to funnel attention toward shrines behind them. Entries on a *shala*'s short axis accommodate a path leading to a square-planned *vimana* at a courtyard's center. Thus that short axis through the *gopuram* confers emphasis on the direction it marks.

Often, as here, *shala*s are built in multiples surrounding a singular square *vimana*, their multiplicity and peripherality subordinating them further to that *vimana*. Mahendra's *vimana* is the largest of four *shala*s radiating out from Rajasimha's *vimana* on axis with its four walls. The other three *shala*s are the shrines to Vishnu and Brahma (see fig. 1.3c, nos. 5 and 6) and the now-sealed *gopuram* to the west (see figs. 1.4, 1.5). Architecture subordinates Vishnu and Brahma to Shiva just as many sculptural triads do throughout the temple complex. By way of his rectangular *vimana*, Mahendra joins Vishnu and Brahma as one more attendant framing the radiant tower that Rajasimha built for Shiva. Mahendra's *shala* is more exalted than their *shala*s, though. His is now the only one of these four *shala*s people can walk through to approach the central tower, the only one to

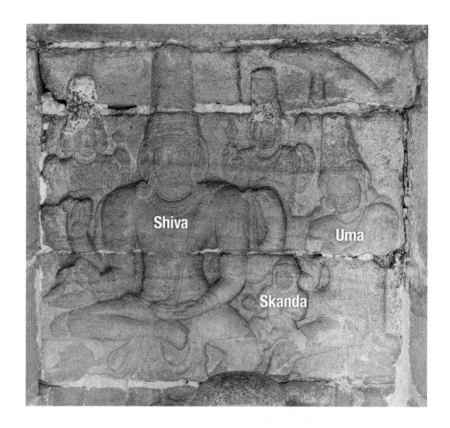

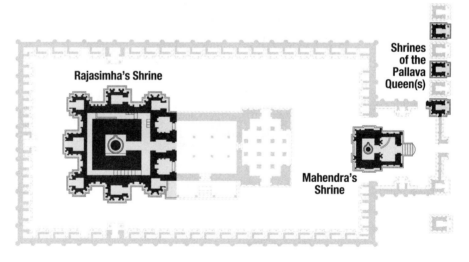

FIGURE 3.10 The layout of Rajasimha's *vimana*, Mahendra's *vimana*, and shrines built by Pallava queens (below) and a Shiva Somaskanda sculptural relief (above). Note that in the relief and the ground plan, the regal father is to the left, the queenly mother to the right, and the son interposed between them. (Graphics by Mark R. Williams)

act as a true *gopuram*. The shrines to Vishnu and Brahma were never permeable. Sealing up the west *gopuram* would give Mahendra's *vimana* that singularity.

These *shala*s are legible as aedicules replicating and emerging from the central tower like offspring from a parent, like the cosmos from its creator, as Adam Hardy's formulation invites us to do.[19] This *gopuram* form is that of a *vimana* that has been split down the center and the two halves pulled away from each other to admit a passageway.[20] Pyramidal towers in the *dravida* mode like Rajasimha's often have *shala* aedicules embedded at the central point of each tier (see fig. 1.2). We can think of this *prakara* as an entire balustrade ("necklace," or *hara*) like those that wrap around each tier of the tower, but as one that has launched outward and downward until it separates completely from the parent tower. Rajasimha's *prakara* at the Kailasanatha is legible as this kind of liberated balustrade, strung with four *shala*s that are offspring of Rajasimha's tower.

Mahendra's *vimana* further engages his father's construction by expanding on a central idea of Rajasimha's *prakara*, the alternation of Somaskandas and royal couples. The oversized couple on the back of Mahendra's *vimana* sits amid the string of alternating Somaskandas and childless couples on that *prakara*'s east wall (fig. 3.5). His shrine nestles there as a "jewel in the crown" of the large *prakara*.[21] The regal couple on his *vimana*'s exterior wall shines forth from the center of this crown, projecting the childless couple motif at an even greater scale onto the open courtyard, three smaller Somaskanda temples on either side of them, and those small temples in turn flanked by royal couples (see fig. 1.4). Face-to-face as well with the Somaskanda relief inside Rajasimha's *vimana*, this supersized king and queen on the outside of Mahendra's *vimana* slip into a crossroads in the flows of back-to-back and side-to-side alternations of royal and divine couples on the monument's earlier buildings. The new arrivals sharpen the comparison and heighten those flows, magnifying principles that were fundamental to the monument's previous layers, continuity and transformation from one generation to another and from divine to royal.

The multiple shrines of the compound's eastern façade can read as the Uma component of this metaphor because they participate in the same idioms as Mahendra's and Rajasimha's *vimana*s. They are small versions of the same kind of building as Rajasimha's *vimana*, east-facing pyramidal towers over cubic inner sancta, each containing a *linga* at its center and a Somaskanda relief on the wall behind that (see figs. 1.1, 3.3). These shrines shrink and multiply the basic elements of his shrine and carry them eastward to receive visitors who would approach the tall tower. Reliefs on their exteriors present many of the same forms of Shiva (see figs. 2.9, 2.10).

Inscriptions on three of these eight little buildings bear the same spatial relationship to the temple that Rajasimha's inscription bears to his *vimana*. They are cut into the single granite layer that crowns the basement moldings (see fig. 4.7). A single line of text begins on the front, east wall just north of the shrine door and then wraps, as the length of the inscription requires, counterclockwise onto the right (north) and then back (west) walls (see fig. 4.5).

Their content is parallel too (appendix 4). Elegant Sanskrit poetry filled with shared metaphors praises the act of erecting temples, identifies temples with those patrons, and praises patrons by name and through their family relations. A general pattern seems to have been in place, available to women as well as men in the Pallava household. The inscription on temple E shares imagery with Rajasimha's inscription. The inscription around temple C repeats the, albeit common, convention for naming the temple ("house," or *griha*) by fusing the names of Shiva and the patron. The inscription around temple G uses panegyric, celebrating the sweetness and beauty of queen Rangapataka and declaring her the sponsor of a temple.

These queenly inscriptions share precise terms of reference with Rajasimha's *vimana* inscription. The poet who composed the former knew the latter. Two verses claim for the royal individual being praised a close connection to king Parameshvara and analogize him to the same aspect of Shiva as the destroyer of Pura (table 3.1). They repeat the image of the crest-jewel, transposing it from Rajasimha's head (where Rajasimha's inscription locates it) to Shiva's head. In praising Rajasimha, they make special reference to his destruction of his enemies. They liken Shiva's world to the Pallavas' through the imagery of the Himalaya Mountains, comparing a queen to Parvati as the "Daughter of a Great King of Mountains" and Rajasimha's *vimana* to Mount Kailasa.

Mahendra's *vimana* "sits" between the *vimana* of his father, Rajasimha, and these little shrines inscribed with the praises of Pallava queens, replicating the spatial arrangement in which baby Skanda sits between his divine parents, Shiva to the left and Uma to the right (fig. 3.10). In architecture too, the fatherly element is on the left and the motherly element on the right for people who regard these buildings from the south, which is the side where a visitor would begin clockwise circumambulation.

Problems with the Open Mandapam *as an Architectural Feminine*

One could read the open *mandapam* as an architectural counterpart of the divine feminine in this temple complex, the Uma component of an architectural Somaskanda. After all, Francis and Schmid call this structure "*Mandapam* of the Goddesses," which describes it well.[22] The only males represented on this *mandapam* are two door guardians on its eastern façade (see fig. 1.5).[23] The largest goddess sculptures in the complex cover its walls. Enormous reliefs of Lakshmi and Saraswati fill the south walls. Durga and Jyeshtha fill the north. All four are larger than their counterparts on the *vimana*, and they are without any of the male companions who accompany them on the *vimana*s. None of these sculptures, however, actually represents Uma or Parvati, the gentle form of the goddess in Somaskanda groups.

From an architectural point of view, the open *mandapam* and Rajasimha's *vimana* could read as a complementary, gendered pair, especially when they were the only structures inside the big rectangular courtyard. The open *mandapam*'s single story and flat roof provide a low, horizontal counterpoint to the emphatic verticality of the multistoried, peaked *vimana* tower. The *mandapam's* hollow core and open forest of columns invert the dense masonry and solid walls of the *vimana*. Sculpture radiates from all four outer surfaces of the *vimana* but concentrates its deities on the north and south surfaces of the open *mandapam*. All four sides of the porous *mandapam* were originally open to crisscrossing flows of light, air, and visitors, whereas the *vimana's* single entry has always led to the dead-end of a tiny, dark chamber.

Mahendra's shrine could enter a dialog between these two older buildings. The large royal figures carved on the exterior of Mahendra's shrine would gaze through an architectural embodiment of the Goddess to one of Shiva, Rajasimha's *vimana*. The foundation inscription that runs beneath that relief meanwhile invites those two deities to come live inside (appendix 3, v. 3). Mahendra's *vimana* is centered along the same east-west axis that bisects Rajasimha's *vimana* and the open *mandapam*. The midway point between the two shrines' *linga*s falls along the rear wall of the open *mandapam* (fig. 3.11), possibly a sign of intentionality, though perhaps a less compelling one than a midpoint falling in the center of the open *mandapam*.

Biomorphism could gender these buildings. The open *mandapam* could present as a vessel or pathway for the seed of lineage to pass through, from the towering, closed *vimana* of the father to the smaller, closed *vimana* of the son. Mahendra's *prakara* offers somatic metaphors as it extends eastward, a canal framing the exiting fertilized seed from the enfolding *prakara*s. Biomorphism, though, can verge quickly into bio-essentialism, from presuming the divine feminine in anything shaped like female reproductive organs to reducing female identity to those organs alone.[24] Such formulations admittedly had flourished in South Asia for centuries before this temple was built, and about male body parts (*linga*) as much as female ones (*yoni*). Some later *shastra*s code the *mandapam* as female and the *vimana* as male, but sexualization of the Goddess was less likely to be that overt before the second millennium CE.[25]

On the whole, however, the open *mandapam* is less convincing than the shrines of the eastern façade as the female component of an architectural Somaskanda. The open *mandapam* would connect to Rajasimha's *vimana* (as Shiva) and Mahendra's *vimana* (as Skanda) through difference and biomorphism, whereas the queens' row of *linga* shrines would connect to those two large *vimana*s through shared literary, architectural, and sculptural references. Each of the little shrines in this row holds a Somaskanda behind its *linga*. The open *mandapam* contains neither. It is not a shrine. Reading any royal analogy into an architectural Somaskanda involving the open *mandapam* would depend on audiences to invent a link between Pallava queens and that building and Uma. Sculpture does not do that. The open *mandapam* bears no Sanskrit foundation inscription on its basement moldings to assert such a link either. Its later Tamil inscriptions include no comparisons between people and deities or buildings.[26] I prefer to identify women with goddesses only when sources close to those women ask people to do that, and that is just what the inscriptions on the little temples of the eastern façade ask people to think about the Pallava queens who built them.[27]

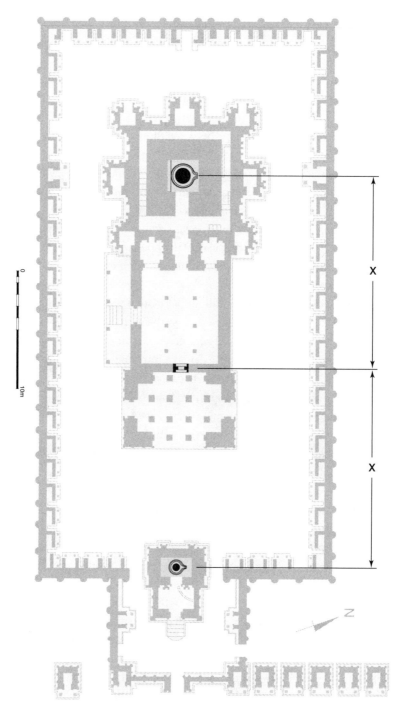

FIGURE 3.11 Ground plan of the Kailasanatha temple complex demonstrating
that the midpoint between the two *vimanas* falls along the back wall
of the open *mandapam*. (Graphics by Mark R. Williams)

Rereading Rajasimha's Prakara

Readers familiar with my previous work will note that I have revised my thinking about Rajasimha's *prakara* since 2005, when I proposed that as the embodiment of an architectural feminine encircling an architectural masculine of Rajasimha's *vimana*, much as a sculptural *yoni* base encircles a stone *linga* inside many Shiva temples.[28] Like those sculptures, these buildings had seemed to me to index female and male divinity by abstracting human genitalia on an architectural scale. Rajasimha's *prakara* shares enough features with later yogini temples from elsewhere in South Asia to have encouraged me to think that it, like them, might embody the *yoni* of the Goddess, a biomorphic reading indeed. I no longer regard the structural similarities with yogini temples as sufficient to characterize that *prakara* as an emblem of female divinity.[29] At most, this *prakara* might be a kind of precursor to yogini temples, a form that served rituals that were becoming more like those enabled later in yogini temples. But that *prakara* seems closer than those later temples do to the design of Buddhist monasteries, much as relief carvings of Shiva Dakshinamurti drew on the visual codes of the Buddha as a teacher in the wilderness.

The more recently formulated design for temples to house deities like Shiva also played a strong role in shaping the units or cells of this *prakara*. Each cell is structured like the region's seventh- and eighth-century temples built in the *dravida* mode.[30] Each cell rises on its own stack of horizontal basement moldings, including a granite one that bears inscriptions. A tiny pyramidal tower caps off each cell. The miniature scale of these cells and their arrangement in multiples strung together around an open-air courtyard would become fundamental to yogini temples built in the ninth to twelfth centuries, but these qualities were already legible in the eighth century as materializations of a divine, expanding presence through the cosmos. These small components of the *prakara* express Hardy's principles of aedicularity as they echo the even smaller components of Rajasimha's central tower and continue their process of replicating, emerging, and growing downward. The *prakara* can read as a string of aedicules that has grown so large, as it were, and flowed so far down the tower that is has broken loose from the central tower and spread outward across the open ground of the courtyard.

The basic regalia of a freestanding Hindu temple that clothes each of these aedicules marks them as temples to Shiva, not to yoginis.[31] It is he who sits inside, against the back wall, and refractions of him that populate the temples' outer surfaces. Reliefs inside every cell of this *prakara*'s east and west walls, and paintings in some of the cells along the north and south walls, show him sitting with Uma and Skanda just as he does inside and outside the *vimana*s of Rajasimha, Mahendra, and the queens (plate 19; figs. 3.1–3.3). Traces of paint in other cells of this *prakara* show other forms of Shiva. All the cells of the north and south walls may have held some version of his presence. Large tableaux of Shiva and other deities acting like or with Shiva still fill the outer walls of these cells, the walls that face onto the large courtyard (see figs. 2.12, 2.13).

Yogini goddesses do not occupy these micro-temples as they do the cells of yogini temples. Other fierce and charismatic goddesses fill some wide recesses and some of the outer walls of micro-temples on the south wall, but may not yet be yoginis. Most of their signs fit within the limits of other, older iconographic categories. Durga appears twice on this *prakara*, Jyeshtha appears once, the seven mother goddesses (*sapta matrika*) show up once as a group, and one of them recurs on her own (see fig. 2.14).

Of the figures of women in the wilderness and perhaps teaching yoginis, one appears on the outer wall of a cell where a deity would (see fig. 2.12, no. 7). The other sixteen sit *between* micro-temples of the north and south walls, on the short span of wall between the back of one micro-temple and the doorway into another (see figs. 2.16, 2.17). Instead of occupying the micro-temples themselves, they sit in view of someone else who might occupy those temples, the deity himself or someone who could look out from the cell's shadow and find their field of vision filled by the figures on this narrow slice of lighted surface just outside. These cells can accommodate a tall person, if seated.[32]

Sculpture suggests they did. On each of the tiny towers over cells 15–29 sits a figure of Shiva in the posture he takes when he meditates over Jalandhara (plate 14 and fig. 3.12). The outer faces of temple towers are also sites from which South Asian temples often signal the identity of a shrine's divine occupants. These figures of Shiva in meditation could mark these cells as micro-temples dedicated to his meditating aspect. That might also have encouraged people who identified with him—a king, for example, whose poets compared him to Shiva or Shiva's son—to follow Shiva in this practice and in the space conveniently provided.

In other words, the micro-temples of the *prakara*'s north and south walls have the shape of meditation cells and sculptural cues that could reinforce that usage. The way those cells fit together around a rectangular courtyard is similar to the layout of *viharas* (dwelling caves) at Buddhist monasteries.[33] At those *viharas* too, cells just big enough to hold one person open onto a common space. At the head of some *viharas* is a larger cell for a divinized master—often a sculpture of the teaching Buddha—who could share in the monks' meditations as well as lead, teach, host, and set an example for them. The cell form likens human and divine occupants and joins them as a band gathered in common purpose around a shared space. The micro-temples along the east and west walls of Rajasimha's *prakara* might correspond to the Buddha's larger cell. They, too, hold sculpture of the divine—Somaskanda reliefs—instead of space for a human body. They open directly onto the courtyard. Their positions along the east and west walls put them opposite the courtyard's entrances. *Vihara* cells that hold sculptures of the Buddha are often directly opposite the main entrance to the cave's central courtyard.[34]

The cells along the north and south walls of Rajasimha's *prakara* could have been simultaneously legible as micro-temples to Shiva and as meditation caves for individual ascetics. By painting rather than sculpting the divine image within, designers could house the divine inside the micro-temple but also leave enough space for a human being to sit inside the cell. People could have had the option to look in and take *darshan* (a mutual,

FIGURE 3.12 Shiva seated on
the roof of cell 16 along the south
wall of Rajasimha's *prakara*.

loving gaze) of the painted deities or to enter this tiny simulacrum of a mountain cave
and sit facing outward to be guided in meditation by yoginis and other divinities sculpted
just outside the cell's portal.

This confluence of choices might reflect a moment of transition or bilingualism, a
solution that simultaneously accommodated ritual action centered on the ascetic practitioner and ritual action centered on a divine image, much as Buddhist worship did. The
ascetic and the divine could be one. The *parivaralaya*, a circuit of small shrines outside
the circumambulatory path of a central shrine, of which several survive from the ninth
and tenth centuries in the central Tamil region, may capture a further step in that transition away from *vihara* modes and closer to spatial organizations one finds at yogini
temples across the rest of the subcontinent by the tenth or eleventh century. At some
temples with *parivaralaya* shrines too, a perimeter wall links them together, absorbing
the shrines' outer walls and enclosing the shrines within a hypaethral court, but the
individual units no longer function as meditation cells. Images of deities occupy the
little shrines, unambiguously directing visitors to stand at their thresholds, looking in.[35]

A Regal Ensemble Facing Many Directions

Compared to the dozens of different subjects that face only north or only south at the
Kailasanatha, only four face east or west. Those four repeat many times. Thirty-one
Shiva Somaskanda groups face east or west. The motif of the childless couple that often
alternates with them appears ten times facing east and six times facing west (figs. 3.4,

3.5) and at magnificent size on the back of Mahendra's *vimana* (fig. 3.7). The other two subjects to dominate the east and west walls are Shiva dancing with straight legs or folded ones (plates 9, 11 and figs. 3.13, 3.14) and Shiva catching Ganga in his hair (Gangadhara) (plate 10 and fig. 3.15). They are quite large in scale and prominently positioned, though they are fewer in number than the Somaskanda groups and childless couples.

Sculptures of all four of these subjects also face in at least one other direction. One Somaskanda image faces south from Rajasimha's *prakara* (see fig. 2.13, no. 51). Nine childless couples face north and seven face south from Rajasimha's *prakara* (see figs. 2.16, 2.17). Shiva Gangadhara faces north and south from that *prakara* and north from Rajasimha's *vimana* (fig. 3.15). Shiva as he dances faces north and south from that *prakara* and south from Rajasimha's *vimana* (see figs. 2.12, no. 25; 2.13, no. 38; 3.13; plate 7). Facing multiple directions could have been a sign in itself, one expressing the concept of the *digvijaya*, the ruler who has "mastered all the quarters" by subduing the rivals around him in every direction. This concept does seem to have mattered to the Pallavas, and to have been their motivation for building temples on all sides of their capital city.[36]

These multidirectional sculptures could be narrative counterparts to the rearing lions that face outward on every wall and corner of Rajasimha's *vimana*, projecting in all four directions and the diagonal angles in between. The regular geometries and fantastic horns of those lions signal some symbolic rather than naturalistic purpose (see figs. 1.2, 3.1).[37] They, too, could express the *digvijaya* concept, the leonine royal presence itself protecting against threats from any angle.[38] It is tempting to read these lions as especially suggestive of their *vimana*'s patron since his name, Rajasimha, meant "lion of kings" or "lion king." The cords hanging across their torsos also suggest protections. The cords are strung with bells like the cords of door guardian figures at other monuments in the region.

These four particular subjects, moreover, carried strong royal connotations. They emphasize qualities on which the success of the Pallavas rested: martial triumph, the guarantee and control of water, ascetic power, and continuous lineage tying the Pallavas to a glorious past and a promising future. Earlier sections of this chapter argue that Shiva Somaskandas and childless couples evoke the continuity of the Pallava lineage and the transformation of sons into fathers and gods into kings. The rest of this chapter describes the spatial dynamics and royal connotations of the Kailasanatha's sculptures of Shiva's dance and Shiva catching Ganga.

Shiva's Dance

The monument repeatedly pairs two versions of Shiva's dance, one on deeply bent knees (which some call Shiva Natesha) and one with straight or erect (*urdhva*) legs (which some call Shiva Urdhvatandava) (plates 9, 11). One pair of each cover the front, eastern face of Rajasimha's *vimana* (fig. 3.13), a fact now obscured by the interpolation of the closed *mandapam* that absorbs the two straight-legged dancing figures and excludes the two bent-legged dancers. Anyone in the eighth century approaching the *vimana* from the east initially saw Shiva's dance as *the* sculptural subject of Rajasimha's *vimana*. This *vimana*'s opposite, west wall reprises these dancing forms, one in each of the wide, deep recesses on that surface. That would have been the first wall people saw if they entered the courtyard through its western gateway.

Shiva again dances with flexed knees in a small frame above Shiva Bhikshatana on the south wall of Rajasimha's *vimana* (plate 7); facing south on Rajasimha's *prakara* (see fig. 2.13, no. 38); and from inside Mahendra's shrine and facing west from two temples on the compound's eastern edge (fig. 3.14). He dances with straight legs on the north face of another temple on the eastern facade and on the north-facing wall of the large *prakara* (see figs. 2.9b, no. III; 2.12, no. 25). Between them, these two dancing postures face all four directions several times over.

Dance becomes ubiquitous at the Kailasanatha if we take into account the many dance-like postures Shiva and other deities take up in scenes of battle. Shiva bends one leg deeply and extends the other in a long diagonal line when he destroys the elephant demon, banishes Garuda, duels with Arjuna, and cuts off Brahma's fifth head (see fig. 2.12, nos. 23, 18, 16, 15). So do Indra attacking Skanda and Narasimha destroying Hiranyakashipu (see fig. 2.12, nos. 11, 10). On a north-facing facet of Rajasimha's *vimana*, Devi performs her own dance, her arm thrown across her torso at the same angle as Shiva's but with her knees less deeply bent and her legs crossed at the ankles (see figs. 2.7, 3.13). Playing music may have shared with dance the special dispensation to face both north and south. Figures of Shiva playing the *vina* face north from Rajasimha's *vimana* and south from his *prakara* (see figs. 2.8 and 2.13, no. 48).

For the Pallavas and the Tamil kings before them, dance was closely associated with war and the king's triumph on the battlefield.[39] Gillet identifies the straight-legged *urdhvatandava* posture as an invention of the Pallava period, and she reads it as expressing royal triumph.[40] Precisely why Shiva dances this way remains a matter of conjecture.[41] The forceful verticality of his raised leg has led some to see this as a posture about virility, and perhaps the story in which Shiva defeats the Goddess in a dance contest by assuming a posture her modesty forbids her to take, but the Kailasanatha reliefs likely predate that story.[42] Gentle females do lean near these figures inside the niches of the *vimana*'s east wall, but not in the deep recess on the west wall where Shiva raises his leg. They also appear beside many other forms of Shiva. No strong narrative connection seems to bind them to Shiva's straight-legged dance. The one representation of a vigorously dancing goddess appears beside Shiva dancing on bent legs (see fig. 2.7).

The form of Shiva dancing on deeply bent knees appears to be unique to the Pallava period. Shiva balances on one foot and one knee, his legs deeply bent, perhaps as a display of dancing prowess (plate 9). This posture is less explosive than Urdhvatandava's, though still quite dramatic with the open placement of the legs and the arm thrown across the chest. The pose has a coiled energy to it that some read as violent. This subject may narrate the wild dance Shiva performs in the charnel ground, one of little consequence in Sanskrit sources but much referenced in Tamil ones. Elements that suggest this topic are the burning torch he waves and the goddess who could be watching the dance.[43] The musicians in a panel on the left and the three dwarves (*gana*s) dancing beneath make it clear that Shiva is dancing.

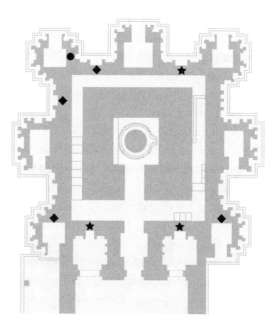

FIGURE 3.13 Diagram mapping the sculptures of Shiva's dance on Rajasimha's *vimana*. Note that the entire east surface is consumed by four embedded shrines holding two pairs of two forms of Shiva's dance. Urdhvatandava (marked with a star) directly flanks the entrance. Natesha (marked with a diamond) directly flanks the pair of Urdhvatandava reliefs. Each repeats on the west wall. Nearby is a dancing form of the Goddess (marked with a circle) (Graphics by Mark R. Williams)

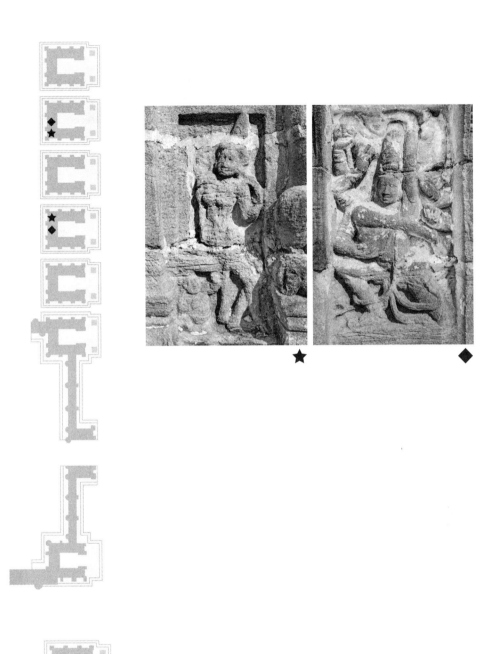

FIGURE 3.14 The Goddess looks on (marked with a star) as Shiva dances with flexed legs (marked with a diamond) on the west side of the shrines along the eastern façade of the Kailasanatha temple complex. (Graphics by Mark R. Williams)

Shiva Gangadhara (The Descent of the Ganga River)

The motif of Shiva holding out a lock of hair to catch Ganga as she falls from the heavens appears twice on Rajasimha's *vimana*, once facing west and once facing north, and twice on Rajasimha's *prakara*, once facing north and once facing south (fig. 3.15). The west-facing figure fills the largest of all the cellas embedded in this *vimana*'s outer shell, a cella stepped forward at the center of the west wall. It bulges toward the *prakara*'s west *gopuram*, an aggressive welcome to anyone who entered that way. Among the figures that face north from the *vimana*, it is exceptional for putting Shiva and his wife together in the frame, touching each other (plate 17). On the *prakara*, it is one of very few motifs to face both north and south.

The prominence of this motif and the exceptionality of its locations suggest that this motif mattered to the Pallavas. Written documents make this even more clear. Poets used it repeatedly as a metaphor for the dynasty. At Rajasimha's temple to Shiva in Panaimalai, an inscription on the granite basement molding reads: "From [the eponymous ancestor, Pallava himself], who had placed his foot on the purifying path, the honorable and great line of the Pallavas descended as the Ganga stream descends from the moon [in Shiva's hair]."[44] The copper plates from Kashakudi (Kaśākūḍi, Kacākūṭi) inscribed under the Pallava king Nandivarman II half a century later again stress purification in this comparison: "The Pallava lineage . . . is powerful like a partial incarnation of Vishnu and, purifying the entire universe, is clean like the descent of Ganga."[45] The Pallava lineage and Ganga's descent to earth are both purifying flows from heaven enriching the earth, both mediators between those realms, and both imports to the Tamil land from points north.[46] These parallels can imply that the Pallavas brought Ganga to the south, making the Ganga local as it were, a claim kings of medieval South Asia commonly staked.[47] Ganga's water pouring on Shiva's hair could also evoke the *abhisheka* bathing ceremony that initiated the transformation of a prince into a king. Gangadhara images put Shiva in the role of Pallava kings, in other words, and assimilate those kings toward Shiva.[48]

Siting the Kailasanatha's largest representation of Gangadhara at the center of the towered *vimana*'s west wall reinforces this motif's identification with the Pallavas by nesting it amid three representations of Shiva Somaskanda on the same building, another motif linking Pallavas to divine descent (fig. 3.15). Skanda and Ganga are parallel kingly analogs in this pairing. Both stories involve water too. Putting the stories together makes even more vivid the similarities between the flowing Ganga and the water pouring over royal princes, youthful Skandas, in the *abhisheka* ritual.[49] Rajasimha's *vimana* sets its largest Gangadhara tableau between the pair of Somaskanda reliefs at either end of this building and addorses it to the Somaskanda relief inside the *linga* shrine at the core of Rajasimha's *vimana*. Gangadhara and Somaskanda stand back-to-back like the twin faces of Roman god Janus, two manifestations of the same principle. The addition of Rajasimha's *prakara* added another eight Somaskanda reliefs to face this Gangadhara panel from its west wall (fig. 3.4).

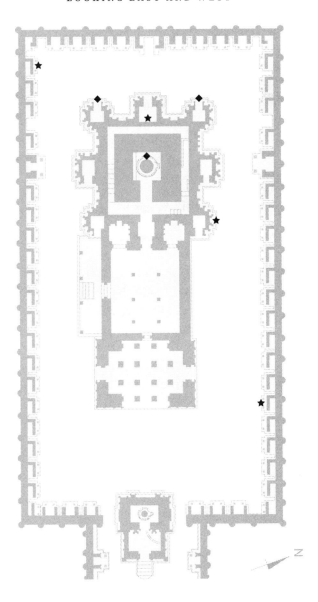

FIGURE 3.15 The locations (marked with a star) on Rajasimha's *vimana* and *prakara* of sculptures of Shiva catching the river goddess Ganga (Gangadhara). Note how the largest of these, on the west wall of Rajasimha's *vimana*, is embedded among sculptures of Shiva Somaskanda (marked with a diamond). (Graphics by Mark R. Williams)

As the only aspect of Shiva to face north as well as south on Rajasimha's *prakara*,[50] Gangadhara seems to offer some resolution between the categories that underpin the shared meanings of sculptures on those walls. The shapes, too, in these tableaux of Shiva Gangadhara suggest a resolution of these two categories. Shiva assumes an open and fiercely energized posture, a jagged silhouette that suits him to the gang facing north

123

in disciplined struggle (plates 13–16). He dominates the center of his rectangular frame (plates 10, 17). But he reaches out his lock of hair to catch—and thus touch—the river goddess. Ganga is visible only in plate 10 (above Shiva's outstretched lock of hair), but Shiva's spouse joins him in both frames. Uma presses against him, her posture closed and soft, her energy mild. Her body stays within the right half of the sculpted frame. Male and female are together, but in struggle. That struggle is heroic and regal, protecting the earth from drought and flood. Their struggle is all about water, the liquid essence of nurture and also lethal in excess.

The West Wall

The center of the west wall of Rajasimha's *vimana* seems to be a pivot point, a synthesis, a space of transition between those two kinds of energy that manifest facing north or south.[51] Shiva Gangadhara resolves north- and south-facing energies at the wall's center. In the shrines embedded at its two ends, Shiva Bhikshatana strolls seductively around from the south wall and Shiva rides his war chariot through from the north wall (plates 8, 12). All three tableaux repeat elsewhere in the monument, but they find their largest realizations on the west wall of Rajasimha's *vimana*.

This is also the wall that holds the densest concentration of signs that could evoke the Pallavas' regal identity. Between Shiva catching Ganga at the wall's center and two Shiva Somaskanda groups capping the wall's ends (fig. 3.15; plate 18), magnificent figures of Shiva's bellicose dancing command the wide and deep recesses (plates 9, 11). Other dancing deities and various musicians crowd around them, expanding the presence of dance to fill every surface of each recess. Below their feet run the first verses of the foundation inscription that praise the reigning king, Rajasimha (appendix 2, vv. 5–8). Further down, the basement frieze that carries gamboling dwarves on other walls carries here a pair of lions flanking an elephant on each of the three projecting facets of this wall (fig. 3.1). These seem to have been royal symbols for the Pallavas. Their inscriptions, including the verse at this *vimana*'s southwest corner, compare the king to a lion and his worthy but vanquished enemies to elephants (appendix 2, v. 11). Amid this blast of royal signifiers, the energies of the north and south walls converge, a spatial mapping of the idea that the Pallavas commanded and resolved those complementary energies.

Conclusions

The analogy so prevalent in Pallava inscriptions between their families and Shiva's family finds material expression in many sculptural, painted, and even architectural versions of Somaskanda at the Kailasanatha temple complex where Somaskanda also manifests in inscriptions praising Rajasimha, his son Mahendra, and the queen who was probably Rajasimha's mother. Patterns organizing the locations of Somaskanda sculptures and interspersing them with childless, royal couples add depth to that analogy. Juxtaposing the two groups in alternation displays their similarities. Embedding the two groups with other figures that recombine their differences plots out a spectrum of continuity between Skanda and Shiva, sons and fathers, gods and kings, baby Skandas and adult kings.

The motif begins with Rajasimha's contributions. Mahendra's contributions intensify it by addorsing the Somaskanda relief inside his shrine to a large relief of a royal couple looking out over the courtyard to the *vimana* built by his father. Mahendra's barrel-vaulted shrine and his inscription on it cast Rajasimha as his Shiva-like father, though Rajasimha's own inscriptions compare him to Skanda, and they recast the row of temples built by Pallava queens on the compound's eastern face into counterparts of Skanda's mother, Uma. Children transform their ancestors, perpetuating lineage through change and continuity.

Somaskanda figures and childless couples are on a very short list of iconographic subjects in this temple complex that face east or west. Shiva's furious dances and Shiva Gangadhara are the others on that list that were important enough to deserve repeating prominently through grand carvings. All four subjects carried strong royal connotations for the Pallavas. They promised mastery of war and water, disciplined struggle, and continuous lineage. Those bodies enacting regal qualities radiate regal presence, command, and protection outward in all directions from Rajasimha's *vimana*.

4

CIRCUMAMBULATING THIS WAY AND THAT
Complementarity Set in Motion

THE PRACTICE OF WALKING AROUND AN OBJECT OF DEVOTION IS SHARED among many traditions, among them Buddhist, Christian, Muslim, and Hindu. The direction of that circumambulation at Hindu temples should be clockwise, *pradakshina*, according to textbooks and Hindus today, who now find counterclockwise movement, *apradakshina*, distressing.[1] (The English term *clockwise* assumes a round clock face, but that such devices in modern times happen to mark the forward progress of time in the same direction as auspicious worship at Hindu temples may be simple coincidence.) Little wonder they find it so, since it is a form of prayer for release from this life and future lives. Fierce proscriptions against such movement are at least as old as the twelfth century.[2] The very existence of proscriptions, of course, signals that people once *did* move that way. Why else make rules against it? Material evidence, too, indicates counterclockwise movement. At Buddhist and Hindu monuments both older and younger than the Kailasanatha, sculptural sequences tell stories that lead visitors counterclockwise around the central object of worship.[3] Some scholars have wondered if the Kailasanatha, too, permitted visitors to move counterclockwise.[4] I believe it did, though I also believe that the people who designed the Kailasanatha temple complex already perceived counterclockwise movement to be transgressive and associated with esoteric practice.

Inscriptions and sculpture at this monument encourage movement in both directions equally and emphatically. The monument's cues to *pradakshina* and *apradakshina*, moreover, mirror each other in many cases: twinned cues point equally in opposite directions.

Their twinning suggests a balancing or counterposing of these two kinds of movement, as if to hold clockwise and counterclockwise circumambulation in dialog, or tension, or to express inversion. One half of the pair balances, flips, undoes, or complements the other. The monument frames clockwise and counterclockwise as reflections of each other, opposite yet identical, and equally accessible.

These paired movements could correspond to the two life modes the Pallavas aspired to, the warrior's asceticism that triumphs over threats, on the one hand, and, on the other, a fecund royal continuity embedded within the cycle of rebirth, persisting back through the ages as ancient lineage and forward in time through the birth of new sons. Poetry woven through with secret allusions and north-facing sculpture embodying ascetic energies cue counterclockwise movement. Declarative words and south-facing sculptures embodying nurturing energies cue clockwise movement. Thus these cues invite visitors to set in motion that pair of complementarities, and the temple complex as a whole offers visitors the chance to enact either kind of energy by walking clockwise or counterclockwise.[5] These twinned cues feature most intensely on the *vimana* and *prakara* built under Rajasimha.

Cues from Landscape and Architecture

Well before visitors enter the Kailasanatha, landscape and architecture give them twinned cues about how to move. From far away, the monument attracts visitors, but close up it holds them at a distance. The temple complex sat out on the western edge of the city in 1980, in what was then a small spur of urbanized settlement surrounded by open fields. A map drawn up then identifies a "burial ground" slightly to the north of the temple, further hinting at the marginality of that neighborhood.[6] In Pallava times, open spaces and water bodies intervened throughout the area understood as Kanchi city, but the city center was closer to the Kailasanatha than it is now.[7] The core of the Pallava city was the royal palace, with one temple marking each of the city's four sides. The Kailasanatha marked the west flank of that core, not far from the palace.[8] A photograph taken by the Archaeological Survey of India in 1900 (fig. 4.1) shows wide-open space to the east of the temple complex, capturing the sense of slight remoteness from the rest of the city that the monument has possessed since perhaps as early as the eleventh century.

The Kailasanatha was well suited to be a royal chapel. The showiest entryway and perhaps a large forecourt open directly toward that space to the east where the palace could have stood.[9] The monument's inscriptions, sculptural program, and grand scale have a royal character. The palace in turn could have shrouded the lower tiers of the temple complex from the town's view. Esoterica would be well sheltered there. The western entrance, facing the once open countryside beyond the town, could have welcomed visitors from the wider kingdom. The tall tower of Rajasimha's *vimana* is easier to see from a distance than it is from nearby. It could act as a beacon across the open fields toward the city center as well as across the flat alluvial plain that opens to the

FIGURE 4.1 Long view of the Kailasanatha temple complex from the east across
an open field. Photo taken by 1900, by the Archaeological Survey of India during
its survey and refurbishment of the monument. (Photo © The British Library
Board, reproduced by permission of the British Library/1008/5[291])

temple's west.[10] That beacon would have been all the more compelling for being the
tallest structure yet to have been built in the Tamil region.[11]

People crossing those spaces toward that beckoning tower would, however, come
up against a mighty enclosure wall that gives the temple complex the look of a fortress
(fig. 4.2).[12] The closer one gets, the more this wall screens out the view of the structures
within. The only carvings on this wall are rearing, horned, leonine creatures ridden by
men who wear cylindrical crowns. Entrances piercing the wall are tiny and difficult to
find. No tall *gopuram* signals their presence. The minute east *gopuram* is lower than
the temples beside it on the eastern façade and dwarfed by the flashier barrel vault of
Mahendra's *linga* shrine behind it (see fig. 1.1).

And yet this fortress-like wall was rather porous, opening to the west as well as to the
east; on the east, the transition between Mahendra's small courtyard and Rajasimha's
large one is doubled. A pair of identical doorways on either side of Mahendra's *vimana*
launch visitors leftward and clockwise or rightward and counterclockwise with equal

force (fig. 1.7). Either of that pair of doorways could be entry or exit. Nothing about their shape limits that choice.

Sculpture cues both directions of movement too. Some contradict the cues to clockwise movement that many later Hindu temples deploy. By the tenth century, figures of Ganesha, a personification of auspiciousness, often mark the start of a clockwise path, and Durga, an emblem of transcendence, often marks its finish. At the twin doors between the Kailasanatha's courtyards, clockwise movement instead takes people past Durga first and past Lakshmi, another personification of auspiciousness, as they exit (see figs. 2.11, nos. 12 and 5; 2.18; 2.19). Sculptures inside Rajasimha's *prakara* could encourage clockwise movement though. Ganesha sits in the southeast corner just to the left of the southern entry into that courtyard (on cell 4; see fig. 1.7), but also on the west wall of Rajasimha's vimana (see fig. 2.6). Chandesha (Caṇḍeśa or Caṇḍikeśvara), a deity who could mark the end of clockwise movement, sits in the northeast just before the northern exit (see fig. 2.13, no. 55).[13]

FIGURE 4.2 The outer surface of Rajasimha's *prakara*, relieved by regal men mounted on rearing leonine creatures (*yali*).

Inside these portals, east and west, buildings and the passageways around them offer equally compelling invitations to move left and right, clockwise and counterclockwise. Each *gopuram* pierces the center of a *prakara* wall. Architectural forms and the spaces around them are bilaterally symmetrical, their northern halves a mirror image of their southern halves (figs. 4.3, 4.4). The only exceptions are the closed *mandapam*, added centuries later, and the row of temples at the monument's eastern edge, which is likely to have been incompletely reconstructed (see fig. 1.7).

Inscriptions

The inscriptions carved onto these buildings in the eighth century also lead visitors who would read them, or listen to them being recited aloud, both clockwise and counter-clockwise. The inscription around the large *prakara* leads clockwise; the inscriptions on five *linga* shrines lead counterclockwise. These five each commence on the east side of their building and then, as their length demands, wind north, west, and south in a steady counterclockwise flow (fig. 4.5).

The tallest of these *linga* shrines is built and inscribed to the same king, Rajasimha, as the large *prakara*. In other words, bidirectionality of movement was part of the plan within that single, early phase of construction. The same people produced the monuments that use text to lead readers in opposite directions.

The content of the clockwise inscription on Rajasimha's *prakara* is grammatically very simple (appendix 1). The text is a long list of nouns, each in the nominative case. The words do not otherwise connect with or modify one another. Each is a laudatory title (*biruda*) for king Rajasimha, and each is a compound word made up of the basic, uninflected roots of several words, as all Sanskrit compounds are. The stack of basement moldings that fifty-five cells of this *prakara* present to the courtyard each carries several of these compound nouns (fig. 4.6). Most cells bear four *birudas*.[14]

On Rajasimha's *vimana*, the inscription is an elaborate poem of complex sentences and fully inflected terms (appendix 2). The poem communicates elliptically through metaphor, allusion, and coded imagery. This text tells, in collusion with the walls' sculptures, a secret story for initiates into esoteric practices (see chapter 5). The other *vimanas*' inscriptions, too, are elegant Sanskrit poems containing double entendres for insider audiences to savor (appendices 3 and 4). They contain metered, poetic verses with fully inflected verbs, nouns, and adjectives and sophisticated literary devices. All are panegyric, lauding members of the Pallava family. Metaphors compare them to Shiva and members of his family, whom they call out with flowery epithets, establishing in this indirect way the intimate linkages between the patrons of these *linga* shrines.

All of these inscriptions encourage movement. They are written in a single, continuous line, and they are long, breaking and resuming for the front of each cell on the *prakara* or bending around every corner of multifaceted *vimanas* (see fig. 3.1). Because Sanskrit is written from left to right, a line of text running around the concave, inside of

FIGURE 4.3 View down the length of the large courtyard,
on the south side of Rajasimha's *vimana*.

FIGURE 4.4 View down the length of the large courtyard,
on the north side of Rajasimha's *vimana*.

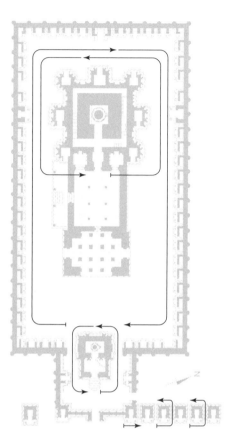

FIGURE 4.5 The directions in which inscriptions encircle buildings in the
Kailasanatha temple complex. (Graphics by Mark R. Williams)

the *prakara*, leads readers in a clockwise direction. A single line of text running around
the convex, outside of a structure like these *vimana*s, leads a visitor counterclockwise.

And these inscriptions ask to be looked at. The letters are ornamental, and they are
incised clear and deep into the one stone layer least likely to erode, the granite course
that cuts through several sandstone basement moldings (plate 7). The granite course is
now just below eye level on Rajasimha's *vimana* and at waist level or lower on shorter
ones (see figs. 1.4, 4.7). All may have been closer to eye level in the eighth century, when
the ground in this alluvial plane was several inches lower. The bright paint that once
covered this monument could have enhanced the letters' visibility.

Designers cared so much about legibility that they copied the verses four times on
each of the cells of Rajasimha's *prakara* (fig. 4.6). The oldest of the four juts forward on
the vertical facet of the octagonal molding.[15] A later copy is on the same molding's upper
facet, which is easier to read from a standing position, but which is also more vulnerable
to weathering. That text has been nearly obliterated. The third copy of the inscription

could have been cut to respond to that problem. That one is cut into the hard granite layer of stone. That text also reached out to another audience: it is written in the *nagari* (*nāgarī*) script used further north, whereas the rest are in a *grantha* script favored in the Tamil south. The fourth copy of this text is on the lowest molding in *nagari* letters so extravagantly florid that all of the words contained in the other copies above cannot fit below. Engravers could indulge in ornamental flourishes presumably because earlier copies provided the full set of laudatory epithets, and legibly.

Being seen is not the same as being understood, of course. Language probably limited who could read these inscriptions, as they are entirely in Sanskrit rather than Tamil, the language spoken locally for several centuries before the Pallavas entered the region. The Sanskrit medium does suggest that these inscriptions staked a claim for the Pallavas' northern identity and were more comprehensible to an elite audience, such as the royal family and their court.

Aurality likely widened the audience beyond those who could read Sanskrit to those who could understand it spoken, as long as they were granted access to the courtyards. The inscribed words could have been recited aloud, as South Indian inscriptions often were.[16] The *vimana* inscriptions are all poems written in metered verse, which implies an aural dimension. In the stone-lined chasms these inscriptions wind through, chanting would have resounded dramatically. Sound thus would likely have been another element encouraging visitors to clockwise and counterclockwise movement.

FIGURE 4.6 The four levels on Rajasimha's *prakara* at which inscriptions are carved. Numbering indicates the sequence in which they were likely cut. (Graphics by Mark R. Williams)

FIGURE 4.7 The inscription on Mahendra's *vimana* is cut into the granite course that runs at roughly the hip level of visitors. Mahendra's *vimana* is seen here from the west.

Sculptural Form

Sculptures could represent circumambulation by enacting it themselves. They could instantiate that sacred action as the spinning of prayer wheels voices prayers. By setting the example, figural sculptures could also inspire visitors to circumambulate, launching a visitor in the same direction by walking or driving or lunging. Sculpture can inspire movement through abstract forms, sculptural composition, posture, and gesture too. Figures at the Kailasanatha complex could inspire motion through all these devices, and in both clockwise and counterclockwise directions. The direction of their motion is consistent, moreover, with other markers of the *mangalam* and *amangalam. Mangalam* aspects of the divine look south and participate in compositions that gesture clockwise. Ascetic warriors look north and their shapes gesture counterclockwise.

This pattern is most emphatic on Rajasimha's *vimana*. At each end of the south wall, Shiva turns and gestures to a viewer's left as he flirts with women (plate 7). When Shiva on his throne faces forward, his wife turns left toward him (plate 3). The figure of Shiva as the teacher leads a visitor to the left by spiraling upward and to the left from one lowered foot through a frontal chest and a smiling face tilting onward (plate 4).

Seductive Bhikshatana provides a particularly clear instance of this intersection of clockwise movement and *mangalam* content. His figure on the south wall is moving to the left (plate 7). The visitor who follows him will round the southwest corner of the *vimana* and then encounter him again, still walking toward the left, this time inside one of the nine aedicules embedded in the *vimana*'s exterior walls (plate 8). Bhikshatana's presence pierces the stone wall, as it were, manifesting on the exterior wall and then the interior heart of the same aedicule. It is as if he walked through the stone wall, or as if his presence radiated through it, manifesting on the exterior as if the intervening wall were transparent (fig. 4.8a).

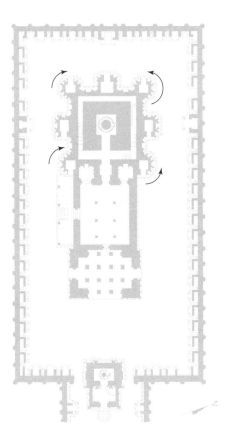

FIGURE 4.8A Diagram of vectors generated by the "wall-piercing" pairs of figures at the western corners or Rajasimha's *vimana*. Figures on the southwest corner move in a clockwise direction. Figures on the northwest corner move in a counterclockwise direction. (Graphics by Mark R. Williams)

This illusion of figures piercing the wall extends to a theatrical level the concept of sculptures circumambulating the temple. The sequence of figures also rewards visitors for following the example of movement implied by the divine body. Their reward is to perceive that theatrical illusion and thus gain a sense of being in the very space through which that deity himself moves. They may also experience a psychological connection to the deity through the sense of eerie familiarity that repetition can induce, that sense of having seen him somewhere before.[17]

FIGURE 4.8B Figures of Shiva moving clockwise (A, B) and counterclockwise (C, D) at the western corners of Rajasimha's *vimana*.

These sculptures of Bhikshatana encourage movement through abstract means as well. The twist of Shiva's torso pulls viewers gaze leftward, clockwise. Viewers see his hips as if they stood a little behind him, his waist as if they had pulled even with him, and his shoulders as if they had moved ahead of him. By collapsing these different perspectives into his single contour, the figure can imply visitors' clockwise movement around him. His body sets the example, rotating down and toward the left, his near leg forming a triangular vector pointing left and clockwise.

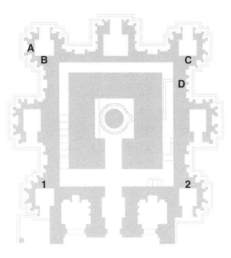

FIGURE 4.8C The locations of sculptures A–D in fig. 4.8a and of the two figures of Shiva dancing with deeply flexed legs (1, 2) on the east face of Rajasimha's *vimana*. The mirror images launch outward in opposite directions.

He looks back over his shoulder, making eye contact with those who stand at his feet, and he rewards them with a beautiful smile, perhaps encouraging them to follow him. That Bhikshatana is also making a hand gesture with his near arm reinforces the sense he means to communicate with those he sees. The object of his pointing gesture also encourages clockwise movement, especially for those who are not seeing the monument for the first time. The "meaning" of the upward gesture could have various significances, but the visuality of it takes the eye to the small figure above him, that of Shiva dancing on one knee (plate 7). That figure, too, will recur around this corner to the left, his feet pointing left as visitors' must if they are to rediscover him (plate 8).

The major figures of this *vimana*'s north wall, by contrast, tilt emphatically to a visitor's right as if they are all about to move west, or counterclockwise. Shiva as he catches Ganga, the Goddess with her lioness, and Shiva riding his chariot lunge deeply in that direction (plates 15–17). Beneath Shiva's symmetrical, meditating form, defeated Jaland-hara sprawls toward the right (plate 14). The crumpled figure, perhaps Kala, at the right end of that wall does much the same, while Shiva above him affirms the right-leaning diagonal with his trident and his splayed thighs (plate 13). Shiva charges into battle, the diagonal line of his torso, foremost arms, and raised leg pulling to the right (plate 15). His face turns in the same direction. Three rotund figures beneath Shiva's chariot charge in the same direction, waving weapons. Just outside the frame, a goddess "ahead of him" rides to the right on a rearing lion.

The wall-piercing dynamic unfolds on the north side, too, of this *vimana*, this time leading counterclockwise. If visitors move in the direction Shiva's chariot points, they round the northwest corner of the *vimana* and find the chariot rider reemerging through the back of the aedicule at that corner (plate 12). The illusion of wall piercing is especially powerful in this case. Shiva on his chariot in profile (on the north wall) has translated into a frontal view on the other side of the stone wall (in the west-facing cella), whereas Bhikshatana's languorous movement stays parallel to the relief plane.

These two wall-piercing pairs of Bhikshatana and Tripurantaka figures are themselves paired by their locations at opposite ends of the *vimana*'s west wall (fig. 4.8). The symmetry of this placement strikes me as a pairing device that sets in dialog, balance, and inversion these sculptures, their *mangalam* and *amangalam* energies, and the directions of movement they enact. Their location also involves visitors in that dialog. When people could still enter the courtyard through the west gateway, the first thing they would encounter was the *vimana* wall these wall-piercing pairs flank. From the right and the left, from the *vimana*'s southwest and northwest corners, these pairs of figures rotated toward those visitors, demonstrating two counterposed options for circumambulation.

The two options also confronted people approaching this *vimana* from the east, though through figures that pulled away instead of converging on them. At the south end of its east wall, Shiva turns to the left, or south, or clockwise, as he dances on bent legs (plate 1). At the north end of this wall, Shiva dances in the same position, but he turns in the opposite direction. These mirror images flank the two ends of the *vimana*'s eastern façade, which would have been easier to see before the insertion of the closed *mandapam* walled them off from each. On each side, Shiva lunges toward the outer end of the wall, a forceful set of diagonal lines carrying visitors' eyes and bodies outward and around the building (figs. 4.8c; 4.9).

Whether people approached from the east or west, the first *vimana* face they encountered offered them at either end a matched pair of sculptures heading in opposite directions. Wherever people began to circle the *vimana*, paired cues to *pradakshina* and *apradakshina* met them.

South-facing figures "cheat" clockwise (to borrow language from the theater), and north-facing ones cheat counterclockwise on the other *vimana*s of this temple complex too. In several cases, this occurs because they echo the compositions and orientations of sculptures on Rajasimha's *vimana*. Shiva the teacher still rotates his body clockwise on the south faces of temples B, C, G, and H of the monument's eastern façade (see fig. 2.10) and Mahendra's *vimana* (see fig. 2.11b, no. 4). Shiva charges counterclockwise as

FIGURE 4.9 Shiva dancing with deeply flexed legs (Natesha). This relief occupies the shrine embedded at the north end of the east wall of Rajasimha's *vimana*. Note that it is a mirror image of the figure of the same subject at the opposite end of this wall (plate 1).

he rides into battle and destroys the elephant demon on the north faces of temples D, E, and G (see fig. 2.9a) and Mahendra's *vimana* (see fig. 2.11b, no. 3). On these smaller buildings with fewer sculptures, though, no sculptural pairs seem to pierce these walls. The drama is less intense at that smaller scale.

Sculptures on Rajasimha's large *prakara* lean in both directions, but most show a pronounced cant to the right. Rather than articulating circumambulation in both directions, these emphasize clockwise movement. This is the same direction in which the *prakara*'s inscriptions track. In other words, figures circle the outer rim of the courtyard in the same direction words do: figures and words collude here about where they ask people to move. North-facing figures surge vigorously to the right, south-facing figures tilt calmly to the right (see figs. 2.12, 2.13). Only their level of energy varies from one side to the other. Bhikshatana actually flips from left to right the posture he takes on Rajasimha's *vimana* (compare plate 7 and fig. 2.13, no. 53) so as to continue moving clockwise on the *prakara*. The direction he walks seems not to have been governed by iconographic rules about his orientation.[18]

Cues to counterclockwise movement on Rajasimha's large *prakara* are infrequent. Few of the fifty-eight tableaux are dominated by left-leaning figures (see figs. 2.12, nos. 11, 14; 2.13, nos. 38, 41, 46). Ten other tableaux balance the vectors by showing two figures clashing from opposite directions (see fig. 2.12, nos. 11, 16, 18) or single figures facing outward in symmetrical postures (see figs. 2.12, no. 6; 2.13, nos. 45, 47, 49, 51, 52, 55).

Sculptural Narrative

Storytelling is surely important at the Kailasanatha. The dramatic sculptural groups read easily in a monoscenic narrative mode, meaning that each tableau can present a single episode or moment from a longer story.[19] That single moment can also function metonymically, a part evoking the whole story.

Some of these reliefs present scenes that are linked together in myth and sculptures elsewhere, raising the possibility that these separate frames may have read to visitors as linked in a narrative sequence. Frame sequencing is a common method for visual narrative in South Asia as well as elsewhere for getting people to move around monuments clockwise and counterclockwise. People have the option to follow a story's temporal sequence by moving around buildings and through space. The monument can make the single line of a story's narrative time bloom into three dimensions. "The one-dimensional, temporal sequence of historical narrative is, so to speak, 'draped' across the spatial dimensions of an actual historical site," as others have put it.[20]

If the sculptural tableaux of the Kailasanatha connect with each other in any narrative way, that way is not a simple, linear sequence. Narrativity here seems multiple and multidirectional, studded with echoes and changes in direction. Sequences wrap back and forth around buildings, letting narrative time fold back on itself or converge into points of stillness.

Where narrative sequences might exist, they lead visitors both clockwise and counterclockwise. Three distinct sculptural compositions could correspond to the clusters of stories now associated with the myth of the Pine Forest. Three others could correspond to the *Devi Mahatmya*. In each case, all three are visible from a single spot or a key episode repeats in several locations, enabling visitors moving in either direction to assemble legible sequences.

These two narrative sequences converge on the temple's grandest relief of Shiva catching Ganga in his hair, a narrative that Pallava culture used to frame the Pallavas as the purifying, heaven-sent Ganga and as Shiva-like ancestors receiving a mythic *abhisheka*. On the second story of the Vaikuntha Perumal temple across town, built some fifty years later, episodes from the *Harivamsha* (*Harivaṃśa*) unfurl in a clockwise direction and episodes from the *Ramayana* unfurl in a counterclockwise direction, and they converge on a scene of royal *abhisheka*.[21] Perhaps the Vaikuntha Perumal's convergence of sculptural narratives was a kind of response text, as it were, to the similar arrangement on the Kailasanatha. In any case, designers of both temples used narrative to encourage people to move clockwise and counterclockwise around the central *vimana* of the temple complex.[22]

The Myth of the Pine Forest

At the southwest corner of Rajasimha's *vimana*, three aspects of Shiva that also feature in the myth of the Pine Forest appear in sequence. The first frame people would see during clockwise circumambulation is Shiva Lingodbhava manifesting in a *linga*-shaped pillar; next is Bhikshatana charming the wives of the sages; then Shiva dances on one knee in a posture some call Natesha (plates 6–9). The building makes strong visual connections between Bhikshatana and Natesha. Both figure types are doubled and paired with each other on either side of that *vimana* corner.[23] On the south face, Natesha dances above Bhikshatana, who points in Natesha's direction (plate 7). On the west face, Bhikshatana walks directly toward the monument's grandest rendering of Natesha (plates 8–9). This kind of stutter around the corner reinforces the importance of those two episodes and of their proximity to each other.

In some versions of this story, the beautiful beggar seducing women in the Pine Forest *turns into* the wild dancer. A causative relationship between these two manifestations of Shiva emerges in literature by the time of the *Chidambaram Mahatmya* several centuries later: Shiva dances with the weapons hurled at him by sages he cuckolded in the Pine Forest.[24] Some verbal narratives lead into this sequence with Shiva Lingodbhava manifesting as a limitless pillar or *linga* of flaming light. Brahma lies, claiming to have found its summit; Shiva in annoyance cuts off his fifth head and must then wander in penance as Bhikshatana in the Pine Forest.[25] But the *Chidambaram Mahatmya* reverses the sequence, casting Lingodbhava's triumphant manifestation as the last episode of these three. After Shiva dances with items the sages hoped to destroy him with, the sages cut off Shiva's *linga*, which falls to the ground and becomes that infinite fiery pillar.[26]

My point is not to "find the text" that could explain the temple's arrangement of these sculptures but to discourage that very project by highlighting the flexibility of narrative in these texts. Resequencing, recasting, and inversion are common among the texts that record these stories. In the voices of different *purana* texts, the hero of one story becomes the goat of the next. A deity's moment of triumph in one *purana* becomes the prelude to his humiliation by another deity in a different *purana*. Episodes serve as chess pieces that multiple narrators variously move into new configurations with new victors. Verbal versions of these myths were too fluid to serve us as reliable "sources" for sculptural narrative, even if South Asian sculptors used verbal stories in that way, which seems unlikely. More likely is that sculptures and verbal texts too arose from a common world of lived experience in which people talked about those stories, saw and heard them performed by storytellers and dancers and puppets, and encountered them in textiles, wall paintings, and other ephemeral materials.

Sculptures at the Kailasanatha of these three episodes are similarly available for resequencing. People moving clockwise first encounter Lingodbhava (plate 6). Shiva's wandering appears next as episode 2, and his dancing form in the panel above can read as episode 3. Pausing at that corner, visitors can see all three reliefs at once and sequence them in any order they choose. They could do this to match up with differing versions of the story they already know or to inspire fresh retellings, new prayers. Sculpture could even have inspired brand-new stories, much as stone sculptures that supported the Buddha's fingers with struts gave rise to the concept of webbing as a distinguishing mark (*lakshana*) of the Universal Ruler.

In the reappearance of episode 2 inside the attached shrine and of episode 3 in the adjoining deep recess of the west wall, visitors might perceive Shiva as passing back and forth between states of walking and dancing during his years of penance. People moving counterclockwise could experience that oscillation just as readily. They would encounter Lingodbhava as the last moment in the sequence, the triumphant outcome of Shiva's seductions and the sages' failure to destroy him. Counterclockwise movement brings that sequence to conclusion in fiery transcendence. Clockwise sequencing spins the episodes more toward the *mangalam*, perhaps, ending the story on the south wall with Shiva's body and smile beside the women who cannot resist them or ending on the west wall with regal dance. In any case, repetitions and the chance to see all three episodes simultaneously make the sequence legible and flexible for visitors moving in either direction.

Seeing the Devi Mahatmya *on Rajasimha's* Vimana

Three reliefs on the north wall of Rajasimha's *vimana* draw on the same well of stories that produced the hymns of the *Devi Mahatmya*.[27] These reliefs exhibit the same strategies of visual narrative as the reliefs that could tell the myth of the Pine Forest.

The first of these three reliefs that visitors see when they walk clockwise shows a goddess chasing a demon. This small relief is above the scene of Shiva kicking the fanged creature who may be Kala (plate 13). The next shows Vishnu sleeping as his personified weapons confront the demons Madhu and Kaitabha (fig. 4.10). This is cut above the doorway to the east-facing cella at the center of the *vimana*'s north wall. The third of these reliefs is the glorious figure that fills that wall's eastern recess, the Goddess resting her foot on the shoulder of her lioness (plate 16). She could embody the transcendent form of the goddess praised in a non-narrative hymn of the *Devi Mahatmya*, the oldest known text to narrate the story of Durga's creation and Mahisha's destruction.

The first of these three reliefs shares the essence of two earlier Pallava reliefs of Durga fighting the buffalo demon Mahisha. One, in Mamallapuram, is about a century older than the Kailasanatha (see fig. 2.2); the other, in Saluvankuppam, is roughly contemporary with the Kailasanatha (see fig. 2.3). She is on foot at Kanchi, fully mounted on her lioness at Mamallapuram, and partway between those postures in Saluvankuppam. In all of them, the Goddess pursues a male warrior. She dominates the left half of the composition, and the retreating warrior cowers at the right. She speeds toward him, weapons flashing all around her, her head held high and her chest extended forward as if filled with energy (*tejas*). In the Kanchi and Mamallapuram reliefs, she holds her sword

FIGURE 4.10 Small relief tableau of Vishnu Anantashayin, Vishnu reclining on a bed formed by the coils of his snake Ananta, as his weapons at left take human form to defeat Madhu and Kaitabha at right. This relief is carved above the doorway to the cella at the center of the north side of Rajasimha's *vimana*. It overlooks the large relief of Durga standing with her lion (plate 16). (Photo by Emmanuel Francis)

across her right thigh at a shallow angle, a strong vector pointing toward him. This is the weapon with which, in the hymn, she decapitates him. He looks back over his shoulder at her as he lunges away, his right leg still a long way behind him. He is serious about leaving, but his chances of escape are fading. In the Kanchi relief, she has already pinned that leg with her trident. In the Saluvankuppam relief, her lioness pins his rear leg with one of her paws. In both, his advanced knee bends as he begins to collapse before her.

There is nothing bovine, admittedly, about the warrior she chases in the Kailasanatha panel (plate 13). He has neither the buffalo head nor the horns that mark Durga's antagonist in the other two reliefs. He has fangs, but so do many figures of Shiva at this temple. Pallava monuments anthropomorphize Mahisha figures more than monuments in central India do, giving them human bodies beneath their buffalo heads and presenting a moment when they still look to have a chance of surviving the battle.[28] It is possible, then, this figure represents Mahisha in a fully human form.

It is also possible the relief tells one of the several stories that appear in the *Devi Mahatmya* of Durga killing demons. In the hand she raises highest, she holds a wavy form that could read as an archer's bow, but her bow in other Pallava reliefs is a single curve, not a triple curve like this one, and she holds it perpendicular rather than parallel to the ground. Because this wavy form also touches her head, it could well be a long, ropey strand of her own hair or an intestine she tears out of the demon Shumbha and wraps in her hair before taking off to kill his brother Nishumbha.[29] The thick strand dances between her upraised hand and the damaged traces of a squashy shape on her head, perhaps the bloody mass of her hair and Shumbha's intestines, intertwined.

Possibly the distinction between the stories of Mahisha's and Nishumbha's demise had not split into two separate episodes for the designers of this relief. Phyllis Granoff concludes that they were still one story up through the fifth century and diverged not long before the tenth century. Even in the text as it now survives, the stories are still close. The demons commit the same offenses (jeering lustfully at the Goddess), and she kills them in the same way (with a trident to the chest and then decapitation).[30]

Another point of connection this relief shares with the *Devi Mahatmya* is the bell the Goddess holds at the left edge of the frame. In the hymns, Durga holds such a bell and it makes a deafening sound.[31]

The second relief on this wall (fig. 4.10) echoes another relief in Mamallapuram widely regarded as narrating a story in the *Devi Mahatmya*, this one of Madhu and Kaitabha's destruction while Vishnu sleeps (fig. 4.11).[32] In both reliefs, Vishnu reclines on the coils of the serpent Ananta as the snake's many heads rise in a protective frame around Vishnu's head. At the right edge of both compositions, two demons swagger, lunge right, and one looks over his shoulder at the sleeping god. Above Vishnu's supine body, small figures personifying his weapons fly toward the demons, sashes fluttering and arms raised. Near Vishnu's feet are respectful figures that may represent donors, a kneeling and bejeweled woman at Mamallapuram and two men at the Kailasanatha, one of whom wears a tall coiffure and holds a staff.

FIGURE 4.11 Large relief tableau of Vishnu Anantashayin. The deity reclines on a bed formed
by the coils of his snake Ananta, as his weapons take human form to defeat Madhu and Kaitabha.
South wall of the Mahishasuramardini cave temple, Mamallapuram, Tamilnadu. Seventh century.

The version of this story in the *Mahabharata* epic, which probably was codified in the
first centuries of the common era, has Vishnu's personified weapons dispatching these
demons while Vishnu sleeps. A few centuries later, the *Devi Mahatmya* interpolates the
Goddess into the story. She is the yogic sleep (Yoganidra) possessing Vishnu. She may
also be the exaggerated sense of power that causes the demons to swagger. It is she who
catalyzes the conflict and she who acts while Vishnu sleeps, dispatching the weapons to
confront Madhu and Kaitabha.[33] Here again, variants of a story demonstrate the fluidity
of narrative in verbal practice, the freedom to tell old stories in new ways.

Durga may be implied in these reliefs of Vishnu's sleep, in other words, even though
no figure in either one represents her. One reason to see her there, and to see the *Devi
Mahatmya* version in both of these compositions of Vishnu sleeping, is that each is
paired by format and location with a relief of another episode in that same collection of
hymns—the scene of Durga pursuing a fleeing male warrior. In Mamallapuram, these
stories actually face each other from the opposite sides of their rock-cut hall (see figs.
2.2, 4.11).[34] On the Kailasanatha, the reliefs narrating Vishnu's sleep and the Goddess's
pursuit of a demon are both diminutive, rectangular panels set high in the north wall just
below the projecting cornice and just above a large niche containing a figure of Shiva.
Composition pairs them too. In both scenes, demons slope off to the viewer's right,
maces dragging at an eighty-degree angle. Avengers pursuing them reach forward with

long arms extended at forty-five degrees, heads thrown back, and legs reaching wide in long strides. The slower diagonals of Vishnu's head and the Goddess's sword tilt down toward the demons.

Pairing is a deliberate device in the *Devi Mahatmya* hymns too, for articulating the supremacy of the Goddess. The close parallels between the *Devi Mahatmya*'s multiple stories of demon slaying bring out the underlying truths, the eternal characteristics, of the Goddess. Multiple narratives echo each other like facets in the jewel that is the devotional text, refracting the myriad forms of the Goddess throughout the cosmos.[35] Sculpture on Rajasimha's *vimana* could use this same device for the same effect.[36]

Those sculptures are close visual counterparts of two other principles of the *Devi Mahatmya* as well—the idea of a supreme goddess who transcends time and the idea that this goddess suffuses others who act in narrative time. Designers of this temple seem to have had direct access to the same thought modes those hymns manifest.

Book 4 of the *Devi Mahatmya* sums up all those multiples in a supreme and transcendent form of the Goddess. Rather than narrating a series of events, this part of the poem praises her glorious nature. She is the goddess who killed not just Mahisha but many demons, a goddess whose identity rises above the achievements of any single battle to embody the very principle of victory itself. She is beyond time. She is also beyond binaries.[37]

This transcendent aspect of the Goddess could inform the large sculpture of the Goddess with her lion (plate 16). As that hymn of praise repeats and magnifies elements from the narrative hymns in the other books of the *Devi Mahatmya*, this big relief repeats and enlarges elements of the smaller narrative relief of the Goddess chasing a warrior (plate 13). In both of these reliefs, the Goddess stands amid her explosion of weapon-bearing arms, leaning her ribs toward a viewer's right and her hips toward the left as she raises one knee higher than her hips. A forward arm holds aloft a curved object, a shield in the large relief, a strand of her hair or Shumbha's intestines in the small relief.[38]

The large relief lifts the Goddess out of a narrative mode and into an iconic one, as book 4 of the text does. Representational strategies parallel the textual strategies. She shifts from a three-quarter profile to nearly complete frontality, and she stops moving. The hipshot pose declares her stasis. She is resplendent in triumph or potentiality. She grows in stature and gets two more pairs of arms and extra weapons to go with them. She no longer holds the trident she wielded with such purpose. It now hovers behind her, "like a standard," its distinctive curved tines stark against one of the few bits of open space in the frame.[39] The hilt of her sword rises behind her shoulder and merges into the contour of the trident's shaft, fusing together the two weapons she uses to finish off all three of the demons who pursue her in the *Devi Mahatmya*, Mahisha, Shumbha, and Nishumbha. Mahisha was a motif to deploy elsewhere in the temple complex (see fig. 2.14), but he does not belong here. Those foes have vanished, and with them the signs that could constrain this relief to a particular story.[40] They persist only in the implements of their destruction, and those have fused together. Trident, sword, and Goddess move outside action and time. They become emblems that transcend particular actions even as they glow with the force of those actions. Those separate actions and moments collapse into synthesis. Repetition folds her narrative aspects into her anachronic truth. She is triumph itself.

This transcendent form of the Goddess echoes, summarizes, or suffuses other deities on Rajasimha's *vimana* much as the Goddess of the *Devi Mahatmya* energizes the rest of the cosmos. The goddesses on either side of Shiva Tripurantaka hold some of her many weapons (plate 15). The trident and the bow recur at the same angles. The lioness one goddess sits astride could be the same lioness the larger Goddess rests her foot on. Between them, these two lion-borne goddesses refract into separate frames, as it were, the Goddess at Saluvankuppam, who seems to stand beside and yet also ride the lion (see fig. 2.3). The lioness pops up once more as a grinning head over the shoulder of another small goddess on Rajasimha's *vimana*, this one to the right of the Goddess beside her lion (plate 16). A breast band (*kuchabandha*) further assimilates all three of these smaller goddesses to the larger figure.[41]

Male deities also repeat the pose and gestures of the transcendent Goddess along the north wall of this *vimana*. In the small panels of the upper register too, Shiva destroying the elephant demon repeats the pose of the raging Goddess pursuing a demon (plate 17). He leans along the same diagonal line. His arms fan out. The trident cuts a strong diagonal toward the lower right. Where Durga displays Shumbha's wriggling intestines, Shiva stretches the elephant's hide. Another way to read that sharing is that she permeates or summarizes them. She surpasses them too. None of them have as many arms or weapons as she does. Immanent and in her subtle form infusing Shiva's postures, Durga could embody and guarantee the victories he achieves. The energy to surge forward could come from her.

Circumambulation and the Devi Mahatmya

People moving clockwise around Rajasimha's *vimana* find themselves standing in the presence of the ten-armed Goddess after they have encountered smaller and narrative reliefs of martial goddesses and demon vanquishing. Then she can stand as the radiant climax encompassing and superseding both narrative themes, a personification of the very principle of triumph. The sculptures present a coherent sequence in the counterclockwise direction too. Visitors begin with the absolute truth in the supreme Goddess. Then they trace her into diverse refractions through which she manifests, visible and invisible, as she emanates through the world of form.

Moving either way takes visitors past reliefs in a sequence that does not match the sequence of their counterparts in the *Devi Mahatmya*, at least as those verses now survive (fig. 4.12a and b). The first episode people pass when they move clockwise corresponds to books 2–3 (Mahisha) or books 5–13 (Nishumbha) in the verbal text. The second episode they pass is now book 1 (Madhu-Kaitabha) of the hymns. They end with book 4 (the Transcendent Goddess). People moving counterclockwise begin with book 4 (the Transcendent Goddess), then move to book 1 (Madhu-Kaitabha), and last to books 2–3 (Mahisha) or books 5–13 (Nishumbha).

Such sequencing does not in itself prove that designers ignored verbal sources: they could have "followed" a text, just a different text. The order of these episodes could have varied among verbal versions of the *Devi Mahatmya*. But if the sequence in modern versions of the *Devi Mahatmya* did matter to eighth-century audiences, and if they looked for narrative links between panels, the building's scrambling of the order of episodes would work to accommodate people walking either clockwise or counterclockwise. Both directions align at least two episodes in the "correct" order. Inversions of a valued sequence could encourage people to double back, splicing together clockwise and counterclockwise movement within one individual's single experience of the monument.

The building also makes two episodes simultaneously visible, the ten-armed Goddess and the destruction of Madhu and Kaitabha. To look at the small narrative relief, people stand in the deep recess reigned over by the Goddess. She is over their left shoulder. This arrangement allows visitors to trace either sequence without moving a step. This would accommodate "readers" moving in either direction.

Simultaneous visibility and variable sequencing of episodes are also strategies that permit tableaux suggesting the myth of the Pine Forest to accommodate visitor movement in opposite directions. The "stutter" or reduplication of imagery also unfolds here, and again as repetition with variation, without variation, and with evocative elision. The two small narrative reliefs present repetition with variation (plate 13; fig. 4.10). Similar compositions align divine heroes challenging from the left and fleeing demons tilting to the right. The demons swap, and so does the shape of the deity (reclining Vishnu replaces charging Durga), but consistent compositional lines suggest that the actions are somehow similar. Repetition implies connection between these episodes or actions, and this bends time into something that need not be a straight line. The time embracing these two events could be cyclical, looping, or echoing, folding or wrapping back around to host the same necessary events of gods defeating demons. If this kind of time is a line, it is not a line that is just about "progress." Rather, it stresses duration, that which stays the same across time. That the Goddess kills demons throughout all time seems fundamental to the core meaning of the *Devi Mahatmya*, and the precise names of demons killed, their number, or the order in which they perish do not.

Repetition with variation recurs between the small relief of Durga chasing a warrior and the large relief of her with her lioness. Selective repetition permits recognition: the large figure's weapons and open, thrusting posture echo her appearance in her narrative scene, letting her read as the same goddess. Strategic omission of the demon can lift the transcendent Goddess out of the particulars of any one episode, permitting her to embody Victory as an anachronic principle. And yet the similarities of form her narrative self shares with her anachronic self suggest that they are not at odds with each other. Repetition assimilates the narrative with the anachronic. The two coexist on the same

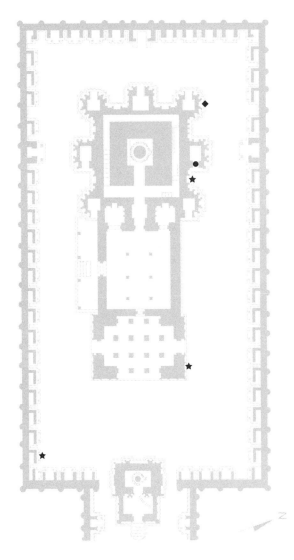

FIGURE 4.12A (*left*) Diagram mapping sculptural reliefs that correspond to hymns in the *Devi Mahatmya*. North-facing surfaces of Rajasimha's *vimana*, Rajasimha's *prakara*, and the open *mandapam*. (Graphics by Mark R. Williams)

FIGURE 4.12B (*clockwise from top left*) The Goddess pursues Mahisha or Nishumbha (marked by a diamond); Vishnu reclines while the Goddess as Yoganidra defeats Madhu and Kaitabha (marked with a circle); the Goddess as Triumph (marked by a star).

physical plane of this monument, and something of her same body carries over between them. Her narrative and anachronic mode may be complementary. Durga transcends Time and she acts in it. Her ability to embrace both ends of apparent polarities like this, or to resolve them into complementarity, is a frequent trope in the *Devi Mahatmya* hymns too.

She then reduplicates without variation and across the space of the large courtyard. Sculptures of the Goddess's anachronic form recur twice more in the temple complex (fig. 4.12a). One occupies the fifth cell of Rajasimha's *prakara*, the first surface to hold a large sculpture that people entering the courtyard see on their left when they walk clockwise, and the last they see on their right when they walk counterclockwise (see fig. 2.12, no. 5). Another figure of her, the largest in the temple complex, fills the east half of the open *mandapam*'s north wall (see fig. 1.3b, no. 3). This is the first figure visitors see on their left as they start moving counterclockwise through the courtyard, or on their right as they conclude a clockwise journey through that space. Visitors moving in either direction see her glorious form on Rajasimha's *vimana* second in the sequence. So people see this goddess at the beginning, middle, and end of their journey around this courtyard, no matter which direction they go. Her form does not change as they pass through that space. She is in their time and she endures outside or beyond it. The supreme Goddess who stands outside time is the alpha and omega, pervading time from its beginning to its end. In this way too, her repeated image can visualize the concept of transcending time.

The same concept is more simply presented at the opposite end of the same *vimana* wall, just beneath her narrative form (plate 13). Time, as Death, may be personified as the humanoid creature in the lower third of this sculptural niche.[42] Above him is the god Shiva. No other figures appear in the frame, though verbal narratives associated with this relief include the boy Markandeya, one of Shiva's devout followers, whom Shiva is rescuing from Death. In this sculpture, Time/Death is tangible, visible, embodied, and concrete. He interacts with deities and with human beings in the realm where humans live. He is overcome in a very physical way with a kick from Shiva.

Visitors moving clockwise would see him as soon as they rounded the *vimana*'s northwest corner. There he is surrounded by other figures that can evoke aspects of time. On either side of him are the large tableaux of Shiva riding his chariot and looking rather like the solar god Surya. Almost directly opposite him is the string of male figures that may represent the planets (see fig. 2.15). In the bodies of these figures, time can appear to circle and cut across the courtyard.

Pallava kings had plenty of reasons to hope to control Time and defeat Death. Like most kings of medieval Eurasia, they bore responsibility for defending the kingdom by leading armies into battle. They were also responsible for the continuity of the royal lineage. The life of the dynasty, as it were, was in their hands. Death does seem to have robbed Rajasimha of his heir, Mahendra III, who probably predeceased his father, precipitating a crisis in the continuity of the Pallava line.

Reducing this monument or this theme to the political, however, surely does not do either justice. A longing to transcend death is nearly universal to the human condition. Deities who can help with that appeal to people everywhere. This temple surely embodied for the Pallavas the powers to realize their dreams, truths that transcended any specific political moment.

Rather than simply telling stories, this temple complex seems to *use* stories to transmit such truths. Narrative could serve those goals through somatic engagement with those visitors in motion. Sequences that could link together these two clusters of three scenes on Rajasimha's *vimana* are elastic and nonlinear. These sculptural narratives accommodate movement clockwise and counterclockwise in pursuit of each story.

All the Way Around

Sequencing links the major sculptural tableaux all the way around Rajasimha's *vimana* into a meaningful sequence for visitors who travel that path counterclockwise. In that direction, they help to reveal esoteric knowledge. How that works is the subject of chapter 5.

A compelling through line is not as clear in the clockwise sequence, however. Perhaps that is just as it should be for movement suited to exoteric worship. Such movement should presumably reveal direct ideas that are widely held. As with many Shiva temples in South Asia, clockwise circumambulation around this *vimana* begins with auspicious images and ends with a figure of Durga. This building inflects that pattern by articulating the auspicious through Shiva loving, ruling, and teaching on the first wall visitors pass and by setting Durga at the head of an army of ascetic warriors in triumph at the close of a visitor's clockwise path. No words on the *vimana* itself add meaning to this clockwise experience. The Sanskrit inscription about Rajasimha (appendix 2) is visible beneath the sculptures, but visitors who walk clockwise encounter it backward, from its last words to its first, which renders it meaningless.

Others have suggested various threads that might connect this *vimana*'s sculptures in a meaningful sequence. Francis proposes the Gangadhara figure on the north side of this *vimana* is a summary of all the other manifestations on that wall, and an invitation to visitors to see all those other forms of Shiva they have just viewed as also being analogs for the king.[43] He reads in the *vimana*'s sculptural program as a whole Shiva's descent to the world of men. Certainly, the tower announces that it is Shiva's mountain, but the sculptural narratives zigzag between multiple and sometimes undefined venues rather than leading in a steady descent or ascent across the worlds of gods, humans, and *asura*s. In the first reliefs visible during clockwise circumambulation, Shiva might be on his mountain or in the world of humans when he relaxes with his consort or sits on a throne. He really mixes with the world of humans when he seduces the wives in the Pine Forest. Perhaps he is still on earth when he dances on the west wall, but he is back up on Kailasa when he catches the Ganga (at the center of the west wall). He is on earth to rescue Markandeya from Death (at the northeast corner), and in the world of the *asura*s to destroy their cities. The north wall ends the clockwise sequence with his return to Kailasa to catch the Ganga one more time.

Gillet ventures that the clockwise sequence might narrate Shiva's "evolution" from "savage" and human to kingly and divine.[44] This idea of savagery, though, runs counter to the admiration this monument and ancient Tamil literature express for kings and gods who dance powerfully on battlefields and in charnel grounds. That seems to demonstrate ideal kingly behavior just as much as sitting on thrones and protecting the earth from flood, drought, and demons do. Shiva is especially regal, moreover, on his throne, which visitors see at the start of their clockwise journey.

Partial clockwise flows of auspiciousness and movement do emerge among the southern sculptures of this building, as in the somatic cues offered by Shiva's energetic dance on the east wall, launching viewers around the *vimana*, and by Bhikshatana seeming to walk through the wall at the southwest corner (fig. 4.8b, A and B). In between, Lakshmi, the embodiment of the *mangalam*, is the first to come into view as a visitor rounds the projecting facet at the building's southeast corner. Other episodes from the myth of the Pine Forest on either side of Bhikshatana could lengthen a narrative chain around the southwest corner. That flow ends at the midpoint of the west wall, however, that pivot between the sculptural themes of the south and north walls. From that point on, visitors walking clockwise are swimming against the visual current, so to speak. Shiva is riding right at them around the northwest corner. Most of the warriors of the north wall and all of their victims and assistants also lunge toward those walkers, countering the direction of their progress.

Rajasimha's *prakara* provides more narrative coherence for clockwise movement as well as somatic and visual rewards. People do follow the direction of the inscribed text when they move clockwise. Its flat pronouncement of honorific titles for Rajasimha, one after another, would match the repetitive tone of the visual imagery on those walls, which presents one divine action after another very like it. This kind of time is cyclic, actions repeat from one cycle to the next, and what makes heroes good are the actions that emulate the actions of their worthy predecessors—the fundamental actions of dharmic kings.[45] The many terms of praise for the reigning king also offer repeated reassurances that the auspicious state of kings sitting on their thrones persists.

Cumulative Patterns

Though they may not tell a single, clear story when viewed in clockwise order, the stories and shapes of sculptures on Rajasimha's *vimana* follow patterns that align them with each other and with the principles of *mangalam* and *amangalam*. Those patterns converge with each other. Table 4.1 summarizes those convergences.

The myth of the Pine Forest and the *Devi Mahatmya* offer contrasting studies in sexual restraint, putting into paired, complementary motion the paired, complementary

TABLE 4.1. Converging patterns of imagery, themes, and movement on Rajasimha's *vimana*

Paired complementarities	
Exclusion	Access
Allusive, indirect inscription texts	Declarative inscription texts
Esoteric	Exoteric
Counterclockwise movement / *apradakshina*	Clockwise movement / *pradakshina*
Austere, protective figures facing north	Nurturing and governing figures facing south
Stories of inviolability, restraint	Stories of seduction, virility

principles of *mangalam* and *amangalam*. The Goddess successfully fends off demons who would rape her. The female protagonist remains inviolable. She faces north and slightly toward her left, which points her toward counterclockwise movement. Her narrative counterpart chases a warrior in the same direction. Shiva faces south and walks clockwise as he successfully seduces the wives of the sages. Shiva turns in the same direction as he dances on one knee. Virile gods move clockwise and inviolate goddesses move counterclockwise, toward the west wall and toward each other.

From the very first, movement toward and through the Kailasanatha temple complex is cued by paired complementarities. From far away the tall structure beckons; closer in, it repels like a fortress. Outside and inside the fortress, bilateral symmetries pull visitors left and right, and originally to the west and east entries. Inside, large sculptures set up paired and opposite cues to movement on the four corners of Rajasimha's *vimana*. Simple texts inscribed into the walls pull readers clockwise. So do sculpted stories about seduction and the gestures of figures who tell them. Elaborate, punning texts inscribed into stone walls pull readers counterclockwise, as do sculpted stories of inviolability and foiled rape.

Movement looks to have been a loaded choice. Circumambulatory movement around Rajasimha's *vimana* integrates consistently with the dialogic pairings of *mangalam* and *amangalam*, exoteric and esoteric. Walking clockwise looks like a form of prayer for fecundities, prosperity, and continuities of lineages from the past and into future generations. Walking counterclockwise looks like prayer seeking protective power, victory, restraint of the self and others, and the transcendence of time.

153

5

WORD-IMAGE TANGO

Telling Stories with Words and Sculptures

MANY STORIES UNFOLD AROUND RAJASIMHA'S *VIMANA*. A POEM INSCRIBED
into the building's stone foundation tells one of these, and sculptures on the walls above
that poem tell others. Together those inscribed and sculpted stories tell yet another story
when they work together, one that was available only to people initiated into a Tantric
form of knowledge.

The inscription is a Sanskrit poem praising the royal patron in the third person
(appendix 2). It does not place its words in the mouth of the king it praises. The text
is panegyric, the kind of praise a courtier might compose for a courtly audience or a
modern host might use to introduce a visiting speaker, rather than the fat-headed puffery
such remarks can sound like if uttered in the first person.[1] The text narrates this king's
descent from gods to sages to valiant Pallava kings; his many virtues; his rescuing the
world from the Age of Strife (*kali yuga*); and his building this temple for Shiva to dwell
in. The sculptures' stories about Shiva and goddesses add extra layers of metaphor to
the verbal narrative in the inscription, and those layers intensify the text's associations
between the Pallavas and divinities. The physical juxtaposition of these sculptures and
this inscription also tell a story neither medium could tell on its own. Together, they
perform a kind of alchemy to proclaim that the Pallavas carried into historical time the
acts the gods performed in the previous age according to the *purana* stories; to imply
that Rajasimha has brought about the return of the utopic age (*krita yuga*) and the start
of a new time cycle; and to demonstrate a convergence between Rajasimha and Shiva,
whom the king has convinced to abide in this *vimana*.

Here is the rare chance to study very early sculpted figures and a verbal text that were created to exist beside each other. Word and image were carved at the same time, on the same structure, executed under the patronage of one king. So here we know there *was* a text linked to this temple *and* we still have it, in its original place. They were a matched pair, created together and created to be seen together. Instead of wondering if verbal texts survive to "explain" the visual imagery on the monument, or debating which form of expression matters more or informs the other, we have the opportunity with Rajasimha's *vimana* to explore more ambitious questions about how narrative worked and how text and image related to each other.[2]

Words and images are fundamentally different things nonetheless, and the monument's designers and earliest visitors would surely have understood them that way. Each of these elements can tell stories, but they do not tell the same stories. The inscription is not a caption for the sculptures, nor do the sculptures illustrate the text. Neither is subordinate to the other, neither is less true or less clever, nor do words and images act in some kind of binary opposition to each other. Rather, they connect across elements of contrast. These images and words work closely together but not in unison, each picking out separate but coordinated rhythmic steps, while the two media periodically peel apart and wrap back together. A fitting metaphor is the Argentinean tango, though that is so distant in time and space from Rajasimha's *vimana*. A closer analogy could be twentieth-century Bharata Natyam, in which the dancer's feet and hands operate in quite separate registers. Her feet keep the rhythm, her hands tell stories upon and across that rhythm, her mouth frames a song, and the separately moving body parts come together in a whole that tells one story.

These meaningful connections between text and image would have been available only to those who could read the inscription or have it recited to them, who could comprehend the sculptures' narrative allusions, and who could experience the monument many times or in the company of someone who had done that. Rajasimha himself probably met all these qualifications. He was a likely target of these verbal and figural messages. They told his story back to him whenever he experienced the monument, reinforcing his identity, deeds, and goals. Surely he had access to teachers and perhaps fellow initiates into ways of knowing that the temple's material patterns embodied.[3] This chapter proposes what initiates could have learned from the *vimana*.

The physicality of the monument's inscription is important to examine first because the physical qualities of this inscription are less ambiguous and potentially more troubling than those of the *vimana*'s sculptures. The *vimana*'s sculptural and architectural forms can then reveal several narrative strategies: telling one story through others, iconicity, simulacra, and a chronogram. These strategies could have functioned as many threads tossed out for visitors to grasp, associations between words and images that worked less like metal staples and more like snowflakes piling up lightly all around until their presence filled the field of experience.

The Inscription

The Pallava inscriptions throughout this monument offer distinct cues that urge their readers to move (see chapter 4). The poem around Rajasimha's *vimana* offers those cues through especially strong and material forms. Its twelve verses run all around the building. The words cling like a tight film to every recess and projection of the molding's staggered planes, often bending in the middle of a syllable to wrap a ninety-degree angle (plate 7 and fig. 3.1). There is, moreover, nowhere one can stand to take in the inscription all at once. Reading the inscription on this *vimana* requires movement. The text unfolds gradually as one walks around the entire building. Because it is written as a single line of text around a convex form—the *vimana*—the only way to read it is by moving counterclockwise. The physical materials of this structure demand that form of movement of those who would read it. These verses begin and end, moreover, just where one might expect counterclockwise circumambulation to do so: they begin just to the right (north) side of the entrance into the inner sanctum (*garbha griha*) and end just before the deep niche adjacent to the left (south) side of that entrance (see fig. 4.5).[4]

And they do demand the gaze. The writing is visual and to that extent deserves the sustained gazing we may grant to images, but this script is especially flamboyant in its appeal to looking. Its elegant version of the Pallava *grantha* script can be tempting to follow for its physical beauty alone. The grand pillars and sweeping curves of its letters can draw and delight the eye (plate 7). This inscription is also very easy to see. It is cut into the vertical surface of a prominent granite course, a material difference that gave special longevity to the inscription. Harder and denser than sandstone, granite holds sharper, deeper cuts and maintains them better against wear. The granite course runs just below eye level.[5] Inscriptions on other *vimana*s in this complex run closer to the ground and require readers to bend down (see figs. 4.6, 4.7).

Sonically, too, this inscription could gather attention to itself. This inscription is a poem, written in metered verse (appendix 2). Aurality is inherent in its basic form. Inscriptions in medieval southern India were often recited out loud.[6] Six of the twelve verses are composed in Sragdhara (Sragdharā) meter, which can have a clashing sonorous quality when recited and seems meant to be shouted or sung loudly.[7] With twenty-one syllables per line, it is showy and grand, a difficult meter both to write and to follow.

Any recitation would have been further embellished by the presence of multiple meters within the poem. Rhythms shift from verse to verse, displaying the complex skills of the poet, offering a performer opportunities to dazzle, and making continual bids for any listener's attention. The pace of metric shifting accelerates as the poem progresses, opening with a five-verse stream of long-lined Sragdhara (vv. 1–5), following with a four-verse cluster of two in Shardulavikridita (Śārdūlavikrīḍita) meter (vv. 7 and 8) set between two in Prithvi (Pṛthvī) meter (vv. 6 and 9), and concluding with three single verses of entirely different meters. A long stream of one rhythm thus gives way gradually to shorter and increasingly staccato bursts.

Shifts in meter align with shifts in content. The stream of five Sragdhara verses asserts something of a spatial pattern, too, as it enfolds all of the north wall and spills symmetrically onto the east and west walls. It carries listeners and readers in stately progress along the north wall, narrating the Pallava lineage from Shiva to the birth of the reigning king. The pace accelerates with two shorter meters at the west wall when the subject shifts to the patron himself, and climaxes at the end—as Indian classical music performances now do—in a rush of three new meters when the patron and Shiva unite. The "sandwich" of two Shardulavikridita verses on the west wall between two Prithvi verses describes exclusively the reigning king's great deeds. The two verses in Shardulavikridita associate the king closely to Shiva; the two verses in Prithvi compare the king to a list of other male deities who play no more than minor roles in inscriptions, sculptures, and paintings throughout the monument. Verse 10 uses a different meter from all the rest to invite Shiva into this temple,[8] verse 11 returns to Sragdhara meter to praise this temple and Rajasimha, and verse 12 uses Anushtubh (Anuṣṭubh) meter for a benediction to that king. These metric shifts surely made the content of this inscription more exciting and meaningful for listeners.

Sculpture and Inscription in Dialog

The figures sculpted above the text on Rajasimha's *vimana* are tall, deeply cut, and dramatically posed (plates 1–17). They tower over the heads of people who are close enough to read the inscription. People who follow the text around the building can look up and down between the sculptures and inscription. The sculptures can draw people close to see their complex details, and then further back to take in the entirety of each grandly carved surface. The inscription reads best from somewhere in between those distances. The multiple, deeply staggered facets of each wall enhance that back-and-forth pattern of movement. Perhaps the paint that once highlighted the sculptures made sculpted forms more vivid from a distance.

Those sculptures and the words of the inscription that run beneath them work together to reward a visitor's counterclockwise movement around Rajasimha's *vimana*. The sculptures make sense in counterclockwise order but not as sequential moments in a single story. A more complex and indirect form of sequencing weaves these sculptures together with each other and through the inscription below them. That dynamic picks up at the very start of the inscription.

The Northeast Corner

Words and sculptures on this building converge around shared meanings even as they stake out quite separate paths of expression. Word and image separate at first. Along this northern half of the eastern wall, sculpture shows Shiva dancing, whereas the inscription mentions him only in reference to Ganga and then moves on to the topic of lineage. The inscription starts on the east wall just to the right, or north, of the entrance to the inner sanctum, invoking the river Ganga (which it calls "maṇḍa[kinī]") flowing through Shiva's hair.[9] As that verse runs northward from the sanctum door, it passes below a sculpture of Shiva, but this shows him dancing rather than catching Ganga in his hair. The sculpture there is a twin of the one just south of the sanctum door (plate 5). The sculpture in the next niche to the north also shows him dancing (see fig. 4.9). By the time visitors see this second sculpture of Shiva dancing, they are before the second verse of the inscription, which ignores the subjects of dance and of Shiva altogether and instead names the first three sages in the Pallava lineage. So far, the two media would seem to have nothing to do with each other.

As soon as visitors round the northeast corner of the *vimana*, though, they do come across a sculpture of Shiva catching Ganga in his hair as his wife clings to his side (fig. 5.1). The composition emphasizes his outstretched lock of hair, framing it with one long arm. That arm and that matted lock fill the entire upper right corner of the niche, where deep shadows isolate them in silhouette, divorced by the composition's midline from the rest of the god's body. Verse 2, meanwhile, has carried on around the *vimana*'s northeast corner. Just as it runs beneath this sculpture, it continues the king's lineage with "the glorious treasure of the Pallava family who was named Bharadvaja." This is where the inscription introduces the Pallava name.

At this corner of the *vimana*, we can begin to see just how sculpture and poem do come together on this monument and how they do not. Stacking a sculptural representation of Shiva catching Ganga above a verse about the same subject would create a situation one could call captioning or illustration. The monument does not do that. Instead, it staggers that verse and that sculpture around the building's northwest corner. The verse directly beneath the sculpture about Ganga instead anchors the lineage recitation in the name of the first Pallava, and this opens up the suggestive realm of metaphor, and a metaphor likely to have been widely legible given its popularity on other Pallava monuments. This sculpture about Ganga and this inscription about kings imply that the Pallava lineage is like the descent of Ganga, descending like her to purify the world, receiving like her favored treatment from the divine, and being central like her to the cosmos.[10] This frames the Pallavas, whereas simply telling and illustrating Ganga's fall would not. Text and image signify more profoundly by reaching across difference in superficial subject matter to a deeper level of purposeful metaphor. Neither medium on its own makes the connection so explicit. The monument's juxtaposition of them is what encourages a visitor to connect them, an involvement that can deepen the visitor's investment in the metaphoric possibilities he or she then discover.[11]

The North Wall

Here again, text and image diverge at the level of subject matter. There is no mistaking these inscriptions as simple captions for the sculptures above them, or the sculptures as

FIGURE 5.1 The relief of Shiva catching Ganga, set into the rich pattern that organizes the walls of Rajasimha's *vimana*. Below Shiva, a crouching elephant gazes out at visitors. Below him, the poetic inscription cut into the light-gray basement molding announces the name of the first Pallava king, Bharadvaja. Leonine creatures (*yali*) rear outward in all directions from octagonal pilasters. Friezes of plump dwarves (*gana*) close the top and bottom of the wall's composition.

mere illustrations of the verses below. Verses 3–5 run the length of the *vimana*'s north wall, tracing the flow of the Pallava lineage onward from Bharadvaja through many fathers and sons, telling of their brave deeds. These sculptures evoke stories about heroic battles deities won.[12]

The first large figure one passes after Gangadhara is the Goddess standing with one foot on the shoulder of a grinning lioness (plate 16). She holds a different weapon of war in each of her ten arms. The potbellied goddess Jyeshtha sits enthroned to her right, a slim goddess to her left. After passing this triad of self-possessed goddesses, a visitor walking counterclockwise encounters the cella attached to the center of the north wall. On the prominent wall facet at the center of this wall, Shiva sits in yogic meditation upon the *asura* king Jalandhara, whose shoulder absorbs the disc that will slice him in half (plate 14). In the next wall recess, Shiva as Tripurantaka rides into battle on a chariot piloted by Brahma (plate 15). A fierce goddess sits on either side of him. At the west end of the north wall, Shiva raises his foot over a fanged creature, probably Kala receiving Shiva's kick for attempting to claim Markandeya (plate 13).

Across these differences in specific content, text and image on the north wall emphasize a similar kind of action—struggles against dangerous forces over which deities and Pallava forebears ultimately exert control. Pallava kings "excelling in the knowledge of weapons, resolute, mighty, full of wisdom and discipline" (v. 4) had "deprived the kings of their firmness and pride . . . [and] crushed the city of Ranarasika" (v. 5). They were "pious, destroyers of . . . arrogance . . . forcibly conquering desire and other enemies within" (v. 4). In the wall's grand recesses, Durga by her lioness and Shiva in his chariot heft weapons with confidence. Triumph looks to be imminent or achieved. That mood persists on the prominent panels at either end of the wall, where Shiva fights off Ganga's deluge and crushes Death himself. Inside the shrine attached to the center of this wall, Shiva dominates Vishnu and Brahma as a king does his attendants (see fig. 3.2a and b), and on the outer side of that wall, he wanders as a renunciant, having fully mastered desire and self (see fig. 1.1). At the wall's center, he displays mastery over himself as well as Jalandhara.

A grand commonality of purpose joins the deities in these sculptures to the kings in this inscription. Deities and men alike battle forces that must be defeated. Again, I suspect metaphor. Shared purpose, action, and success liken these royal ancestors to triumphant gods and goddesses and contextualize the achievements of Pallava forebears on a cosmic scale. Frequent repetitions of the same basic posture at the center of similar compositions can also imply that these figures are locked in what is fundamentally the same struggle. It is as if abstract visual elements have piled these quite separate narratives against each other in a series of translucent layers. Each is visible individually and through the others, displaying their commonalities amid their many small differences, a nice example of expressive capacities peculiar to visual narrative.

Against these convergences between word and image, an asymmetry emerges around the feminine. In sculpture, goddesses are warriors at least as fierce as the gods, but females enter the inscription only as objects of male control, seduction, and protection—the

PLATE 1 Shiva dancing with deeply flexed legs (Natesha). This relief occupies the shrine embedded at the south end of the east wall of Rajasimha's *vimana*. (Photo by Emmanuel Francis)

PLATE 2 (*facing page*) Shiva touches Uma's chin tenderly. A heavy coat of
lime plaster from perhaps the nineteenth century still coats this relief.
East end of the south wall, Rajasimha's *vimana*. (Photo by Emmanuel Francis)

PLATE 3 (*above*) Shiva and Uma sit enthroned (Shiva Umasahita). Lakshmi/Shri
is on the left in the posture adopted by kings during their consecration
(*abhisheka*). Two elephants pour water over her head. The goddess on the right
may be Saraswati. East recess in the south wall, Rajasimha's *vimana*.

PLATE 4 Shiva Dakshinamurti sits under a tree. Deer, lions, sages, and a royal male figure surround him. Central projection on the south wall, Rajasimha's *vimana*. (Photo by Emmanuel Francis)

PLATE 5 Shiva dancing with extended legs (Urdhvatandava). This relief occupies the shrine embedded just to the south of the single entrance into Rajasimha's *vimana*. A figure in exactly the same pose—not a mirror image—occupies the shrine embedded just to the north of that entrance. Both shrines are now sealed by wooden doors that the temple caretakers seldom open.

PLATE 6 Shiva Lingodbhava manifests in an endless pillar of flame. Below is visible the crown and hand of Vishnu as he takes the form of a boar to dig down to find the pillar's root. At the upper left, Brahma flies up to find the pillar's top. At the lower left and right, Brahma and Vishnu in human form salute Shiva. At the upper right, the moon and sun salute Shiva. West recess in the south wall, Rajasimha's *vimana*.

PLATE 7 Shiva Bhikshatana with two wives of the sages in the Pine Forest. At the upper left, a sage waves his fist in anger. Above, a small panel presents Shiva dancing with his legs deeply bent (Natesha). West end of the south wall, Rajasimha's *vimana*.

PLATE 8 Shiva Bhikshatana carved inside the shrine embedded
at the south end of the west wall of Rajasimha's *vimana*.

PLATE 9 (*facing page*) Shiva dancing with his legs deeply bent
(Natesha). South recess in the west wall, Rajasimha's *vimana*.

PLATE 10 (*above*) Shiva catching the river goddess Ganga in his hair
(Shiva Gangadhara). Other deities attending this miracle line the
three walls inside this especially large shrine embedded at the center
of the west wall, Rajasimha's *vimana*.

PLATE 11 Shiva dancing with both legs extended,
and the toes of his right foot pointing to the sky
(Urdhvatandava). North recess in the west wall,
Rajasimha's *vimana*. (Photo by Emmanuel Francis)

PLATE 12 Shiva driving a horse-drawn chariot
into battle (Tripurantaka). This tableau occupies
the interior of the northernmost shrine embedded
in the west wall of Rajasimha's *vimana*.

PLATE 13 (*facing page*) Shiva kicking or leaping on a crumpled enemy, perhaps Kala/
Time (Kalarimurti). Above, a goddess armed with a spear and trident pursues a fleeing
warrior who has dropped his mace. West end of the north wall, Rajasimha's *vimana*.

PLATE 14 (*above*) Shiva sits deep in yogic meditation above the king
Jalandhara, who is dying from the disc (*chakra*) Shiva has thrown into his
shoulder. Central projection on the north wall, Rajasimha's *vimana*.

PLATE 15 (*top*) Shiva riding into battle on a chariot with Brahma (Tripurantaka). Three armed dwarves (*gana*s) below and a lion-riding goddess at the right charge in the same direction. At left, a heavily armed goddess sits enthroned, her face haloed by a mass of unbraided hair. West recess in the north wall, Rajasimha's *vimana*.

PLATE 16 (*bottom*) The Goddess stands at her ease, one foot on the shoulder of her lioness. To the right, an enthroned goddess poses regally with one leg resting on her bench as a deer and a lion peer over her shoulders. To the left, Jyeshtha sits in the posture adopted by Lakshmi and by kings being consecrated (*abhisheka*). Her adult children look over her shoulders. East recess in the north wall, Rajasimha's *vimana*.

PLATE 17 Shiva catches the heavenly Ganga River in his hair as she falls from the heavens (Gangadhara). Parvati leans into him, perhaps helping to bear the strain of his task. East end of the north wall, Rajasimha's *vimana*. The small panel above portrays Shiva conquering the elephant demon (Gajasamharamurti).

PLATE 18 Relief carving of Shiva Somaskanda, Shiva seated with Uma and their baby
Skanda between them. Rearing leonine creatures (*yali*) frame the back of their wide
throne. Brahma and Vishnu stand behind Shiva, saluting him. A female attendant
stands behind Uma. An umbrella shelters Skanda and Uma. This relief is high on the
north end of the west of Rajasimha's *vimana*, above the doorway into the attached
shrine housing a relief of Shiva Bhikshatana. (Photo by Emmanuel Francis)

PLATE 19 Traces of a painted representation of Shiva Somaskanda on the east-facing
wall inside cell 43 in the northern side of Rajasimha's *prakara*. From the top left: the red,
matted locks of Brahma; Shiva's taller matted locks, frontal face, and torso; golden Vishnu
standing behind Shiva's shoulder, his wheel (*chakra*) and conch on either side of his
crowned head; the red-faced baby Skanda seated at Shiva's elbow; the crowned head of
Uma, in front of Vishnu's elbow and beneath a tilted umbrella. (Photo Emmanuel Francis)

Ganga in Shiva's hair, beautiful women charmed in secret by the king, Bhu rescued by Vishnu from the monster. Gender had distinct connotations in the divine and the human registers for the Pallavas. Devotion to mighty goddesses is seldom a guarantee of a high regard for human women.[13]

Thematic continuities between the deities in these sculptures and the kings in this inscription set up a chronogram, which is to say that visitors could understand themselves to be enacting time itself as they moved counterclockwise around the *vimana*. They could have that experience if they understood time in the way that Daud Ali finds embedded in *prashasti* (eulogistic poetry) written for kings of medieval South Asia.[14] He discerns a world view in which kings in historic time carried on the flow of time and great deeds that deities had enacted in Puranic (Purāṇic) time. The events narrated in the *purana* texts did not serve as parables or as otherwise divorced from historic time. They told of an earlier age continuous with historic time, and their divine agents were earlier versions of the human agents who have ruled since. Demonstrating these continuities on a royal monument could thereby articulate a royal patron's sense of responsibility and relevance to the present as well as to the past and its divine heroes.

Ali finds this conception of time and South Asian kingship in sources produced over many centuries, including the eighth.[15] He finds them in many kinds of sources, but especially in *prashasti*, a literary category to which the first half of the inscription on Rajasimha's *vimana* belongs. The visual and material evidence of this temple is, I would argue, yet another useful kind of source to integrate into the widely synthetic method of intertextuality that Ali demonstrates.

The inscription on Rajasimha's *vimana* marks time through the Four Ages (*yuga*s). These markers get clearer with each age. Walking around the north side of the *vimana* and reading these verses in counterclockwise order would thus take the visitor forward in time through the Four Ages in sequence. At the center of the north wall, verse 4 anchors Pallava kings in the Age of Strife (*kali yuga*), the last of the four ages, struggling against its vicissitudes. Verse 3 names Drona and his son Ashvatthaman, Brahmin/warrior heroes of the *Mahabharata* epic, which took place in the third of those ages, the Age of Trey (*treta yuga*).[16] Verses 1 and 2 trace the Pallava lineage back through virtuous sages to the time of Shiva. These can indicate the second age, the Age of Deuce (*dvapara yuga*), and the first age, the Age of Completeness (*krita yuga*), respectively.

As time progresses through these four ages on the *vimana*'s inscribed basement molding, sculpture on the walls above carries forward the earliest age instead of shifting into later times and human events. It portrays divine acts in a continuing Puranic time. Thus, the monument visually superposes eternally divine time above the steadily deteriorating conditions in historic time below. This contrast renders all the more impressive the ability of Pallava ancestors, as they struggle through the darkening cycle of the Four Ages, to live up to feats of deities in a better time. Sculpture and the three-dimensional space of the monument in this way add a significant measure of intensity to the basic claims the inscription stakes.

This *vimana* functioned as a chronogram, mapping out the time of world history and permitting a visitor to reenact that time through movement. It shares some elements of the architectural chronogram John S. Hawley finds at Ellora's Kailasanatha monolith. He argues that the reliefs narrating the *Mahabharata* and *Ramayana* epics articulate the *treta* and *dvapara yuga*s along the staircases that lead from ground level (where the *kali yuga* unfolds) up to Shiva's shrine (in the *krita yuga*). Movement on those stairs past these reliefs carries visitors through time in either direction. Climbing takes them back through the ages to "Shiva's constancy atop Mount Kailasa, . . . the unchanging, foursquare stability of the *krita yuga*, the first eon of world history."[17] Narrative reliefs spool time back and forth into and out of the *kali yuga* below and the *krita yuga* of Shiva's abode above.

The chronogram at Kanchi would not have required climbing, though like one at the Ellora temple it places the realm of Shiva higher above the earth than the realms of men. Both monuments enabled visitors to enact time by moving through space and to move through the very space-time in which deities also move. The horizontal, circumambulatory course at Kanchi was another path through time and space to Shiva. People at Ellora could approach Shiva himself by climbing upward. The Kanchi temple kept that divine, sculpted world above the text about kings, letting the visitor's eyes track up and down at any point to take in that spatial arrangement. This inscription spread time laterally, and in a counterclockwise flow.

The Northwest Corner

The northwest corner of the *vimana* presents the theme of Shiva's family through a text-image arrangement like the one at the northeast corner. A sculpture and inscription about the same subject are spatially staggered around the building's corner, with the inscription raising the topic first. When visitors walk counterclockwise and turn these corners, they encounter an opportunity to participate in the interaction of text and image. If they can supply a piece of information they just heard or read from the inscribed poem, they can link the gods in the sculptural register above to a Pallava name inscribed in the verbal register right below. Those who make the connection can associate the Pallavas with other good things that had descended from the divine realm to benefit the earth.

Verse 5 deploys the theme of Shiva's family to bring the inscription's lineage recitation to a crescendo in the birth of the subject of this panegyric, saying he was born to king Parameshvara, just as Guha (alias Skanda or Subrahmanya) was born to Shiva. This verse initially bears no obvious connection to the sculptural register above it. Shiva kicks Kala above the first half of this verse (plate 13). But when the verse reaches onto the west wall, it emerges below a sculpted panel of Somaskanda, Shiva beside his wife and their baby son, Skanda (plate 18). Thus the same divine baby Guha/Skanda whom the inscription identifies as Shiva's son appears in sculpture with his parents at the top of the wall, just above those inscribed words (see fig. 3.1). These parallels have a chance to sink in when visitors stand before both, looking up and down between Guha in his verbal and visual contexts or hearing the verse recited as they see the sculpted form. And since the words beneath the Somaskanda relief compare Guha to king Rajasimha, the inscription inserts a layer of meaning about kings into what sculpture could present as a purely divine matter. The Pallava Rajasimha has literally descended from his alter ego in sculpture at the top of the wall into the inscribed layer at the foot of the wall.[18] Visitors see the king's physical as well as genealogical descent from the heavens—the same associations sparked for the Pallava dynasty's founder at the *vimana*'s northeast corner by the superposition of Shiva catching Ganga over Bharadvaja's name. The monument thus employs the same narrative strategies at two successive corners of the building to present Shiva Gangadhara and Shiva Somaskanda, the two metaphors that Pallava panegyrists most favored in their monuments and inscriptions.

The West Wall

While the sculpture of Somaskanda peels out just the divine half of the divine/royal simile in verse 5 below it, the inscription severs the generations instead, and it does so at that corner of the building. Verse 5 names only fathers (Shiva and Parameshvara) on the north wall, and only sons (Guha and Narasimha II) on the west wall. In other words, the architectural corner marks a precise break in the inscription between the recitation of Pallava ancestors and the appearance of the panegyric's hero. The inscriptional space of the north wall was only for Pallava ancestors: the hero himself does not belong in those grim times.

Rather, he is the star of the poem for the length of the west wall. He arrives like a thunderclap. The words on which verse 5 turns onto the west wall are the names of the god (*subrahmaṇya kumāro guha*) whom this king resembles (*iva*).[19] Next follow praises of the king's qualities. These persist through verses 6 and 7 and halfway through verse 8. Verse 8 shifts topics from praise to benediction just as it turns the southwest corner (see appendix 2).

At both ends of the west wall, these verses wrap and break around the building's corners in a way that creates an intriguing rupture between the poem's form (verse structure) and its content (praises of the king). The neatness with which those corners clip verses 5 and 8 to exclude other topics from the west wall forms a tight equation between that wall and that king.

Sculpture supports this dedication of the west wall to Rajasimha's praises. The Somaskanda composition at the north end of this wall (plate 18) recurs at the south end of the wall. Thus Somaskanda panels bracket the west wall (see fig. 3.15). The pair can act as visual framing devices around the wall that features praises of that Guha-like son in its inscription. They are small sculptures, however, and set high in the wall above the doorways into attached shrines that contain much larger and more dramatic sculptural groupings. They are not that easy to see.

The large sculptures of that wall diverge from the inscription in their overt content. As the verses compare Rajasimha to Guha, Indra, Krishna, and Kubera, visitors reading them pass reliefs of Shiva fully armed and riding in his chariot; Shiva as a dancer pointing one leg to the sky; Shiva catching Ganga; Shiva in a dance of deep flexion; and Shiva as the naked mendicant, Bhikshatana, before whom the sages' wives fall in desire (plates 8–12). The wall's two north-facing facets introduce new images, one of Shiva playing a *vina* (see fig. 2.8) and one of a goddess dancing (see fig. 2.7).

Some qualities the inscription praises in Rajasimha appear in some of these sculptures, but through rather formulaic imagery about kings and gods. The words running beneath Shiva as he catches Ganga retail that the king was like the god Kubera in "gratifying good men by giving them riches" (v. 6). That verse also says of the king, "In secretly seducing women skilled in the arts, (he is) Manmatha (i.e. Kama)," and Bhikshatana enacts seductions, but at a point on the wall quite distant from that verse.

Word and image on this wall connect in more dramatic and suggestive ways through the concept that time cycles through the Four Ages (*yugas*). Verse 7 invokes the *krita yuga* as the ancient time when kings could hear "a bodiless voice coming from the sky." It names the *kali yuga* as the present, and wonders that the hero of the poem can hear that voice even now. Rajasimha, in other words, has a capacity that is distinctive to the *krita yuga*, the utopic age at the start of a time cycle, even as he exists in the *kali yuga*. The verse remarks on the wonder of this ability.

The world view Daud Ali traces through many panegyrics from medieval South Asia frames the goal of kings as being to end the wretched *kali yuga* by defeating the rival kings who divide the earth among them in constant strife. By uniting the world into a single, harmonious kingdom, one king would win the goddess Earth as his beloved and return the world to the utopian *krita yuga*.[20] Ali invites us to see the battles fought among kings in medieval South Asia as in this way purposeful and idealistic action.[21] Thanks to the actions of a single king, the horrors at the end of a cycle of the Four Ages could give way to the joys of the start of a new cycle.

The inscription on Rajasimha's *vimana* does not explain that idea in a direct way. But those who understood kingship and time in these ways could catch the inference that Rajasimha had enacted what all kings strove to do. He had united the entire world under his domain and thereby caused the end of strife and the start of a new cycle of time, with all of the bliss attendant on that happy first *yuga*. Perhaps only a limited audience could catch these meanings, but the poet seems to have been confident such an audience did exist.

Sculpture plays into this world view, too, though not with anything so literal as someone listening to disembodied voices. What it does offer is a visual counterpart to the poem's recollection of the glorious *krita yuga*. The grand sculptures filling the recesses of the west wall reprise the sculptures of the eastern façade, and in the same sequence. On the west wall too, visitors pass first a figure of Shiva dancing with one leg pointing straight up and second a figure of him dancing with one knee touching the ground (see plates 9, 11; fig. 3.13). Reprising the eastern façade can signify return of the *krita yuga*, because the poem on that wall began its tracing of time with the act of Shiva catching Ganga in his hair. Sculptures that loop visitors' memories back to that wall could also loop time back to the utopic time the inscription constructed for that eastern space.

The architecture sets up light effects that enhance that impression. Deep shadow blankets the north wall for most of the year. At any moment except morning in midwinter, the sun hits the west wall much harder than the north wall, which lies in the shadow of the *vimana*'s tall tower. Strong light splashes the west wall every afternoon of the year. Before the construction of the closed *mandapam* nearly a thousand years after this *vimana* was built, the *vimana*'s east wall, too, would have caught more sunlight than the north wall.

By circumambulating counterclockwise, people passed from the east wall's bright *krita yuga* into the north wall's darkness of the *kali yuga* and back into the bright new day of the *krita yuga* on the west wall. Thus the building could help visitors experience that light of a golden age shining on either side of a dark time. The earth renews. The effect would be theatrical, the building a simulacrum enfolding visitors in a re-creation of the cosmic cycle.

Architecture, inscription, sculptures, and stories on this *vimana*'s east, north, and west walls further contributed to the experience of the revival of a past golden age after a time of grim struggle. Visitors who had access to the inscription's contents could understand this monument as a word-image chronogram. Circumambulating could reenact or speed up time, which is also to turn back time if one perceives time as a cycle.

When the king performed that circumambulation, perhaps he could hasten or relive the struggles of his ancestors as well his own restitution of the *krita yuga*.[22] Those who had access to the poem could locate these transformations in the agency of the king. The poem's recitation of lineage unfolds on the shadowy north wall, but light returns as soon as Rajasimha's name appears around the northwest corner. Light and word herald the same man.[23]

The Southwest Corner

Yet again, a momentous declaration is inscribed around a corner of this building. The building's corners do seem to serve as "turning points" on a figurative as well as a literal level in the story this inscription tells about its hero. Major ideas on those spots shift the course of narrative action and build especially freighted layers of metaphor.

Just beyond the point at which verse 8 rounds this corner, it intimates that the living king is born to rescue his people from the *kali yuga*. The returning *krita yuga* that unfolded in poetry, light, and sculpture just before this corner could take place because this king acted to bring it about.

Verse 8 connects the west wall's verses about a *king* who has arrived on earth to the south wall's verses that implore *Shiva* to come to earth. Vishnu is the point of connection the verse forges, a kind of a hinge between the king and Shiva. The text does not

165

directly mention Vishnu. It implies him by framing the king's rescue of his people "from the ocean" after they had been "swallowed by the terrible *makara* [crocodilian beasts] that the Kali age is," an allusion to Vishnu rescuing Earth (Bhu) from a monster at the bottom of the sea. The king is another Vishnu, come down to renew the world. And in coming down to earth, both of them realize the same action that the following verses will implore of Shiva.

Daud Ali finds even in Shaiva environments this trope of kings as Vishnu. Vishnu plays the role of Shiva's chief devotee. Vishnu is a god of this world, here to create, protect, and dissolve, whereas Shiva is a god of the next world, which can be achieved only by transcendence (*moksha*).[24] Ali's model structures a place for Vishnu in Shiva's temple, and this monument bears the model out.

The inscription on Rajasimha's *vimana* brings Vishnu into its story just where it shifts topic from the king to Shiva, and just where the physical inscription turns an architectural corner. Vishnu supplies a marker that maps the king into Shiva's world as another Vishnu.

Ali notes that other royal panegyrics make much of the erotic element of Vishnu's possession of his two wives (Fortune/Lakshmi and Earth/Bhu) and of the king's union with the earth as a "loving embrace"; a king who loses his kingdom is "cuckolded" by his conqueror.[25] Verse 8 contains those pieces: the kings Rajasimha has humbled were arrogant because they had "attained" Kamala (Kamalā, Lotus or Lakshmi); she became his when he humbled them; he was born to rescue the earth (Bhu).

Sculpture participates in this hinging and eroticism as well. Directly above the stones inscribed with both halves of verse 8 are two sculptures of Shiva Bhikshatana that transform into a Shaiva idiom the erotic component of the Vaishnava analogy in that verse. This motif appears twice in succession, on either side of this southwest corner (plates 7, 8). Seduction is a central concept of the moment portrayed. Shiva approaches two women who kneel in submission, overcome by the beauty of his naked body as a cuckolded husband rages behind them. The twist of the god's body turns his perfect backside and his smiling gaze to the visitor, expanding the sphere of his seduction. A shared language of seduction and eager surrender marries this sculpted form to the king-like Vishnu of the inscription rescuing his fecund wife from a monster. And further along the south wall, a figure of Harihara, Shiva hybridized with Vishnu, looks back toward the southwest corner from the west side of the cella at the center of the south wall (fig. 5.2). Vishnu's presence recurs in multiple elements at this western end of the south wall.

The South Wall

Imagery of Rajasimha and Shiva drawing steadily closer to each other permeates the words and figures of the *vimana*'s south wall. Architecture backs up the inscription's imagery, and sculpture once again offers indirect corroboration with the central idea of the verses on that wall.

FIGURE 5.2 Shiva Harihara enthroned, his right side showing Shiva's signs, his left side showing Vishnu's signs. This relief is on the east surface of the shrine embedded at the center of the south wall of Rajasimha's *vimana*.

Rajasimha's construction of this shrine is the chief topic of the three verses that extend along this wall. Verse 9 adds that the temple is a home for Shiva; verses 10 and 11 express the wish that Shiva settle there for a long time. The inscription thus connects the king and Shiva more directly than it does on other walls, and through this temple building itself—its name, its creation, and its purpose of bringing Shiva to live in this king's capital city. The south wall is the first spot where, since the start of the inscription on the east wall, the inscription, and not just the sculpture, describes Shiva.

Poetry joins king and god on other levels as well. These verses pair king and god as host and guest (v. 10) and pair the two homes, this temple and Mount Kailasa, as rivals for Shiva's presence (v. 11). The Sanskrit words zigzag between descriptions of Rajasimha and those of Shiva. The interweaving is closest in the names the poem gives the temple, Rajasimhapallaveshvara (v. 10) and Rajasimheshvara (Rājasiṃheśvara) (v. 11), welding the king's coronation name to Ishvara, a name for Shiva—a common device across South Asia for naming temples, to be sure, but also one that fits into a larger verbal pattern at this monument.

Architecture reinforces associations the inscription sets up between Shiva's mountain home and the home Rajasimha has built for him. The *vimana*'s shape can evoke Shiva's mountain through its *shikhara* peak and its small, simple interior like a hermit's cave. Its orderly stack of aedicules along the tower are decorative motifs that can read with equal facility as the huts of the ascetics who live near Shiva on Mount Kailasa and as palaces of the gods on the mount of heaven.[26] Many temples across South Asia have shapes that encourage these same metaphoric readings, but the Kailasanatha *vimana* is the largest— and therefore an especially vivid—realization of that metaphoric form to have survived from its time. The inscription does boast that the temple's "summit licks the sky" (v. 11).

Sculpture diverges from the inscription on a literal, superficial level. Above verse 8, visitors see not Varaha's rescue of Bhu but Shiva as the naked mendicant, Bhikshatana (plate 7). Further along the south wall, the inscription tells of Rajasimha building the temple, but the large sculptures above it present Shiva in the eternal flaming pillar or *linga* (plate 6); Shiva as Harihara, half Shiva and half Vishnu (fig. 5.2); Shiva sitting underneath the banyan tree, performing yoga, and lecturing (plate 4); Shiva enthroned with his wife (plate 3); and Shiva flirting with her (plate 2).

These sculptures and the inscription collaborate to join king to god through a theatrical staging of Shiva's progress toward the king's home for him, making visible the convergence that the inscription expresses through words of prayer. That staging could begin with the first three sculptures a visitor passes while moving counterclockwise along the south wall. All of these can evoke narratives about Shiva coming to this earth and interacting with humans.[27] Shiva enters the Pine Forest (located variously by myth in particular Tamil towns including Alandurai [Ālanturai] or Tillai), where the sages were dwelling with their wives. He manifests in a pillar of fire that plunges infinitely deep into the earth and rises above the clouds. He sits under the banyan tree, lecturing to kings, sages, and the wild animals of the forest. The *vimana* wall makes him manifest in the visitor's physical field in the form of sculptures. The verse beneath the sculpture of Shiva under the banyan tree, verse 10, is the first to invite Shiva to make this temple his home. Verse 11 repeats that invitation. In the recess above verse 11, Shiva sits on a throne with the Goddess (plate 3). The scene might help visitors imagine Shiva having accepted Rajasimha's invitation to take up residence in this stone house. He is enthroned before their eyes.

Directly beneath that scene are carved the words "rājñā rājñām" (king of kings) (v. 11) to describe Rajasimha. As on the north wall, then, implied metaphor can here join kings in inscriptions and deities in sculpture. Verse 11 praises the king for defeating proud enemies, while sculpture shows Shiva defeating first the arrogant sages of the Pine Forest and then Vishnu and Brahma.

The same verse also deploys a convention common in Pallava inscriptions that identifies the king with a lion and his humbled enemies with elephants.[28] This offers an intriguing option for thinking about the building's many elephant and lion sculptures as more than mere ornaments. The elephants kneel beneath major sculptural tableaux of Shiva, their forelegs bent as if crouching in supplication or bearing Shiva on their backs (fig. 5.1; plates 4, 7). Lions crouch beneath the fierce goddesses of the north wall (plates 15, 16). These and the lions carved on attached columns are rearing up and lunging forward. They burst with an energy these docile elephants do not display. Lions rise above the register the elephants occupy, surging into the register that carries sculptures of Shiva and goddesses. The lions against columns are explicitly male—their posture displays their genitals toward visitors—in contrast to the female lions who accompany the Goddess.

Sculpture and inscription on the south wall also coordinate to frame a tone for the entire wall, as they do on the west wall. On both surfaces, paired sculptures bracketing the far ends of the wall summarize a concept raised by the first words of the inscription on each wall. On the west, words pronounce the king is like Shiva's son Guha; sculptures of Shiva and Guha bracket the wall. On the south, words proclaim that the king has won over fortune and earth. Sculptures of Shiva's seductive conquests frame the south wall's sculptural array. The sculpture of Shiva tenderly chucking his wife under the chin forms a pair with the sculpture of Shiva Bhikshatana. The two compositions mirror each other loosely in the crook of Shiva's forward arm and leg, the supple twist of his ribs, and the gentle tilt of his head (plates 2, 7). Each group consists of erotically charged interaction between seated and standing figures. An angry husband or an attending dwarf fills the corner they leave empty.

The Southeast Corner

After Shiva's journey on the south wall to the stone house Rajasimha has built him, that convergence intensifies around the next corner, at the southern end of the east wall. There a superposition of text and image could express that the king himself has merged with his god.

Yet again, the building corner is a site for the proclamation of a major idea in the inscription. Verse 12 begins just centimeters before the east end of the south wall, then wraps two right angles and passes under the threshold of the niche attached to the east wall's southern end. In that niche is a sculpture of Shiva dancing on one knee (plate 1). Just as the inscription passes underneath that figure, it describes the king as Shivachulamani (Śivacūḷāmaṇi), meaning one "who wears Shiva for his crest-jewel."[29] In other words, the king wears the god on his head like a jewel in his crown. South Asian inscriptions could serve the function of making donors physically manifest in the space where their name was cut. Having one's name carved on a stone kept one's presence at that place and put one's presence in juxtaposition with the deity to whom one gave.[30] Words could make the king present directly beneath this sculpture that could make the god present. The sculpture of Shiva dancing could thus look to ride on the king's head like a jewel in the king's crown. Sculpture makes these words of the inscription concrete, though not in any way that I would consider "illustration," because sculpture and text are not equivalent. Sculpture makes suddenly tangible what might have sounded like a mere figure of speech in the inscription. Words embed sculpture in a layer of meaning it would not enter on its own.

Subject matter could further weld together Shiva and the king at this spot. Shiva dances here with an expansive energy that could read as violence.[31] Verse 12 opens by characterizing Rajasimha as Ranajaya, "he who is victorious in battle." This would per- petuate the kind of loose overlap between text and image that occurs along the north and south walls, between qualities the poem praises in the king and qualities the sculptures present in Shiva.

Shiva's deeply flexed dance is the penultimate sculpture a visitor would see before entering the *vimana*'s interior. The last letters of verse 12 are incised at the right end of the threshold in front of him. So the joining of king and god, text and image, unfolds for visitors just as they are about to complete counterclockwise circumambulation and enter into Shiva's very home, the inner shrine, or *garbha griha*, a zone charged with potential for direct encounter with the divine.

Identifying Narrative Devices

Telling one story through other stories is the largest-scale narrative device apparent on Rajasimha's *vimana*. Separate stories about gods (told by sculptures) and kings (told by the inscription) tell a larger story about integrating Rajasimha and Shiva. Narrative also performs at least three other functions there: chronogram, iconicity, and simulacrum. All employ narrative unfettered by pedantic, story-driven sequence, using narrative instead toward dramatic effects and transformative experiences.

Narrative makes the *vimana* a chronogram. By following the inscribed narrative coun- terclockwise and comprehending its meaning, a person moves through a complete cycle of the Four Ages of time, from one utopic age to the next. The visitor's body enacts time by moving through the space of the monument. Perceiving parallels between the royal time of the inscription and the Puranic time of narratives in the sculptures above it engages a circumambulating visitor in stitching together those two flows of time. The person moving through the Four Ages of the inscription is also looping back to the time of the gods every time he or she looks up to the sculptural register.

Another kind of magic that narrative could perform was to make the divine present in the visitor's space. This "iconicity" can occur when sculpture makes the divine somati- cally manifest before the visitor. The divine looks to be present in the visitor's own space and to share with the visitor the vivid state of being in a human body. These divine bodies signal the idea of iconicity through narrative by referencing stories about exactly that act of manifestation. As Lingodbhava and as Kalarimurti, for example, Shiva makes himself present to those who, like the monument's viewers, hold him in awe. This repetition of the idea of manifestation through multiple images can also signal that he is prone to making such appearances and that manifesting in the human sphere is fundamental to his nature. The sequence of images along the south wall could imply that Shiva was manifesting right in Kanchi to live in that *vimana*, precisely what the inscription there beseeches Shiva to do.[32]

Storytelling in itself could have brought the divine into the visitor's presence. This dynamic may have operated at Amaravati in sculptures telling stories that brought listeners peace of mind and understanding, just as the living Buddha had done centuries before. Sight of the story could catalyze transformation in the viewer, just as sight of the Buddha himself had done.[33] This mode of constructing and engaging visual narrative could have been yet another Buddhist tradition that the Kailasanatha inherited or appropriated. Indeed, Shiva's very Buddha-like Dakshinamurti at the center of the south wall, his hand raised in the *chin mudra* of discoursing, could well read as a teacher telling stories to visitors who stand before him as well as to the men seated around him on the temple wall.

Processes of evocation this complicated would surely have worked best with audiences who knew the stories deeply. The succinct quality of sculptural narrative on this *vimana* suggests just such audiences. A single, monoscenic panel could apparently suffice to conjure entire stories, a signal that the expected audience already knew the story well.[34]

Visual narrative can also collapse time to create simulacra, environments that enfold visitors and virtually transport them to other spaces and times. This could happen on Rajasimha's *vimana* through a clustering of monoscenic reliefs whose stories share their setting to some degree. On the north wall, several scenes could take place on battlefields. Shiva rides into battle on a chariot (plate 15); a goddess pulls an arrow from her quiver as the lion she rides rears up (plate 15); Shiva sits meditating on the dying Jalandhara (plate 14); the Goddess, who embodies battlefield triumph itself, lounges against her steed, a different weapon ready in most of her ten arms (plate 16). By sharing this wall, all these battlefields can become one paradigmatic, cosmic realm of divine combat enveloping visitors in its grim, dark, and thrilling atmosphere. Narrative can thus generate a three-dimensional experience for the visitor.[35] Repetition can enhance the "reality effect" of this environment, cloaking its fictions in an air of certainty.[36] This effect takes hold with yet more force on the north-facing wall of Rajasimha's *prakara*, where so many more reliefs portray sites of divine combat (see fig. 2.12).

Something comparable seems to operate on the south-facing walls. There, repetition can take visitors to this sunny earth honored by Shiva's presence. On Rajasimha's *vimana*, he comes as a wanderer, his thick sandals anchoring him to earth that appears at a visitor's eye level (plate 7). He manifests in fire to humble Vishnu and Brahma (plate 6). He sits among the beasts of the forest, his back against a tree, one foot planted on the ground (plate 4). He and his partner sit or flirt on Mount Kailasa or in Kanchi (plates 2 and 3). Rajasimha's *prakara* spins this out to a dozen scenes of the divine couple enthroned at home, dispensing grace to all sorts of petitioners and, through the angles of their bodies and gazes, to anyone who stands before them (see fig. 2.13).[37]

Conclusions

Verbal and sculpted stories on Rajasimha's *vimana* have very little in common on an overt level, but when these many stories bounce off each other, they open up a different story of this king carrying world history forward, a worthy successor to the divine heroes of Puranic time, as he moves steadily toward convergence with Shiva. The story builds over the course of a counterclockwise journey around the *vimana*, from the north wall, where shared actions unite Shiva and goddesses with the king's ancestor; through the west wall, where luminous Rajasimha comes to earth, matches the achievements of other gods, and brings about the return of the utopic Age of Completeness (*krita yuga*); until the south wall, which brings Shiva to earth and to Kanchi and intertwines him with this king in this very building; to the east wall, where this king joins his god to his own body. A fusion of word and image tells the story of fusion between Rajasimha and Shiva, a simile the inscription never makes on its own, comparing this king only to other gods.

Word and image here are complementary but not identical. They work together, though not through simple, hierarchical processes of illustration or captioning. They connect to generate metaphor, a chronogram, iconicity, and a simulacrum staging divine responses to royal prayer. Each medium can add extra layers of meaning to the other. Their points of most significant connection are indirect and abstract.

These relationships emerge through a variety of visual and physical devices. They require the materiality and spaces of architecture to work their magic. Continuous phrases in the inscription are split or staggered around adjacent sides of a building corner to allow associations to different sculptures, or to hinge together meanings on adjacent walls, or to isolate a single topic on a single surface. Sculptures are stacked above words to imply connections. The north wall reprises a single posture among different figures to imply commonality; the west wall reprises the sculptural groupings of the east wall to portray cyclic time. Natural light creates adjacent walls as separate worlds. Paired sculptures signal a common idea among the forms they bracket. The text before the first member of the pair heralds that idea. Corners are turning points in stories as well as in space.

How was this coordination planned and achieved? Perhaps the beautiful reliefs inspired the poet to tailor his, albeit rather formulaic, panegyric to them. Perhaps the temple's designers adapted their program to the poem, although that program does follow formulae widely used at Pallava temples. And the results are not so neat as to indicate the inscription drove the design: words may break perfectly at the corners, but the last verse ends an entire niche before the doorway into the temple.

In any case, the precise coordination between these two media was probably realized by carving the text into the wall after the reliefs were carved. Working from the top of the wall downward protected finished work from the dangers of falling debris and busy feet. Sculptures had to fit in the exact center of each surface, according to the design templates of this monument. Letters could be chalked onto the granite to rough out the fit. Adjustments in the size and spacing of letters would have been easier to make than changes to the location or the subject matter of the sculptures.

In this convergence of stories, neither images nor text serves as handmaid to the other. Neither is less subtle. Neither is simple truth to the other's deceptions or imitations. Together they can generate further layers of meaning. Though scholarship may be often logophilic, and though we may now live in a mostly scopophilic world, this monument invites us to consider that such hierarchies have not always shaped vision, and may foreclose our perceptions. And for those of us biased toward visual expression, this monument teaches that to ignore text is to miss out on good secrets.

CONCLUSIONS

WHAT SOME MIGHT CALL THE ORNAMENT ON THE KAILASANATHA TEMPLE complex—its sculptures, paintings, and architectural forms—was made with a plan and with the purpose of carrying important meaning. The plan was complex, thorough, very consistent, and designed to be comprehensible. The monument yields up particular categories of thought through which the elite of the Pallava court understood the world and their place in it. Those categories can remind us how distant the past can be, even as they inspire admiration for the wisdom of people so long ago.

Comprehending is tough now, centuries later, but many pieces of the plan still lie where we can interpret them. They are there thanks to the particular blend of love and neglect these stones received during and since the eighth century. These pieces are the data of this book, the documents. They include the words inscribed into these buildings about their patrons, the sculpted reliefs and traces of painted murals on the buildings, the buildings themselves, and the spaces they carve out that guide light, shadow, sound, and people's movements and gazes.

Material Patterns

The plan that organizes these pieces coordinates multiple complementary pairs of ideas through a series of strong patterns. Using haptic and aural as well as visual experience to transmit those pairs to visitors, the monument aligns imagery of nurture and triumph, prosperity and austerity, with clockwise and counterclockwise movement to convey secret and public meanings. A clockwise path through the compound could activate what south-facing sculptures make visible, the energies that encourage the prosperity of kingdoms and the continuity of lineages (table C.1). A counterclockwise path could lead toward ascetic practice and victory over forces of darkness, the themes of north-facing sculptures. Perhaps only initiates into the esoteric had access to that counterclockwise path and its lessons. Rajasimha was such an initiate.

The mystical and the overt underpin the system organizing into two distinct groups all the figural imagery that faces north or south on all the eighth-century buildings in the temple complex—the vast majority of the monument's imagery, that is. Vigorous, struggling figures hardened by ascetic discipline and heroic struggle face north in deep shadow and lean counterclockwise. They gaze across courtyards and pathways to meet the gazes of the same gods and goddesses but in gentler, interactive bodies enacting grace, warmth, seduction, and marriage, drenched in sunlight, facing south, and leaning counterclockwise. The two groups stand back-to-back as well as face-to-face around this temple complex, completing each other, two sides of the same coin. Nurture and continuity face conquest and renunciation, twining together in cycles of birth, death, and rebirth in our world of form. These two forms of energy, woven together, constitute the power and responsibility of rulers. They embrace battlefield triumph and spiritual transcendence as well as peaceful governance and continuous lineages.

These complementary energies merge in figures that face east and west, divine couples with sons and royal couples in which husbands are grown sons who do not yet have sons of their own. The pairing of these two kinds of couples signals continuities and transformations across generations and from kings to gods. The Skanda-like king in one inscription becomes a Shiva-like father in his son's inscription. Sons become fathers. Pallavas become Skandas. Deities become kings.

Representations of Shiva Somaskanda dominate east- and west-facing sculpture and painting. The theme appears in inscriptions too, and in architectural metaphor. Mahendra's *vimana* interposes itself, Skanda-like, between architectural emblems of his progenitors, the *vimana* built by his father and the row of *vimana*s built by Pallava queens.

TABLE C.1. Patterns aligned with Shaiva Siddhanta categories at the Kailasanatha temple complex

Paired complementarities	
Triumph over outer and inner threats	Nurture, fecund energies
North-facing	South-facing
Austerity, battlefield triumphs	Prosperity, teaching, couples
Counterclockwise movement	Clockwise movement
Mystifying poetry, complex grammar	Overt content, simple grammar
Esoteric experience	Exoteric experience
mumukshu asceti	*bubhukshu* worldly

These *vimana*s all share a common idiom as towered, east-facing *linga* shrines presenting Somaskanda reliefs behind those *linga*s, and girdled by inscriptions comparing their patrons to members of Shiva's family.

Complementary energies merge in the royal sphere. This is articulated by the very few image types that face in more than two directions in the temple complex. They may evoke the *digvijaya*, the royal presence that conquers all directions. One of these image types is the childless royal couple. Another is the yogini, who is both human and divine and who teaches kings, who are warriors and ascetics, in the wilderness. Figures of Shiva dancing and catching Ganga in his hair, subjects that Pallava inscriptions invested with strong royal metaphors, also face in multiple directions. Those two image types synthesize the visual qualities of north-facing warriors as well as south-facing teachers. They also join together to dominate the west wall of Rajasimha's *vimana*, a space thick with royal signs.

Shiva manifests in deeply royal colors throughout the monument. He is the king of a court peopled by the other Hindu deities like the Goddess, Skanda, Vishnu, and Brahma. He is also a new version of the Buddha and of Jinas. Shiva appears with or as these other deities, their signs absorbed into his body. Their signs provide a vocabulary to manifest him in material form. Together, these many elements along with the unprecedented scale of this monument demonstrate the grand kinds of material traces that often distinguish the products of royal patronage from those of other, less well-resourced donors.

The pattern distinguishing north-facing from south-facing sculptures throughout the Kailasanatha temple complex is a static one. So are the patterns among sculptures facing east and west, and those facing all four directions.

Other patterns are activated by visitors' movement through the temple complex. Architectural spaces, sculptural form, and visual narrative lead visitors on twinned paths clockwise and counterclockwise around the temple complex. So do words inscribed on buildings. People moving clockwise can read and sing a list names for king Rajasimha. People moving counterclockwise can read elaborate poetic constructions, cryptic allusions to the cycle of cosmic time, and an announcement that Rajasimha took esoteric initiation. Inscriptions introduce layers of reference to royal history to the resonances the sculptures can carry. Sculpted narratives enrich those references by engaging plays of time, space, and light. Together, verbal and visual narratives collude to tell a secret story through other stories, a secret story that leads to a confluence of devotee and divine.

Shaiva Siddhanta Meaning

Taken together, these patterns signal the importance of esoteric as well as exoteric practice at this site, and they offer evidence about what that practice was. That practice shares several ideas with the Shaiva Siddhanta practice that Richard H. Davis documented in the late twentieth century. On one level, this is not a surprise. Verse 5 of Rajasimha's *vimana* inscription is the oldest surviving physical record to contain the phrase "Shaiva

Siddhanta," and it does so to declare that the king had "destroyed all his impurities by following the path of Shaiva Siddhanta," meaning he took initiation into that esoteric, Tantric, renunciant practice.[1] On another level, the connection can seem surprising because that practice now carries quite exoteric connotations.

That Rajasimha followed this path was important enough for the poem to tell this before it lists his other characteristics. That he was also the temple's patron indicates that on some level, this *vimana* was a Shaiva Siddhanta monument, according to whatever that term meant in the eighth century.[2] That meaning appears to have valued esoteric as well as exoteric practice, and to have held the two in a close dialog.

Announcing Rajasimha's initiation is, unfortunately, all the inscription says about Shaiva Siddhanta. Most of the information we now have about its character derives from younger texts and twentieth-century observations of its practices. Those do articulate some core principles that resonate closely with strong patterns governing the material forms of this monument: the significance of counterpoised clockwise and counterclockwise movement as expressions of engagement with or transcendence of this world of form; the goal of convergence between the devotee and Shiva; and the view that everything is always in the process of being emitted from or absorbed into the divine source. Emission and reabsorption are "the primary organizing logic" of recent Shaiva Siddhanta ritual practice and temple design.[3]

In contemporary Shaiva Siddhanta practice, ascetics seeking purification, liberation, "a reunification of [their] soul as similar to Shiva," are termed *mumukshu* and perform a ritual called *karanyasa* by moving their concentration from the thumb of the right hand, one finger at a time, until they reach the pinkie finger. Those who choose the path of engagement with this life (*bhoga*), seeking "things that come about through differentiation of the cosmos," are called *bubhukshu*. They will perform *karanyasa* in the opposite direction, starting with the right pinkie. The first movement, the one performed by ascetics, is counterclockwise and moves inward to the heart of the temple. The second, the one performed by those engaged with this life, is clockwise and flows outward from the temple.[4]

These rituals use only the hands, but given the symbolic power that invests ritual, they could also index Shiva's activities on a cosmic level. The worshipper often acts "as a Shiva" in Shaiva Siddhanta practice. Ritual mirrors Shiva's activities of emission and absorption. The metonymic nature of ritual would permit hands and entire bodies to serve equally well as indices or connections to cosmic action.

Thus twentieth-century Shaiva Siddhanta meditation practice holds in dialog the clockwise path of the householder (*mumukshu*) and the counterclockwise path of the renunciant (*bubhukshu*) seeking transcendence. These correspond so closely with the physical structures of the Kailasanatha as to suggest that these aspects of modern Shaiva Siddhanta may be fourteen hundred years old. Having the two options for efficacious movement set in such close dialog with each other and in the same monument, quite possibly a Pallava family chapel, suggests that those same royal people had open to them both options for movement and the larger life choices that movement could have entailed. The environment could have offered usable wisdom to rulers who aspired to be master ascetics and victorious kings embedded in a long, continuous lineage.

Davis finds the ideal of a convergence between worshippers and Shiva at the heart of eleventh- and twelfth-century *agamas* on Shaiva Siddhanta. Through Shaiva Siddhanta ritual, the worshipper is "acting as a Shiva," and makes his body into a Shiva-like form.[5] A king can be the archetypal worshipper pictured in these sources, though even his convergence with Shiva is not a joining of equals.[6] The king is expressing "fealty" to Shiva.[7] This would suit the inscription on Rajasimha's *vimana* that grants him the virtues of several gods, but never of Shiva himself.

Later Shaiva Siddhanta sources present the cosmos as oscillating between energies of emission and reabsorption. Shiva's motion downward to the temple is an act of emission outward into the universe from the creative source; the worshipper's entry into the temple is an act of reabsorption, of moving back toward that creative source. Shiva and the worshipper converge at the temple as they move along these paths and through the act of worship.[8]

When the poem on the Kailasanatha *vimana* asks Shiva to live in this stone house (vv. 10, 11), it could be asking for Shiva to move downward along the path of emission. When verse 5 notes that the king has chosen the Shaiva Siddhanta path, it could identify him as someone who seeks reabsorption upward into the divine source. These verses would place Shiva and the king on converging paths, which the monument materializes by uniting verse 12 with the dancing figure of Shiva above it at the *vimana*'s southeast corner. That convergence occurs near the door to the inner shrine.

Verse 5 and verse 12 occur at opposite corners of the *vimana*, bracketing the building on the diagonal. The phrase "Shaiva Siddhanta path" is cut just south of the *vimana*'s northwest corner. The remark about the crest-jewel is just north of the southeast corner. The two points frame the architectural form of the *vimana*. Thus, reflections of this Shaiva Siddhanta concept physically frame the building, much as Somaskandas bracket the west wall and erotic compositions bracket the south wall. They also frame the king by bracketing everything else this poem has to say about him (vv. 6–11).

The counterclockwise flow of this monument's inscription about a king who takes Shaiva Siddhanta initiation and attains reabsorption into the divine suggests that counterclockwise movement already carried associations of renunciation and reabsorption. Recent Shaiva Siddhanta literature and practice, too, associate counterclockwise movement with liberation, renunciation, and the worshipper's assimilation toward Siva.[9] Those permitted to walk that path at the Kailasanatha may only have been those who had taken initiation into Shaiva Siddhanta. Certainly, that is the audience most likely to have been capable of understanding the story of convergence between Rajasimha and Shiva. Perhaps only Pallavas were expected to read this story, in the monument that was their personal temple. The courtyard narrows considerably around the *vimana* that carries this inscription, making for an intimate viewing space.

178

And yet the existence of an esoteric level of meaning suggests the coexistence of an exoteric one as well, a public counterpart that gave value to the secret one by contrast. The *vimana*'s high tower could be seen for miles across the alluvial plains where Kanchi lies. Anyone who got inside the temple courtyard would be dazzled by the intensity of ornament that surrounds one on all sides, so unlike the sleek minimalism of rock-cut Pallava monuments from the preceding century. The Kailasanatha temple complex energetically participates in an aesthetic of display, a robust invitation to feast the eyes. Thus it seems Rajasimha's *vimana* was designed for clockwise as well as counterclockwise motion. Each direction enables opposite versions of progress. Both have their uses. The two kinds of motion are exact opposites in their direction, but they are also mirror images and they tread the same ground. They are bound together dialogically.

Rajasimha's *prakara*, moreover, plays directly to an exoteric audience through a text-image relationship rather like the one outlined here on his *vimana*. The inscription and most of the sculptures lead in a clockwise direction. In sculpture, deities act out heroic and grace-bestowing deeds in Puranic time; below run the titles (*birudas*) of the king who lives in the current age. Sculptures and inscriptions share a broad swath of references to victory, fame, beauty, passion, heroism, prosperity, grace, restraint, wisdom, and protection. The inscriptions ascribe these virtues to the king. The sculptures embed them in gods. The combination can support what the *vimana* makes more explicit: this king acts as the gods acted.

This pairing of highly charged, complementary pathways could have served well the dual identity the Pallavas sought as warriors and ascetics, rulers simultaneously engaged in the work of this world and the spiritual quest. Shaiva Siddhanta practices, too, seem to have empowered rulers to integrate these two modes of engagement. Temple building was not a task just for kings "in their dotage" but rather an aspect of their worldly engagement, part of their quest of "completion of [their] 'conquest of the quarters.'"[10] Rajasimha may have taken initiation and built this *vimana* as he continued to govern and perpetuate the lineage, and otherwise sought to perpetuate this world of form. His fellow initiates, and the family who amplified his temple's themes with their own buildings, may have kept those ideals alive. They may have expressed both ideals by moving in both directions around this structure, resolving these two dialectic and counterpoised opportunities within their own practice and their own listening, gazing, moving bodies.

APPENDIX 1

Inscriptions on Rajasimha's Prakara

TRANSLATED BY EUGEN HULTZSCH

These inscriptions line the inner face of Rajasimha's *prakara*, cut into the granite band in the basement moldings of fifty-five of the small cells that make up that structure. The numbering below begins directly to the left of the southern entrance into the large courtyard from Mahendra's *prakara*. Several titles (*birudas*) are carved on each cell. The same titles were later recut into three other courses of these basement moldings. These recapitulate the contents of the granite course, except the highly ornamental text on the lowest molding, which is so large that some of the titles do not fit.[1]

1. The illustrious (*shri*) Rajasimha. He whose desires are boundless. The conqueror in battle. The lovely.
2. The unconquered. The wrestler with his foes. The fearless. The mighty.
3. He who is eager for conquest. The excessively fierce in battle. The bearer of prosperity. The great statesman. (He who resembles) the sun in rising.
4. The cloud (which showers) wealth. The granter of safety. The ornament of his race. The destroyer of his enemies.
5. He whose power is rising. He whose fame is rising. He who boasts of the bull (as his sign). He whose sign is the bull.
6. He who possesses terrible prowess. He who is rising ever and ever. The exalted and lovely. He who is endowed with terrible bravery.
7. The extremely noble. He who is to be conquered (only) by submissiveness. The lion in battle.
8. The spotless. The great jewel of Kanchi. He who possesses harsh valor. The emperor.
9. He who is compassionate to the distressed. He whose companion is the bow. He whose doubts are solved. The guileless.
10. The thunderbolt to his foes. The unrivalled wrestler. He whose deeds are wonderful. He who possesses the knowledge of elephants.
11. The fulfiller of wishes. He whose refuge is Ishana (Shiva). (He who resembles) the moon in rising. He who resembles the cloud (in showering gifts).
12. The destroyer of hostile empires. The crest-jewel of princes. He who is continually showering (gifts). The king of kings.
13. He who possesses the knowledge of musical instruments. The wonderful archer. The lion among heroes. He who is desirous of prosperity.

14. The altogether auspicious. The crest-jewel of warriors. He who is sporting with the goddess of prosperity. (He who resembles) Arjuna in battle.

15. The favorite of the goddess of prosperity. (He who resembles) Rama in war. The ruler of the whole earth. The dispeller of warriors.

16. He who is fearful in battle. He who possesses unbounded power. The lord of the three worlds. He who showers gifts.

17. The fulfiller of desires. He who is compassionate to the poor. He whose gifts never cease. He who is endowed with brilliant courage.

18. He who goes to war (only in order to procure the means) for gifts. The constantly just. He whose heart is pure. He whose (only) armor is justice.

19. The conqueror of wealth in battle. He whose bow excites terror. The invincible. He who is modest (in spite of his) virtues. The sun of the earth. The spotless. The ocean of arts. He who is firm in battle. He who goes to anger (only) at the proper time. The subduer of the wicked. The sun of the Pallavas.

20. The omnipotent. The benevolent. The constantly active. The lion among men.

21. He whose fame is pure. He who resembles Partha (Arjuna) in valor. The terrible and lovely. He who is liberal (at sacrifices).

22. The fearless. The great wrestler. The madly excited. The madly passionate.

23. The possessor of the world. He who resembles Mahendra in heroism. The powerful. He who resembles Manu by his deeds.

24. The diplomatic. The favorite of Shripati (Vishnu). The hero in battle. The sun at the end of the world.

25. He who is firm in battle. The jewel of protection. The fierce in battle. (He who shows) valor in battle.

26. He whose strength is unequalled. The destroyer of his enemies. He whose valor is unbounded. He who is fond of horses.

27. The matchless. He whose commands are unbroken. The sudden thunderbolt. He whose valor never fails.

28. He to whom the provinces bow. The unopposed. He whose power is wonderful. He who likes (to issue) orders. The wonderfully brave.

29. The irresistible in attacking. The conqueror of (all) quarters. He who is unrestrained in battle. (He who resembles) the king of Vatsa (in the knowledge of) elephants.

30. He whose commands are blazing. The supreme lord of the earth. He whose punishments are terrible. The highly proud.

31. The highly brave. The highly rising. He who rises higher and higher. He whose commands are terrible.

32. The abode of virtues. (He who resembles) spring in rising. He whose beauty is unrivalled. The majestic.

33. He who resembles Upendra (Vishnu) in valor. The fulfiller of hopes. The ornament of his race. He who is exalted by virtues.

34. He whose desires are lofty. The destroyer of rebels. The unrivalled archer. The famous.

35. The religious. The refuge of the distressed. He who is kind to refugees. The destroyer of plagues.

36. (He who resembles) Tumburu (in the knowledge of) musical instruments. He whose authority is the (Shaiva) doctrine. He who is adorned with (the power of issuing) orders. He who is fond of legends.

37. The daring. The unimpeded. The follower of the (Shaiva) doctrine. The restless. The highly rising. The subduer of rebels. The unrivalled king. He who resembles Death in valor. The receptacle of victory. The black-robed. The subduer of the haughty.

38. The naturally profound. He whose eyes are his spies. He whose goad is knowledge. The refuge of the distressed.

39. The subduer of villains. He who showers gifts. The devotee of Devadeva (Shiva). He whose speed is unrestrainable.

40. The graceful. The highly brave. He whose anger is fierce. He who is making conquests (only for the sake of) justice.

41. The wood-fire. The bestower of prosperity on his country. The sinless. The barrier of justice.

42. The far-seeing. He whose commands are proud. The follower of polity. He who pleases the eyes.

43. He whose deeds are blameless. He whose profundity is unfathomable. He who showers (gifts) without clouds. He who possesses no small prowess.

44. He is afraid (only) of injustice. The destruction of his enemies. The possessor of the earth. The irresistible.

45. He whose anger is not fruitless. The destroyer of his foes. He whose power is unresisted. The unreproached.

46. The death of his enemies. The unimpeded. The daring. The gentle-minded.

47. The ocean of safety. He whose good qualities are well-known. The constantly active. He who is skilled in expedients.

48. The scent-elephant. He who possesses the grace of Cupid. The reviver of poetry. He who goes to anger (only) with good reason.

49. He whose punishments are fierce. He whose anger is unbearable. The shading tree. The ornament of the earth.

50. The noose of Varuna. The ocean of firmness. The emperor. He who is fond of elephants.

51. He who has no enemies (left). The unbarred. He who distresses his enemies. The crest-jewel of the world.

52. The lion among princes. The destroyer of armies. The liberal. The formidable.

53. He whose valor is terrible. The elephant among kings. He whose grace is pleasant. He whose eyes are the sciences.

54. (He who resembles) Bhagadatta (in the knowledge of) elephants. He whose grace is extraordinary. (He who resembles) the lion in valor. (He who resembles) Narada (in the playing of) the lute.

55. The devotee of Shaṃkara (Shiva). The foremost among heroes. He who knows the truth. The devotee of Ishvara.

The Foundation Inscription of the Rajasimheshvara,
Rajasimha's Vimana

TRANSLATED BY EMMANUEL FRANCIS

This inscription is engraved in one line on the course of granite slabs of the base of the Rajasimheshvara, that is, the central shrine in the Kailasanatha complex.

1. [in Sragdhara meter]
    . . . tainted with (literally: bearing) (black)ness (. . . *tva*) by his (i.e. Shiva's) tresses, with blue from the brightness of his throat, with red from the rays of jewels in the serpents' hoods, flowing from Sthanu's (i.e. Shiva's) jewel, filling the ponds of the three worlds, may (Ganga), the foaming stream variously coloured, purify you . . .

2. [in Sragdhara meter]
    . . . after him (i.e. Brahma), (there was) that ascetic Angiras, born of his own spirit; (then) his (i.e. Angiras') son, the minister of Indra and teacher of the gods (literally: those who enjoy *amrita*)[1] (i.e. Brihaspati); his (i.e. Brihaspati's) son was Shamyu; from him, of formidable might and celebrated in the three worlds, took birth the best of ascetics, the glorious treasure (or source) of the Pallava lineage who was named Bharadvaja.

3. [in Sragdhara meter]
    From this delightful one (was born) Drona, the highly respected preceptor of the Pandavas and Kurus; then there was the great Ashvatthaman who deprived the kings of their firmness and pride; his son, called Pallava, (was), like Manu, the first of the valiant kings who governed the entire world and the originator of a line of conquerors.

4. [in Sragdhara meter]
    The Pallava kings who were pious, destroyers of the arrogance of the haughty and mighty Kali (age), truth-speaking, profound, with a spirit dexterous in sustaining the three *varga*s,[2] unmatched in service to the elders, forcibly conquering desire and other enemies within, excelling in the knowledge of weapons, resolute, mighty, full of wisdom and discipline.

5. [in Sragdhara meter]
    In their lineage, begotten from Ugradanda, the supreme lord who crushed the city of Ranarasika, a pious prince took birth—like Subrahmanya Kumara Guha took birth from the supreme lord Ugradanda (i.e. Shiva) who crushed the bellicose Pura—the glorious Atyantakama, chief of the Pallavas, by whose spear power the

multitude of the enemies has been destroyed, who was known as Bahunaya whose great political savvy was celebrated, who, on the path of the Shaiva Siddhanta, destroyed all his impurities.

6. [in Prithvi meter]

In secretly seducing women skilled in the arts, (he is) Manmatha (i.e. Kama); in constantly protecting those following the triple path (i.e. the three Vedas), (he is) Vasava (i.e. Indra); in splitting the hearts of the enemies of ascetics, twice-borns, and gods, (he is) Madhava (i.e. Krishna); in gratifying good men by an abundance of riches, (he is) Vittada (i.e. Kubera).

7. [in Shardulavikridita meter]

That in the Krita (age), a bodiless voice coming from the sky had been heard by kings—foremost among them Dushyanta—who were familiars of the gods and accepted by Kanva and by other sages, this is no wonder; but that in the Kaliyuga which is deprived of true virtues he, the king Shribhara ("he who bears prosperity"), again heard that voice, this is a great surprise!

8. [in Shardulavikridita meter]

He who humbled kings full of arrogance because they had attained wealth (*kamala*) by means of their political savvy and heroism, destroying their intelligence in just the lapse of a frown, this Purushottama, victorious in combat, born to rescue from the ocean of sin (his) sinking subjects swallowed by the terrible *makara* that the Kali age is, may he be victorious for a long time.

9. [in Prithvi meter]

At the order of this king who rules the entire world—which he acquired by his valor and fortified by his political savvy, in which he killed his enemies and humbled the kings—this haughty and wonderful residence of Hara (i.e. Shiva) has been erected, worthy of (or resembling) his own glory, resembling the smile of Shiva.

10. [in Aryagiti meter]

In the Rajasimhapallaveshvara,[3] in (this) place where a host of kings of gods and *asura*s reveres (him), may Shankara (i.e. Shiva), who has the coils of the king of serpents as terrifying ornament, be abiding for a long time.

11. [in Sragdhara meter]

In this house of stone which has been built by him who is a Rajasimha (lion-king) for the dense crowd of elephants that are his arrogant enemies, the king of kings to whose orders all the directions submit and who reveres *dharma*, (in this house) which robs Kailasa of its charm, which bears the name of Rajasimheshvara, whose summit licks the sky, may Vrishanka ("he whose mark is the bull," i.e. Shiva) always manifest his presence!

12. [in Anushtubh meter]

May Rajasimha, Ranajaya, Shribhara, Citrakarmuka, Ekavira, Shivaculamani[4] protect the earth for a long time.

APPENDIX 3

The Foundation Inscription of the Mahendravarmeshvara, Mahendravarman III's Vimana

TRANSLATED BY PADMA KAIMAL

The inscription is a single line of text cut into the granite band crowning the basement moldings of the *vimana* of Mahendravarman III Pallava, the oblong shrine just inside the east *gopuram* in the Kailasanatha complex. The text is four verses of Sanskrit, written in *grantha* script.

1. [in Sragdhara meter]
   May the motionless, the lord, the first of the gods forever joyfully dwell in this matchless (temple of) Mahendreshvara, which was constructed near the Rajasimheshvara (temple) by Mahendra who sprang (from) the chief of the princes of the holy Bharadvaja-gotra, from that Urjita, whose bravery frightened the elephants of rival kings.

2. [in Sragdhara meter]
   May the skin-robed (Shiva), surrounded by a troop led by Skanda,[1] be present at this dwelling, the holy Mahendreshvara, which was constructed (near) the temple of the holy Rajasimheshvara by the illustrious Mahendra, the son of king Rajasimha, who sprang from that Lokaditya ("the sun of the world") whose valor dried up the army of Ranarasika just as the heat of the sun does the mud.[2]

3. [in Sragdhara meter]
   May Isha together with Uma graciously take for his permanent dwelling this temple of Mahendreshvara, which was erected near the Rajasimheshvara by Mahendra, the son of king Rajasimha, the lion among the heroes of the earth, creator of another Golden Age (*krita yuga*) thanks to his sinless virtues.[3]

4. [in Vamshasta meter]
   May Maheshvara, the refuge of all the gods and demons, who puts an end to time and has made an end of (the demon) Pura, always (take up) his residence . . . the temple of Mahendravarmeshvara.

Other Pallava Inscriptions on and about the Mahendravarmeshvara

Emanuel Francis has found several more fragments of stone inscriptions about this patron reused in this building and walls nearby. One is a fragment of a verse about the

Pallavas' mythical genealogy written in Sanskrit *grantha* on two superimposed stones set in the south wall of Mahendravarman's shrine.[4] He surmises they say something about the Pallavas' mythical genealogy, and perhaps Rajasimha, though the breaks obscure much. The breaks are disruptions he finds consistent with renovations to that portion of the complex that seem to have taken place during Rajasimha's lifetime.[5] A second inscription, embedded in the *prakara* around Mahendra's *vimana*, is in ornamental *nagari* script. Francis suggests it could be a *biruda*, a title of praise.[6] Third is a single line of Sanskrit prose, in *grantha* script, on the north and south sides of the stairs leading up to the entry of Mahendra's *vimana*. This gives the name of the sanctuary as Mahendravarmeshvaragriha.[7] Fourth, a stone bearing the name of the shrine as "Mahendravarmeshvaragriha" is "fixed at the far north of Okkapirantankula St in Kanc(h)i." The text is in Sanskrit prose, *grantha* script.[8]

APPENDIX 4

The Foundation Inscriptions around Vimanas C, E, and G, Marking Donations by Pallava Queens

TRANSLATIONS COMPILED BY PADMA KAIMAL

These inscriptions are each a single line of text cut into the granite band crowning the basement moldings of three of the eight *vimana*s along the eastern side of the Kaila-sanatha temple complex. They begin on the east wall. The longer inscriptions wrap around to the north and west walls. The texts are Sanskrit prose lines or verses written in *grantha* script.

Vimana C

1. The house (or temple) of the auspicious (shri) Nityavinita's lord (Ishvara).

Vimana E

1. [in Vasantatilaka meter]
   Of a husband whose bow revealed its force in destroying cities and whose emblem is a bull, of a supreme lord whose unblemished glory spread with the name of Kalakala, she was the most profoundly beloved darling, like the daughter of the King of the Mountains was to Shiva (Parameshvara), he whose bow revealed its force in murdering Pura, whose emblem is a bull, and whose unblemished glory spread with the name of Kalakala.[1]
   or
   (Her) husband's well-merited fame being widespread as "Kalakala" on account of his bow's power (having been made) manifest in the destruction of cities, (thus) like the "Daughter of the Great King of Mountains," (she,) the dearly beloved wife of Parameshvara, the "Bull-bannered One,"[2]

2. [in Vasantatilaka meter]
   For being able to win the deep affection of the lord Narasimhavishnu (or, of the god Vishnu Narasimha), who is devoted to the protections of the circle of the earth and who shattered the breast of his enemies, she shines as if she had humbled the pride of the goddess of the lotus (i.e., Lakshmi).[3]
   or
   attaining supremacy (as Queen Mother), shines with surpassing splendor,

subduing, as it were, the pride of Pushkaradevata, while god-like Narasimha-vishnu, true to his sacred vow, is protecting the encircling world, tearing out the hearts of his enemies.[4]

Vimana G

1. [in Vasantatilaka meter]
   Prosperity (Shri)! She who, from the first Creator whose address, after the uninterrupted creation of a thousand beautiful, charming, and gracious women, had long ago attained perfection, is like the most accomplished work—utterly full of attractions, kindness and grace,[5]

   or

   (She) who, full of loveliness, gentleness, grace, and purity, seemed to be the masterpiece of the primeval creator, Brahma, whose craftsmanship had attained perfection at last, after he had created thousands of good-looking women,[6]
2. [lost][7]
3. [in Anushtubh meter]
   This is she who caused to be built this beautiful temple for the god who wears the moon as his diadem: Rangapataka, who among women is like the banner of the stage/scene.[8]

   or

   That Rangapataka, who was, as it were, the banner of women, caused to be built this lovely dwelling of (Shiva), whose crest-jewel is the moon.[9]
4. [in Upejati meter]
   She whose endless sweetness seduces, adorned with its charm, its coquetry, and its emotions, like the science of seduction.[10]

   or

   (She) who was so appealing because of (her) genuine sweetness, adorned with sentiments (both) charming (and) fascinating, (who) like the art of attraction . . . [text missing][11]

GLOSSARY OF SANSKRIT TERMS

*Parenthetical romanization includes diacritical marks providing full
phonetic representation of original terms in the Devanagari script.*

abhaya mudra (abhaya mudrā) Open-palmed gesture of reassurance

abhisheka (abhiṣeka) Lustration ceremony in South Asia through which men became kings

acharya (ācārya) Teacher, often a teacher of sacred knowledge

agama (āgama) Body of textual literature outlining rules for various practices, among them carving sculpture and building architecture

Alakshmi (Alakṣmī) Another name for Jyeshtha

amangalam (amaṅgalam in Tamil; amaṅgala in Sanskrit) The complement of *mangalam*. A mode of being that seeks transcendence. *Amangalam* things include infertility, asceticism, renunciation, and celibacy. Alakshmi is a synonym for *amangalam*.

Andhakasamharamurti (Andhakāsaṃharamūrti) Form of Shiva in which he destroys the demon Andhaka by piercing his torso and catching the blood before it falls to earth to grow into new demons. Andhaka is also an embodiment of blindness.

anjali mudra (añjali mudrā) Gesture of respectful address, with palms pressed together in front of chest

apradakshina (apradakṣiṇā) Circumambulation in a counterclockwise direction; literally, "moving away from the south (*dakshina*)"

Ardhanarishvara (Ardhanārīśvara) See under *Shiva*.

Arjuna Son of Indra; the third Pandava brother in the *Mahabharata* epic

Ashvatthaman (Aśvatthāman) Ascetic warrior born to Drona, the Pandava brothers' teacher in martial arts, in the *Mahabharata* epic

Bharadvaja (Bhāradvāja) First Pallava king, according to lineages recited in inscriptions on Pallava monuments

Bhikshatana (Bhikṣāṭana) See under *Shiva*.

Bhu (Bhū) Goddess who is Earth, often shown in sculpture and painting as one of Vishnu's two wives

Bhuta (bhūta) See *gana.*

biruda Praising title or epithet

Brahma (Brahmā) Male deity in the Hindu pantheon associated with the process of creation. At the Kailasanatha, he is frequently paired with Vishnu as attendants waiting on Shiva.

bubhukshu (bubhukṣu) One who chooses the path of engagement with this life and the *mangalam* mode of being

chakra (cakra) Circular blade, usually held or thrown by Vishnu, but also by Shiva to kill Jalandhara

chakravartin (cakravartin) Ideal ruler as bearer of the law

Chalukya (Cālukya) Known by later historians as the Western Chalukya, this dynasty was powerful in the southern Deccan in the sixth to eighth centuries CE

Chamunda (Cāmuṇḍā) Fiercest of the seven mother goddesses (*sapta matrika*), she comes to be worshipped on her own after ca. 700 CE

chin mudra (cin mudrā) Close-fisted gesture, with palm held forward, signifying teaching and communication

Dakshinamurti (Dakṣiṇāmūrti) See under *Shiva.*

Dandin (Daṇḍin) Poet sponsored by the Pallava court. Author of a cleverly monitory poem on good kingship.

darshan (darśan) Intense, devotional, and even tactile gaze exchanged between devotees and the divine

Devi (Devī) The Goddess in her singular or supreme form as the source of all other goddesses

Devi Mahatmya (*Devī Māhātmya*) Collection of Sanskrit hymns celebrating the victories of the Goddess over various demons and her transcendence over Time

digvijaya Command of all directions. Nature of power sought by kings of medieval South Asia.

dikpala Guardian of the directions. *Dikpala* figures were carved in many temples to ward off danger from all directions.

dravida (drāviḍa) Architectural mode featuring pyramidal towers, split pilasters, and strings of axially aligned halls. Found most commonly but not exclusively in southern India. Sanskrit for "Tamil."

Drona (Droṇa) Father of Ashvatthaman. Pandava brothers' teacher in martial arts, in the *Mahabharata* epic. Becomes a warrior, defying his birth into the priestly caste.

Durga (Durgā) Name for the supreme form of the female divine; often a synonym for Devi. Male gods generate Durga and give her their weapons to destroy the buffalo demon Mahisha, whom they cannot control.

dvapara yuga (dvāpara yuga) Age of Deuce, second of the Four Ages (*yuga*s) of cyclic time

Gajasamharamurti (Gajasaṃharamūrti) See under *Shiva.*

gana (gaṇa) One of the dwarf minions who attend on Shiva, often providing a plump comic foil to his imposing grandeur

gandharva Musician who plays and sings music in the world of the gods

Ganesha (Gaṇeśa) Elephant-headed god who embodies *mangalam*. May accompany yoginis and *matrika*s. Often cast as one of the sons of Shiva and Parvati.

Ganga (Gaṅgā) Goddess who personifies the river that flows from Shiva's home in the Himalayas across northern India and into the Bay of Bengal. "Ganges" in British English.

Gangadhara (Gaṅgādhara) See under *Shiva.*

garbha griha (garbha gṛha) "Seed house" or "womb." Term for the inner sanctum of Hindu temples.

Garuda (Garuḍa) Man-bird who transports Vishnu

gopuram (gōpuram) Barrel-vaulted gateway that pierces the *prakara* walls surrounding temples in southern India. A common element of a temple in the *dravida* mode.

Govardhana Mountain that Krishna lifts to shelter Braj villagers from the deluge Indra sends down when they worship Krishna instead of him. Also the name of the form of Krishna lifting that mountain.

grantha An early script for writing Sanskrit

Hiranyakashipu (Hiraṅyakaśipu) Evil king killed by Vishnu in his incarnation as Narasimha, the man-lion

Jina (jina) One of the twenty-four teachers revered as perfected beings in the Jaina tradition. Synonym for *Tirthankara*, literally "one who has crossed over" to a higher level of being.

Jyeshtha (Jyeṣṭhā) The "oldest woman," this round-bellied goddess is a mother of adult children. A deity favored in the Pallava period but denigrated in more recent times.

Kailasa (Kailāsa, Kailāśa) Himalayan mountain that is Shiva's mythic home

Kailasanatha (Kailāsanātha) "The Lord of Mount Kailasa," an epithet for Shiva. The Pallavas' Kanchi temple by this name is one of many named after this aspect of Shiva.

Kala (kāla) Sanskrit for "time," "death"

Kalakala (Kālakāla) Death of Death; another name for Shiva Kalarimurti. See also *Shiva*.

Kalarimurti (Kālārimūrti) See under *Shiva*.

kali yuga Age of Strife; literally the "black age"; last of the Four Ages

Kama (Kāma) God of love

karanyasa (karanyāsa) Ritual in which practitioners move their concentration from the thumb of the right hand, one finger at a time, until they reach the pinkie finger; or they move in the opposite direction, starting with the right pinkie. The movement is a microcosm of circumambulation around a temple.

Kotravai (Koṟṟavai) Beautiful goddess of the battlefield in early Tamil literature. A deer is often her companion.

Krishna (Kṛṣṇa) Cowherd, lover, heroic king, naughty child, and deity often described as an incarnation of Vishnu

krita yuga (kṛta yuga) Age of Completeness; the first and happiest of the Four Ages. A utopia.

kshatriya (kṣatriya) Caste of kings and warriors

Kubera God of wealth, treasure, plenty

Lakshmi (Lakṣmī) Goddess who embodies the *mangalam*. Another name for her is Shri. She is associated with good fortune, plenty, fecundity. Vishnu is her husband. She is often shown seated in the same posture as kings receiving *abhisheka* with elephants pouring water over her.

linga (liṅga, liṅgam) Columnar emblem of Shiva. Some early *linga* sculptures are explicitly phallic in form. Later *lingas*, more abstract in form, have come to be regarded as aniconic emblems of Shiva.

Lingodbhava (Liṅgodbhava) See under *Shiva*.

Madhu and Kaitabha (Kaiṭabha) Disruptive forces who threaten the world while Vishnu sleeps. Vishnu's weapons defeat them while he continues to slumber.

Mahabharata (*Mahābhārata*) Epic of the massive war between the Pandava brothers and the Kauravas, their cousins

Mahisha (Mahīṣa) Water-buffalo demon whom the Goddess kills in the *Devi Mahatmya*

Mahishasuramardini (Mahīṣāsuramardiṇī) Form of the Goddess in which she kills Mahisha

mandala (maṇḍala) A geometric diagram that maps an orderly cosmos centered on its chief deities. Mandala drawings make good objects for meditation because of their regular forms. One meditation practice is to picture the mandala unfolding as a three-dimensional, heavenly palace.

mandapam (maṇḍapam) Hall, often supported by pillars

mangalam (maṅgalam in Tamil; maṅgala in Sanskrit) The complement of *amangalam*. A mode of being that seeks to sustain life and the cycle of rebirth. *Mangalam* things include fecundity, nurture, water, procreation, marriage, prosperity, and kings on their thrones. Shri and Lakshmi are synonyms for *mangalam*.

Markandeya (Mārkaṇḍeya) Young devotee of Shiva whom Shiva rescues from Death

matrika (mātṛka) Mother-goddess; South Asian sculpture emphasizes her martial qualities more than her maternity

mumukshu (mumukṣu) In contemporary Shaiva Siddhanta practice, ascetics who seek purification, liberation, and a reunion with the divine

naga (nāga) Snake or mythical creature that is part snake, part human

Narasimha (Narasiṃha) Incarnation of Vishnu who is half man, half lion

Natesha (Naṭeśa) See under *Shiva*.

Nishumbha (Niśumbha) Demon the Goddess kills in the *Devi Mahatmya*. First she kills his brother Shumbha and ties intestines from his corpse into her hair.

parivaralaya (parivārālaya) Shrines lining the outer side of the circumambulatory path around a central shrine. These were common in the ninth and tenth centuries in the central Tamil region.

Parvati (Pārvatī) Form of the Goddess who is Shiva's wife. Another name for Uma.

pradakshina (pradakṣiṇā) Circumambulation in a clockwise direction; literally, "to the south"

prakara (prākāra) Structure that surrounds temple courtyards. At least one story high; its inner surface may be lined with small shrines or cells, as are the *prakara*s at the Kailasanatha.

prashasti (praśasti) Eulogistic poetry written for South Asian kings and frequently preserved in stone inscriptions

puranas (purāṇas) "The old ones"; Sanskrit texts that record the myths of the deities

Ramayana (*Rāmāyaṇa*) Sanskrit epic narrating the journeys of Prince Rama

ratha "Chariot"; also used to describe any of the five rock-cut temple-shaped monoliths carved from a single boulder at the south end of the Pallava port-city, Mamallapuram

Rati Wife of Kama, the god of love

Ravana (Rāvaṇa) Ten-headed, twenty-armed warrior whom Shiva imprisoned beneath Mount Kailasa

samhara (saṃhara) Destruction

sapta matrika (sapta mātṛka) "Seven mothers"; the heptad form in which *matrika*s are most commonly worshipped in South Asia

Saraswati (Sarasvatī) Goddess personifying the Saraswati River. Sometimes described as the wife of Brahma.

194

sarvatobhadra Facing in all directions

Shakyamuni (Śākyamuni) "The sage of the Shakya clan." Another name for the Buddha.

shala (śāla) Hall; architectural form rectangular in plan with a barrel-vaulted roof

shastra (śāstra) Treatises containing instructions for various practices such as building, carving, painting, and dance

shikhara (śikhara) Mountain-like tower on a temple

shilpa shastra (śilpa śāstra) Treatises containing instructions for making visual art

Shiva (Śiva) A male deity in the Hindu pantheon associated with yoginis, the sun, and the cycle of creation and destruction. Shiva in many forms has been the central object of worship at the Kailasanatha temple.

Shiva Ardhanarishvara (Śiva Ardhanārīśvara) Shiva with a body that is half female and half male

Shiva Bhikshatana (Śiva Bhikṣāṭana) Shiva wandering naked and penitent, charming the wives of the sages

Shiva Dakshinamurti (Śiva Dakṣiṇāmūrti) Shiva as a teacher in the forest

Shiva Gajasamharamurti (Śiva Gajasaṃharamūrti) Shiva destroying the elephant demon

Shiva Gangadhara (Śiva Gaṅgādhara) Shiva catching the Ganga River in an outstretched lock of his hair as she falls from the heavens

Shiva Kalarimurti (Śiva Kālārimūrti) Shiva kicking and defeating Death (Kala) to defend his young devotee Markandeya

Shiva Lingodbhava (Śiva Liṅgodbhava) Shiva manifesting from within an infinite flaming pillar or linga. Vishnu as a boar is unable to find the base of the pillar. Brahma as a goose is unable to find its top.

Shiva Natesha (Śiva Naṭeśa) One of the many dancing postures in which sculptures represent Shiva. In this posture, both his knees are deeply bent and one knee touches the ground.

Shiva Somaskanda (Śiva Somāskanda) Shiva with the goddess Uma as his wife and the god Skanda as his baby son. In most representations, they share a wide throne and Skanda sits between his parents.

Shiva Tripurantaka (Śiva Tripurāntaka) Shiva riding a chariot into battle against the three cities of the *asura*s, lower beings

Shiva Umamaheshvara (Śiva Umāmaheśvara) See *Shiva Umasahita*.

Shiva Umasahita (Śiva Umasāhitā) Shiva seated comfortably with the Goddess in her form as Uma

Shiva Urdhvatandava (Śiva Ūrdhavatāṇḍava) Shiva dancing with unbent legs. He stands on one fully extended leg. The other leg rises straight up past his shoulder, toes pointed to the sky.

Shiva Vinadhara (Śiva Vīṇādhara) Shiva playing music on the *vina*

Shiva Yogishvara (Śiva Yogīśvara) Shiva as a master of yoga

Shri (Śrī) The female divine embodying the *mangalam*, the energy that sustains life on this earth. A synonym for Lakshmi.

Shumbha (Śumbha) Demon king who proposes to Devi in the *Devi Mahatmya*. She kills him and ties intestines from his corpse into her hair. Then she kills his brother Nishumbha.

Silappadigaram (*Cilappatikāram*) Ancient Tamil epic, written by Ilango Adigal, in which a virtuous and wronged woman transforms into the goddess Kotravai

Simhavahini (Siṃhavāhinī) Lion-borne form of the Goddess. Variant of Durga's Mahishasuramardini aspect.

Skanda See *Subrahmanyam*.

Somaskanda (Somāskanda) See under *Shiva*.

sthapati Chief artisan who directs other members of his guild

Subrahmanyam (Subrahmaṇyam) Princely and often martial young god also known as Murugan, Skanda, Kumara, Karttikkeya, and Shanmuga (who rides a peacock). Myths and the visual arts often cast him as a son of Shiva and Parvati/Uma.

tandava (tāṇḍava) A fierce dance or energy. Shiva's famous dance as Nataraja with one leg lifted across his body fuses *tandava* energy with tranquil, or *ananda*, energy. See also *Shiva Urdhvatandava*.

tejas Energy

treta yuga (tretā yuga) Age of Trey, third of the Four Ages (*yuga*s) of cyclic time

Tripurantaka (Tripurāntaka) See under *Shiva*.

Trivikrama Dwarf incarnation (avatar) of Vishnu, who covers the worlds in three steps. Visual representations often show him raising a long, straight leg into the air at a high angle.

Uma (Umā) A form of the Goddess that is a gentle wife to Shiva. Often a synonym for Parvati.

Umamaheshvara (Umāmaheśvara) See under *Shiva*.

urdhva linga (ūrdhva liṅga) Erect phallus signifying a state of self-control

Urdhvatandava (Ūrdhavatāṇḍava) See under *Shiva*.

Vaishnava (Vaiṣṇava) Of or pertaining to Vishnu

Varaha (Varāha) Boar incarnation Vishnu assumes to rescue the goddess Earth (Bhu) from the ocean.

vastushastra (vāstu śāstra) Collective term for the body of Sanskrit treatises on architecture

vihara (vihāra) Structural or rock-cut building in which residents of a Buddhist monastery slept, meditated, and perhaps assembled. The latest form consists of a central hall surrounded by small cells, on three sides, and one large cell, on axis with the entryway, for a seated image of the Buddha teaching.

vimana (vimāna) A building containing a shrine to a deity. Often square in plan; usually carries a tower.

vina (vīṇa) A stringed musical instrument that resonates through one or two hollow gourds

Vinadhara (Vīṇādhara) See under *Shiva*.

Vishnu (Viṣṇu) A male deity in the Hindu pantheon associated with preserving the earth. This he often achieves by descending to earth in physical form (avatar).

Vishnu Anantashayin (Viṣṇu Anantaśayin) Vishnu reclining on a bed formed by the coils of his snake Ananta

yali (yāli) Composite leonine creatures, often with horns, that are frequent architectural ornaments on South Indian temples. At Pallava monuments, they sit at the base of columns or rear up from them. Later, they form a running frieze beneath the roof cornice or among the basement moldings.

yogabandha Strap that enables yogi practitioners to hold certain postures

Yoganidra (Yoganidrā) The deep yogic sleep possessing Vishnu when the demons Madhu and Kaitabha threaten the world. The *Devi Mahatmya* hymns identify this as an invisible form the Goddess takes.

yogini (yoginī) A divine or human female practitioner of yoga; in temple sculpture, a goddess joined by many other yogini goddesses to express the multiplicity and ubiquity of Shakti

Yogishvara (Yogīśvara) See under *Shiva*.

yoni (yonī) Female reproductive organs; these may be abstracted in sculpture as a circle with a single opening

NOTES

ABBREVIATIONS

EI	*Epigraphia Indica*
IA 1978–79	*Indian Archaeology 1978–79: A Review*
IA 1994–95	*Indian Archaeology 1994–95: A Review*
SII	*South Indian Inscriptions*

INTRODUCTION

1   I use the name Kailasanatha to signify the entire temple complex. R. Nagaswamy prefers to call the monument Rajasimheshvara after the name used in the *vimana* inscription (Nagaswamy, *The Kailasanatha Temple*, 1). Inscriptions on other shrines within the complex, however, give each of them separate names: Mahendravarmeshvara (Mahendravarmeśvara) and Nityaviniteshvara (Nityavinīteśvara). Even the inscription on Rajasimha's *vimana* uses other terms for the temple: Rajasimheshvara (v. 11) and Rajasimha-Pallaveshvara (v. 10). See appendices 2–4.

I prefer therefore to follow K. R. Srinivasan and Emmanuel Francis, using Rajasimheshvara to refer to the *vimana* alone and Kailasanatha to refer to the larger complex in which that *vimana* stands (K. R. Srinivasan, "Pallavas of Kāñcī," 59; Francis, "Le discours

royal," 394). They note that Kailasanatha is the name by which this temple has been known locally for the past century. This popular usage may be a holdover from Narasimhavarman III Pallava's ninth-century Vēlūrpāḷaiyam plates, which recognize Rajasimha for building "of stone a house for the moon-crested (Śiva) which was comparable with the (mountain) Kailāsa" (H. K. Sastri, *SII*, 2.5.98, v. 13, 511). Francis notes that the comparison with that mountain is key to the temple's iconography.

2   On those phases of neglect and the changes made to the building during phases of revival, see Kaimal, "Loved, Unloved, Changed: Afterlives of the Kailasanatha Temple in Kanchipuram," *Artibus Asiae* 81.2 (2021).

3   The ground plans in this book are designed by Mark R. Williams of Colgate University. They are informed by my visits to the site as well as

197

the plans by Francis, "Le discours royal," 638; Gillet, *La création d'une iconographie*, flyleaf insert; L'Hernault, *L'iconographie de Subrahmanya*, plan 1; Rea, *Pallava Architecture*, plate 24; and K. R. Srinivasan, "Pallavas of Kāñcī," fig. 41 (which replicates Rea).

Édith Parlier-Renault's plan identifies the figure inside the large *vimana*'s northeast shrine as Parvati, but that goddess is only an onlooker from the right wall; the central figure is Shiva dancing. On the open *mandapam*, Jyeshtha sits where her plan says "Durga" (Parlier-Renault, *Temples de l'Inde méridionale*, plan 30). The plan in Susan L. Huntington and John C. Huntington's survey depicts all the small shrines of the large *prakara* opening directly onto the courtyard (Huntington and Huntington, *The Art of Ancient India*, fig. 14.32). Those of the north and south walls, however, open to the east.

4 For photos, see, for example, Raman, *The Dharmarāja Ratha*.

5 Art historian Pia Brancaccio proposes that Buddhist *vihara*s (dwelling caves) in fifth-century Ajanta disoriented visitors to allow them to feel transported to the divine realm. Brancaccio, "The Cave as a Palace."

6 Because the shrine interior is under active worship, I have been permitted to view it but not to photograph it for publication.

7 Margaret Darby of Colgate University, personal communication, 2011.

8 Romita Ray of Syracuse University, personal communication, 2012.

9 As Caroline Walker Bynum finds to be true of medieval visual culture in Europe. Medieval History seminar, Institute for Advanced Study, Princeton, NJ, December 2011. See, too, Granoff, "Heaven on Earth"; Meister, "Navigating Hudson," 46-47.

10 Crispin Branfoot makes this point for South Indian temples in general. Branfoot, *Gods on the Move*, 41–61, 129–43.

11 On the newness of this Shiva, see Schmid, " Bhakti in Its Infancy"; Gillet, *La création d'une iconographie*.

12 On the monument's diverse audiences, see Gillet, *La création d'une iconographie*, 65–71. Emma Natalya Stein finds Buddha sculptures from all over the city in styles of the sixth to twelfth centuries. The present site of the Kamakshi (Kāmākṣī) Amman temple was

once a cluster of Buddhist and Jaina shrines, which included an early Buddha figure now in the Chennai Government Museum. Stein, "All Streets Lead to Temples," 218–25; fig. 3.71. On the persistence of multiple religious traditions in much of Tamil history, see Orr, "Sacred Ground"; Orr, "Identity and Divinity." The city's southeastern extension is still called Jina Kanchi. Heitzman, "Secondary Cities," 311.

13 Orr, "Sacred Ground"; Schmid, "Au seuil du monde divin."

14 Stein posits that the Pallava palace stood to the northeast of the Kailasanatha complex, just to the southeast of the Ekambaranatha complex. Stein, personal communication, 2020. This idea is a revision of her hypothesis in her dissertation: that the palace was just east of the Kailasanatha complex. Stein, "All Streets Lead to Temples," 91.

15 Nagaswamy, "Innovative Emperor and His Personal Chapel"; Nagaswamy, *The Kailasanatha Temple*, 17–19.

16 Robert DeCaroli argues that the Pallava court sponsored the poet Dandin and his cleverly monitory poem on good kingship. DeCaroli, "An Analysis of Daṇḍin's *Daśakumāracarita*." Francis is skeptical that Dandin and Bharavi were patronized by the Pallava court, but he finds Mahendravarman I Pallava the likely author of the *Mattavilasa* (*Mattavilāsa*). Francis, "Le discours royal," 79–113. So, too, is Srinivasan. K. R. Srinivasa, *Cave Temples of the Pallavas*, 8. For translations of the *Mattavilasa*, see Lorenzen, "A Parody of the Kāpālikas"; King Mahendravikramavarma Pallava, *Mattavilasa Prahasana*.

17 Devangana Desai, too, perceives that an *acharya* (teacher) or architect-priest and his disciple or the *sthapati* (chief artisan) worked together to design the monuments at Khajuraho. Desai, "Textual Tradition," 62.

I share with Emmanuel Francis, Valérie Gillet, and Charlotte Schmid a discomfort with seeing temples only through the eyes of a learned priest (*acharya*), as they find Dennis Hudson doing in his study of the Vaikuntha Perumal. Francis, Gillet, and Schmid, "Chronique des études 'Pallava' I," 604; Hudson, *The Body of God*. Richard H. Davis has similar reservations and contrasts that approach with the focus on architects and the goal "to understand the logic of the temple itself" in the *Encyclopaedia of Indian Temple Architecture*. Davis, "Hudson Rethinks Bhagavata Thoughts," 31–35; Meister and Dhaky, *Encyclopaedia of Indian Temple Architecture*, vol. 1, pt. 1.

18 In believing that the people ultimately responsible for what this deluxe monument looked like and how it occupied space were smart and successful in their own terms, I follow the innovative art historical interventions of Molly Emma Aitken, in her interpretations of Indic manuscript painting, and Catherine Becker, in her interpretations of Andhra sculpture. Aitken, *The Intelligence of Tradition*; Becker, *Shifting Stones*, 21.

19 Gillet documents the same north/south pattern organizing sculpture at the other temples built in the Pallava realm until the second half of the eighth century. Gillet, *La création d'une iconographie*, 318–25. On the shift in that pattern after that, see ibid., 326–28. On these other Pallava temples, see also K. R. Srinivasan, "Pallavas of Kāñcī"; Dumarçay and L'Hernault, *Temples Pallava construits*; Parlier-Renault, *Temples de l'Inde méridionale*; Francis, Gillet, and Schmid, "Chronique des études 'Pallava' I"; and Mahalingam, *Kāñcīpuram in Early South Indian History*, 109–32.

Inscriptions verify that Rajasimha himself patronized the Shore Temples at Mamallapuram, the Talapurishvara (Tālapurishvara) at Panaimalai, the Airavateshvara (Airavateśvara) in Kanchi, and the Adiranachanda (Atiraṇacaṇḍa) at Saluvankuppam. Architecturally, too, these temples share much with Rajasimha's *vimana* at the Kailasanatha. Mamallapuram's Shore Temples, for example, repeat the aedicular components of its spires, and the Talapurishvara at Panaimalai embeds subshrines in the outer surface of its *vimana* as Rajasimha's *vimana* does.

But I do not subscribe to R. Nagaswamy's bold attribution of all Mamallapuram's temples to Rajasimha. That relies on identifying one royal epithet (*biruda*) as Rajasimha's alone. Nagaswamy, "New Light on Mamallapuram." I find the high value Pallavas placed on their long shared lineage makes it unlikely a king would have one *biruda* all to himself. For other convincing counterarguments, see K. R. Srinivasan, "Pallavas of Kāñcī," 76–78; Gillet,

La création d'une iconographie, 57; Lockwood, Siromoney, and Dayanandan, *Mahabalipuram Studies*, chap. 5.

20 On the Kailasanatha as the oldest of the Pallava-period temples in the city, see Gillet, *La création d'une iconographie*, 57; and Soundara Rajan, "Rajasimha's Temples," 182. Francis, however, sees the Shore Temples as older. Francis, "Le discours royal," 390, n. 354.

21 Francis, Gillet, and Schmid, "Chronique des études 'Pallava' I," 598–601.

22 Ibid., 601–2; Minakshi, *The Historical Sculptures at the Vaikuṇṭhaperumāḷ Temple*, 52; Asher, "Historical and Political Allegory"; Hudson, *The Body of God*, 18. Pallavamalla's emulation of Rajasimha also manifested in an inscription on copper plates issued by the later king. Hultzsch, *SII*, 2.3.73. On Pallavamalla's admiration for Rajasimha, see Mahalingam, *Kāñcīpuram in Early South Indian History*, 76.

23 Becker frames the challenge by citing W. J. T. Mitchell: "The academic probing of images as vessels of the sacred has the tendency 'to pose as an iconoclastic practice, a labor of demystification.'" Mitchell, *What Do Pictures Want?*, 8; Becker, *Shifting Stones*, 234.

24 This strategy I borrow from Becker's empathetic reading of Buddhist sculpture from ancient Andhra. See Becker, *Shifting Stones*, chap. 2.

25 Michael Baxandall theorized this mode of seeing and called it a "period eye." Baxandall, *Painting and Experience in Fifteenth-Century Italy*. I share with Richard H. Davis a desire to see and tell history "from the inside," as opposed to a recitation of dates and events. Davis, "Hudson Rethinks Bhagavata Thoughts," 28, characterizing R. G. Collingwood's view of history.

26 British archaeological surveys begin in the early twentieth century with Rea, *Pallava Architecture*; and Longhurst, *Pallava Architecture*, pt. 3, 10–17. It receives mention in 1920 by Jouveau-Dubreuil, *Ancient History of the Deccan*, 46–74; and then Gopalan, *History of the Pallavas of Kanchi*. Art history takes up the monument with Soundara Rajan, "Rajasimha's Temples"; Nagaswamy, *Tantric Cult of South India*; K. R. Srinivasan, "Temples of the Later Pallavas"; K. R. Srinivasan, "Pallavas of Kāñcī"; Lockwood, Siromoney, and Dayanandan, *Mahabalipuram Studies*;

Lockwood et al., *Mamallapuram and the Pallavas*; and Dumarçay and L'Hernault, *Temples Pallava construits*. Surveys of South Asian art history feature it too, including Huntington and Huntington, *The Art of Ancient India*; and Dehejia, *Indian Art*.

27 T. V. Mahalingam puts Rajasimha's accession in 691; DeCaroli sees the reign as extending from 695 to 722. Mahalingam, *Kāñcīpuram in Early South Indian History*, 109–32; DeCaroli, "An Analysis of Daṇḍin's *Daśakumāracarita*," 675. On the variety of dates assigned to Rajasimha's accession and death, see Gillet, *La création d'une iconographie*, 37. On the difficulty of fixing such dates with certainty, see Francis, "Le discours royal," 27–32.

28 Nagaswamy saw this as evidence of "highly developed concepts of [a] Devi cult." Nagaswamy, *Tantric Cult of South India*, 167. Francis, Gillet, and Schmid note that women have been central to the worship of Shiva. Francis, Gillet, and Schmid, "Chronique des études Pallava III," 288–95.

29 Lockwood, Siromoney, and Dayanandan, *Mahabalipuram Studies*, 35; Francis, Gillet, and Schmid, "Chronique des études 'Pallava' I," 592–93, 596–97, 606; Parlier-Renault, *Temples de l'Inde méridionale*, 146–63; Gillet, *La création d'une iconographie*, 318–19; Francis, "Le discours royal," 393–98; Schmid, "Au seuil du monde divin," 78–84.

30 Francis, "The Genealogy of the Pallavas"; Francis, "Le discours royal," 433–34; Schmid, "La Prospérité."

31 On the presence of explicit mountain imagery in Indic temple architecture evoking Mount Meru and the mountain of heaven studded with palaces for each god, see Granoff, "Heaven on Earth"; Nagaswamy, "The Brihadīśvara as Paramākāśa"; Meister, "Forest and Cave"; Meister, "Prāsāda as Palace"; Meister, "Symbol and Surface."

32 See also Meister, "The Hindu Temple." The temple can be read as a palace as well as Mount Meru.

33 See Hardy, *The Temple Architecture of India*, 37–43; Hardy, *Theory and Practice*, 27; Desai, "Temple as an Ordered Whole."

34 On the hut analogy, see Meister and Coomaraswamy, "Early Indian Architecture"; Meister and Rykwert, "Adam's House and Hermits' Huts."

35 On the tree analogy, see Meister, "Forest and Cave."

36 Granoff, "Heaven on Earth."

37 Kaimal, "Learning to See the Goddess."

38 Vasudha Narayanan observes that Vishnu is never without Shri, though he dominates her when they are together. Narayanan, "Śrī."

39 On the importance of attending to distinctions people made between women and goddesses, see Hiltebeitel and Erndl, "Introduction: Writing Goddesses, Goddesses Writing"; Menon and Shweder, "Power in Its Place"; Ochshorn, "Goddesses and the Lives of Women," 396; and Goodison and Morris, "Beyond the 'Great Mother.'" On the dangers of assuming that maternal imagery for the divine "reflects an increasingly positive attitude toward women in medieval society," see Bynum, *Jesus as Mother*, 139.

40 On the importance of grounding understandings of the distant past in the specifics of material culture, see Goodison and Morris, "Beyond the 'Great Mother'"; and Tringham and Conkey, "Rethinking Figurines."

41 Compare Becker's demonstration of sight catalyzing transformation in a viewer through Amaravati sculptures of the "Man in the Well." Becker, *Shifting Stones*, chap. 2.

42 To paraphrase Yve-Alain Bois, faculty member of the Institute for Advanced Study, Princeton, NJ, in his lecture "Materialist Formalism," delivered at the institute in 2011.

43 Ibid.

44 On the importance of acknowledging the physicality of inscriptions, see Orr, preface to *Pondicherry Inscriptions*, pt. 1, v.

45 On visual material supplying information that the textual record cannot, see Francis, Gillet, and Schmid, "Chronique des études Pallava III," 301. On the complementarity of text and image, and a challenge to the assumption that visual material is only for the illiterate, see Mostert, "Reading Images and Texts."

46 R. Nagaswamy argues that sculptures of the directional guardians, solar deities, and others in the monument's outer regions demonstrate that "the *vāstumaṇḍala* concept is fully developed in the Kailasanatha temple of Kanchi." Nagaswamy, *The Kailasanatha Temple*, 28–29. And again Nagaswamy, "Innovative Emperor and His Personal Chapel," 53. Here he borrows a chain of associations between temple,

mandala, and organizational grid planning proposed by Stella Kramrisch's *Hindu Temple*: that temple sculptures and walls follow *agama*s and *shastra*s in using a grid diagram mapped out beneath the ground plan, a diagram thought to associate the temple above it with the concept of the primordial man, Purusha (Puruṣa). Sonit Bafna challenges this chain of associations between mandala, grid, and temple. Bafna, "On the Idea of the Mandala."

47 Scholars date the *Bṛhat Saṃhitā*, which contains architectural theories, to the sixth century. Hardy, *Theory and Practice*, 22; Mosteller, "The Problem of Proportion," 389; Bafna, "On the Idea of the Mandala," 45. Meister notes that people began composing such treatises around the same time they began building temples in stone. Meister, "Vāstupuruṣamaṇḍalas," 253–55. Such knowledge became more urgently needed for actual building practices. On these early texts as compilations of even older knowledge, see Hardy, *Theory and Practice*, 22; Mosteller, "The Problem of Proportion," 389.

48 See Davis, "Hudson Rethinks Bhagavata Thoughts," 39. Davis is critical of Hudson's assumption that sacred texts reflect an unchanging theology. Davis regards texts, even when they compile much older elements, as reliable sources of the beliefs in operation only at the time of compilation.

49 Desai, "Textual Tradition," 59–61; Desai, "The Location of Sculptures." Mary Beth Heston finds Padmanabhapuram conforming to a mandala and thus following rules laid down in the Mayamata. Heston, "The Nexus of Divine and Earthly Rule," 101.

50 Mosteller's quotation of B. N. Goswamy on the translation of *shastra*. Mosteller, "The Problem of Proportion," 389, n. 385.

51 On preferring this flexibility to perceptions of *shastra*s as straitjackets of tradition or as simple instruction manuals, see Bafna, "On the Idea of the Mandala"; Hardy, *Theory and Practice*; Mosteller, "The Problem of Proportion"; Parker, "Text and Practice"; Thakur, "Application of Vāstupuruṣamaṇḍala"; Chanchani and Sears, introduction to "Transmission of Architectural Knowledge."

Mehmet-Ali Ataç, historian of ancient Near Eastern art, warns: "One of the main problems is that the long-standing text-based methods of iconographic interpretation have usually been employed too rigidly. Some sort of direct semantic coherence between texts and images has often been assumed—either a relation of parallelism, or, when that does not work, one of complementarity." Ataç, "'Time and Eternity,'" 164.

52 Hardy, *Theory and Practice*. Samuel K. Parker cites examples of mismatches between sculpture and *shastra*s. Parker, "Text and Practice," 34. Gift Siromoney and his collaborators find that the proportions of sculptural figures at the Kailasanatha do not correspond to the recommendations in the *Shilparatnam* (*Śilparatnam*) treatise. Siromoney, Bagavandas, and Govindaraju, "An Application of Component Analysis," 34–35.

53 As Ataç puts it: "We should also acknowledge, however, that in ancient art images may hold special information that texts do not immediately preserve. . . . [Visual representations may] constitute a system of communication in their own right . . . a system not parallel or complementary but independently hinged, as it were, from textual systems of codifying information." Ataç, "'Time and Eternity,'" 164–65.

54 Hardy, *Theory and Practice*, 266–69.

CHAPTER 1.
ORDER AND IMPROVISATION

1 My sense of the sequence in which these components were built was significantly refined by Francis, "Le discours royal," 391–93; and Schmid, "Bhakti in Its Infancy," 118–20. On the process of expansion at other South Indian temples too as a series of oscillations rather than a steady growth outward from the center, see Branfoot, "Remaking the Past," 22–26.

2 Meister, "Ethnography and Personhood."

3 A *linga* was most likely part of this monument from the start, even if the current stone was added later. See Dumarçay and L'Hernault, *Temples Pallava construits*; Lockwood, Siromoney, and Dayanandan, *Mahabalipuram Studies*, 27–32, 42–61; K. R. Srinivasan, "Pallavas of Kāñcī." They dispute K. V. Soundara Rajan's suggestion that the Somaskanda reliefs in these shrines were initially the sole objects

of worship. Soundara Rajan, "'Cult' in the Pallava Temples," 144–46.

4 Lockwood, Siromoney, and Dayanandan, *Mahabalipuram Studies*, 27–32, 42–61; Gillet, *La création d'une iconographie*, 279.

5 Hudson thought the initial purpose of that passageway was structural—perhaps to lighten the weight of structure held the same view. Hudson, "Kanchipuram," 23–25. Stein notes that circumambulation through this passage has not been easy for some time. Stein, "All Streets Lead to Temples," 58. The path was presented on October 23, 1999, to Anuradha Nambiar, who found the cramped passageway very difficult to crawl through (personal communication, February 2002).

6 Phyllis Granoff notes parallels to literary descriptions of heaven in which every god is master of her or his own heaven, and each heaven contains all the other deities in a subordinate location. Granoff, "Heaven on Earth." Diana L. Eck writes about the multiplicity of deities as "kathenotheism," the worship of one deity at a time within the acknowledgment that a great many deities exist. Eck, *Darśan*, 26.

7 Francis, Gillet, and Schmid, "Chronique des études 'Pallava' I," 592; Gillet, *La création d'une iconographie*, 170.

8 Schmid brought this to my attention on-site in 2011. For photos of other Surya sculptures, see Huntington and Huntington, *The Art of Ancient India*, 161; Gopinatha Rao, *Elements of Hindu Iconography*, vol. 2, pt. 2, plates 88–95.

9 Mallmann, *Les enseignements iconographiques*, vol. 67, 80, 93, 95–107. On Shaiva appropriations of Surya's iconography, see also Hatley, "The Brahmayāmalatantra."

10 For a photo, see Kaimal, "Playful Ambiguity," fig. 20.

11 Ibid., fig. 3. On Govardhana and Gangadhara being linked at the Vaikuntha Perumal, see Francis, Gillet, and Schmid, "Chronique des études 'Pallava' I," 600, figs. 9–10.

12 Kaimal, "Playful Ambiguity," figs. 10, 13.

13 Among those who have observed this connection are Francis, Gillet, and Schmid, "Chronique des études 'Pallava' I," 595, 599.

14 Gillet offers this convincing reading of the figure type. She interprets this frontal figure as a walking form of the ascetic teaching form of Shiva, Dakshinamurti. She notes that

L'Hernault read this as a form of Shiva's fierce Bhairava aspect and that Parlier-Renault linked it to Shiva's forms as Bhikshatana, or the destroyer of the elephant demon, or the destroyer of Jalandhara. Gillet, *La création d'une iconographie*, 109–13. Gillet also notes affinities with images of Lakulisha (Lakulīśa) and wandering mendicants since the Upanishads: ibid., 98–100. See also Parlier-Renault, *Temples de l'Inde méridionale*, 215; and Adicéam, "Les images de Śiva dans l'Inde du Sud: III et IV." On similarities with the *chakravartin* (ruler as bearer of the law) of Buddhist sculptures, see Francis, Gillet, and Schmid, "Chronique des études Pallava III," 103–4, 137–39, and figs. 69, 70.

15 On close parallels between Buddha and Krishna around the concept of *viraha*, Tracy Coleman writes: "*Viraha-bhakti* is found in Sanskrit and Pāli literature much earlier than the Āḻvārs because it originates in the heterodox traditions of Buddhism and Jainism, when the beloved saviour, embodied in human form, departs or dies, and devotees subsequently suffer and long for the saviour's return." Coleman, "Dharma, Yoga, and Viraha-Bhakti," 57.

16 In coining this new name for the building, I aim to sidestep confusing terminology in the earlier scholarship. Alexander Rea calls this the *mahamandapam*; the closed *mandapam* he calls the *ardhamandapam*. Rea, *Pallava Architecture*, 19, 36–38. Eugen Hultzsch calls this simply the *mandapa*, reserving the term *mahamandapam* for what Rea calls the *ardhamandapam*. Hultzsch, *SII*, 1.VI, 111–16. A. H. Longhurst calls the open *mandapam* "the ancient mandapa." Longhurst, *Pallava Architecture*, pt. 3, 12. Srinivasan calls it "Rajasimha's *mandapa*." K. R. Srinivasan, "Pallavas of Kāñcī," 63. Francis and Schmid call it the "*mandapam* of the goddesses." Francis, "Le discours royal," 390; Schmid, "Bhakti in Its Infancy," 114.

17 Emma Natalya Stein got me to see that the open *mandapam* could be the oldest surviving structure in the complex, when we visited the site together in 2015. Rea thought so too, referring to its "archaic details," the massive stone piers and heavy square capitals. Rea, *Pallava Architecture*, 36–38.

18 For examples, see K. R. Srinivasan, *Cave*

Temples of the Pallavas, plates 4–34.

19 See, for example, the unfinished caves in Viḷāppākkam, Aragaṇḍanaḷḷur, and Mamallapuram. Ibid., plates 1 and 26. See also the caves at Tiruppāmalai and Mēlcēri. Pattabiramin, *Sanctuaires rupestres*, vol. 42, plates 18 and 35.

20 See the later pillars at Kōnēri Mandapam and Mahishasuramardini Cave in Mamallapuram and Srinivasan's typology for pillar form change. K. R. Srinivasan, *Cave Temples of the Pallavas*, 41 and plates 39.A, 45.

21 What Rea assumed to be a foundation inscription was instead cut a few centuries later as part of the donation campaign that sustained the temple. Rea, *Pallava Architecture*, 11, n. 77. The inscription is No. 85 in Hultzsch, *SII*, 1.VI, 116–17.

22 On the Skanda temple, see Badhreenath, *Śāluvankuppam Excavations*.

23 For this brilliant rereading of the Shore Temples, see Francis, Gillet, and Schmid, "Chronique des études 'Pallava' I," 587–90. Other monuments in Mamallapuram bear other signs of forceful rededication to Shiva. Imprecatory verses praising Shiva and cursing the worship of other gods occur at several monuments previously dedicated to Vishnu including Mamallapuram's Dharmaraja Ratha, Ganesha Ratha, Ramanuja Mandapam, and Adivaraha cave temple, suggesting a widespread program of appropriation. See Raman, *The Dharmarāja Ratha*, 78–79, 96. In further acts of appropriation, Somaskanda reliefs are inserted where earlier sculptures indicate Vaishnava iconographic programs at the Varaha cave and the Mahishasuramardini cave. Dehejia and Davis, "Addition, Erasure, and Adaptation."

24 Lockwood et al. see the Somaskanda sculptures in this *prakara* as contemporary with sculptures of that subject at other monuments patronized by Rajasimha. Lockwood, Siromoney, and Dayanandan, *Mahabalipuram Studies*, 30.

25 R. Champakalakshmi perceives that the centrality of Shiva and the marginalization of Vedic deities articulates the transition from Vedic to Puranic deities in the Kailasanatha. Champakalakshmi, "Iconographic Programme and Political Imagery," 224.

26 On these *gopuram*s and analysis of the form throughout the south, see Harle, *Temple Gateways*, especially 15.

27 Francis, "Le discours royal," 391; Schmid, personal communication on-site, 2013.

28 For identifications of these sculptures, see Gillet, *La création d'une iconographie*, 285. Compare Nagaswamy, *Tantric Cult of South India*, 50–56; Rea, *Pallava Architecture*, 29–35.

29 Schmid, "Bhakti in Its Infancy." Schmid finds this iconographic merger assimilates these figures of Shiva to the Skanda of the *Mahabharata*, the *Skanda Purana*, and Kushāna sculpture and to the Murugan of the fifth- to seventh-century Tamil texts of the *Tirumurukārruppaṭai* and *Paripāṭal*.

30 As at Elephanta, Cave 1, for example. L'Hernault reads this relief, too, as Shiva's wedding. See L'Hernault, *L'iconographie de Subrahmanya*, 100, photo 48.

31 Schmid, "Bhakti in Its Infancy," 109–10.

32 Rea, *Pallava Architecture*, 19.

33 Ibid., 22–25. I follow Gillet's labeling of these shrines alphabetically from south to north.

34 On the complete anastylosis of the small *prakara* around Mahendravarman's *vimana* and temple A on the eastern façade of the temple complex, see *IA 1978–79*, 147; and *IA 1994–95*, 136.

35 Rea shows the bricks there in 1903. Rea, *Pallava Architecture*, plate 25. Hultzsch knew they were not original. Hultzsch, *SII*, 1.24, 10.

36 Hultzsch, *SII*, 1.24, 10.

37 For analysis of the conflicting literature around this attribution, see Francis, "Le discours royal," 391–92, nn. 361–63; Hultzsch, *SII*, 1.28–30, 23–24; Lockwood et al., *Pallava Art*, 149–53. Pallava women built, but they transferred the merit to their husbands, in contrast to Bana princesses and those of the tenth century. Francis, Gillet, and Schmid, "Chronique des études Pallava II," 41.

38 James C. Harle puzzled over the *shala* shape of this temple and the expectations this set up to be a gateway, which it clearly was not. He concluded that the *shala* shape was a function of being either in the middle of an enclosure wall or in direct line with the *garbha griha*. Harle, *Temple Gateways*, 15–16. Mahendra's temple baffled Longhurst, who thought it might have been built before Rajasimha's *vimana*. Longhurst, *Pallava Architecture*, pt. 3, 13.

39 Rea, *Pallava Architecture*, 20; K. R. Srinivasan, "Some Aspects of Religion," 154–55. Gillet and

Schmid drew my attention to these collisions on-site in 2011.

40 On these as iconographic shifts manifesting at later temples in the area, see Gillet, *La création d'une iconographie*, 320–22.

41 Mahalingam, *Kāñcīpuram in Early South Indian History*, 133; Mahalingam, *Readings in South Indian History*, 31–32; K. R. Srinivasan, *Cave Temples of the Pallavas*, 8–9; Schmid, "Bhakti in Its Infancy," 120; Francis, "Le discours royal," 645.

CHAPTER 2.
LOOKING NORTH AND SOUTH

1 The iconographic identifications in this chapter's endnotes draw heavily on the following resources: Adicéam, "Les images de Śiva dans l'Inde du Sud: II–XV"; Dessigane, Pattabiramin, and Filliozat, *Les légendes çivaïtes*, chaps. 40, 44; Divakaran, "Durgā, the Great Goddess"; Gillet, *La création d'une iconographie*; Nagaswamy, *Tantric Cult of South India*; Gopinatha Rao, *Elements of Hindu Iconography*; K. R. Srinivasan, "Pallavas of Kāñcī"; K. R. Srinivasan, "Some Aspects of Religion"; Tartakov and Dehejia, "Sharing, Intrusion, and Influence." Rather than citing them repeatedly, the endnotes call out only additional references.

2 On the pattern then shifting, see Gillet, *La création d'une iconographie*, 323–28.

3 Compare that subject as it is sculpted on the second tier of the Dharmaraja Ratha in Mamallapuram. Raman, *The Dharmarāja Ratha*, plate 15(a). Some versions are less violent. On overlaps between this and the iconography of Shiva's dance, see D. Smith, *The Dance of Śiva*, 201–2. On the sweetening of Shiva in the south, from Death itself to the Death of Death, see Shulman, "Notes on the Kālantaka Myth."

4 On this identification, see also Mevissen, "Political Geography."

5 The umbrella above and the fighting *ganas* below are other distinctive elements of this version of the subject. A more frequently employed form for evoking this narrative is the solitary figure of Shiva standing at his ease with one foot crossed in front of the other (*pratyalidha*), one hand on his bow and another plucking the string. This is commonly rendered in bronze. See Banerjea, *The Development of Hindu Iconography*, 487.

6 In a local Kanchi version of Jalandhara's story, Vishnu tries to rape the demon's chaste wife, Brinda, while Jalandhara is fighting Shiva, but she outwits him. Though her only escape lies in self-immolation, she takes that action, assumes power, and remains chaste.

7 For other Pallava examples, see Gillet, *La création d'une iconographie*, figs. 135–37.

8 Schmid and her colleagues make a strong case that Kotravai looms large in this iconography and that the bloody goddess and the goddess of auspiciousness are one and the same goddess. Francis, Gillet, and Schmid, "Chronique des études Pallava III," 301; Schmid, "La Prospérité." Gary Michael Tartakov and Vidya Dehejia point out that the *Silappadigaram* refers to "Korravai, the Victorious Goddess who . . . stands upon the neck of a defeated buffalo losing its blood through its fresh wounds" and kills a buffalo demon with a sword. Tartakov and Dehejia, "Sharing, Intrusion, and Influence," 330. See also K. R. Srinivasan, "Some Aspects of Religion," 152–54.

Gillet, by contrast, entertains the option that the *Devi Mahatmya* is relevant only to the seven mothers (*sapta matrika*) and several goddesses around them on the south wall of the large *prakara*. Gillet, *La création d'une iconographie*, 307–9.

9 These Pallava syntheses are discussed in Francis, Gillet, and Schmid, "Chronique des études 'Pallava' I," "Chronique des études Pallava II," and "Chronique des études Pallava III"; Champakalakshmi, "Iconographic Programme and Political Imagery," 223–25; and Kanaganayagam, "Reading the Pallava Period." On Kotravai's transformation into Parvati, see Schmid, "Bhakti in Its Infancy," 128–30.

Nagaswamy sees signs of Durga already present in early Tamil texts describing goddesses. Nagaswamy, *Tantric Cult of South India*, 6–20.

10 Schmid sees this iconography as also having roots in Vaishnava iconography as a kind of female avatar from the *Mahabharata* that Shaiva traditions appropriate. Schmid, "Á propos des premières images." Tartakov and Dehejia classify this as the Simhavahini

(lion-borne) variant of Durga's Mahishasura-mardini aspect and see this figure as stressing the Goddess's association with the lion and her supremacy over other gods by wielding their weapons, rather than the bloody aspects of sacrifice and destruction associated with Kotravai. Tartakov and Dehejia, "Sharing, Intrusion, and Influence," 331.

11 On the long history across the subcontinent of the motif with the buffalo, see Mitterwallner, "The Kuṣāṇa Type." For examples elsewhere in the Pallava kingdom, see the seventh-century Ranganatha cave at Shingavaram and, in Mamallapuram, the Trimurti cave, the Adivaraha cave, and the Draupadi Ratha. For photos, see K. R. Srinivasan, *Cave Temples of the Pallavas*; and Schmid, "La Prospérité," figs. 6–11.

12 Francis, "Le discours royal," 425–26.

13 On Gangadhara's iconography, see also Lockwood et al., *Pallava Art*, 47–52; and P. R. Srinivasan, "Gangadharashtakam." Rea mistook these as depictions of Shiva destroying the elephant demon, reading the lock of hair as the elephant's skin. Rea, *Pallava Architecture*, 40–41.

14 Michael Lockwood et al. and Marguerite E. Adicéam observe that these are the earliest known representations of Shiva's wife (Parvati/Uma) supporting him as he catches Ganga. Adicéam notes that this and other Pallava examples are unusual in that they make no apparent reference to Parvati being jealous of Ganga and place Parvati and Ganga on the same side of Shiva, not in opposition. The Pallava version may indicate that her power contributes to the task at hand. In later representations and those further to the north, the jealousy theme can overwhelm the descent theme, and Adicéam wonders if Kalidasa, the fifth-century playwright in the Gupta court, invented the jealousy subplot. She notes that the *Tēvāram* mentions this jealousy only twice. Adicéam sees the resulting imagery as characterizing the female divine as a mediator between Shiva and others. Adicéam, "Les images de Śiva dans l'Inde du Sud: XV"; Lockwood, Siromoney, and Dayanandan, *Mahabalipuram Studies*, 4. See also Francis, "Le discours royal," 415, n. 502.

15 Ganga's corporeal form is absent from both cliffs in Mamallapuram that depict this subject. Adicéam wondered if this figure of Ganga

on the Kailasanatha *vimana* might be buried under plaster, but the plaster is now gone and no Ganga is there. It is possible that the river goddess was represented in paint on the now-lost, original layer of plaster. Ganga is presented in a mermaid-like form in the earliest known Pallava instance of this subject, the relief in the cave halfway up the great rock in the center of Trichy. For photos, see Kaimal, "Playful Ambiguity."

16 Lockwood et al. wonder if the dog is an illusion Shiva conjures as he catches Ganga or an emblem of the Kadamba "feudatories." Lockwood, Bhat, and Siromoney, "A Mystery Dog in Sculpture" and "Dhvani in Epigraphy and Stone."

17 On these qualities in the hymns, see Humes, "Is the *Devi Mahatmya* a Feminist Scripture?" Compare Shulman, "The Murderous Bride."

18 On the goddess of the *Devi Mahatmya* as specifically undermining a gender binary, see Humes, "Is the *Devi Mahatmya* a Feminist Scripture?"

19 On Pallavas cherishing this dual identity and on Ashvatthaman as an expression of that, see Francis, "The Genealogy of the Pallavas," 346–47; Francis, "Le discours royal," 184–90, 440–41, 497, 544. There is a sense in the *Mahabharata* that this duality of Ashvatthaman's identity is problematic. In a similar vein, DeCaroli reads Dandin's poem as a lesson to Rajasimha on the qualities of a good king, among them fighting well, strategizing, and setting aside his own pleasure—in short, the qualities of an ascetic warrior. DeCaroli, "An Analysis of Daṇḍin's *Daśakumāracarita*."

20 My iconographic sources identify her variously as Bhairavi (Bhairavī), the Chandi-Bhairavi form of Tripura Bhairavi, or Maheśvari, though she does not match existing sculptures of any of them.

21 See Minakshi, *The Historical Sculptures at the Vaikuṇṭhaperumāḷ Temple*.

22 The creatures over her shoulder look to be Kotravai's deer or stag and Durga's lion. Some iconographers suggest Yogeshvari (Yogeśvarī) or Kaushiki (Kauśikī) as her names.

23 Schmid makes a convincing case for this position in "La Prospérité," 475. She argues that Lakshmi served as a reminder of how similar were the processes through which divine *tejas* (energy) generated goddesses and kings. She

makes the case for figures of Lakshmi especially, at seventh-century Vaishnava monuments. I am extending this to the identically
posed figure of Jyeshtha and proposing that
this eighth-century Shaiva monument could
have appropriated and transformed that
Vaishnava sign for Lakshmi on this Shaiva
monument, much as Rajasimha's Shore Temples appropriated and transformed a Vaishnava site into a Shaiva temple complex in
Mamallapuram. On that appropriation, see
chapter 1, note 23. On Shri and Durga as complementary aspects of the king at the Kailasanatha, see Parlier-Renault, *Temples de l'Inde
méridionale*, 190.

24 Caroline Walker Bynum, personal communication, Institute for Advanced Study, Princeton, NJ, 2011. As examples, Bynum cites
Cistercian monks who understood themselves
as feminine and maternal when they aspired to
honor "a need and obligation to nurture other
men, [and] a need and obligation to achieve
intimate dependence on God," and nuns of
Helfta who saw themselves as princes leading
armies. "Twelfth-century monks sometimes
call themselves women, [and] early medieval women sometimes call themselves men."
Bynum, *Jesus as Mother*, 138, 168, 251.

25 Samira Sheikh argued that martial masculinity
was forged in the Devi temple. Sheikh, "Taming the Goddess."

26 Apffel-Marglin, "Kings and Wives," 156,
170–71.

27 The goddess Mariamman can manifest in a
man. Harman, "Introduction: Fierce Goddess." Male devotees as well as female ones
visualize the self as the Goddess and the Goddess as the self. Preston, *Cult of the Goddess*.

28 Ferro-Luzzi, "The Female *Liṅgam*"; Guha and
Ferro-Luzzi, "More on the Idea of the Female
Liṅgam."

29 A sexually active state also had a consistent
effect on both, softening both kinds of bodies.
Apffel-Marglin, "Female Sexuality."

30 Leslie, "Śrī and Jyeṣṭhā." Leslie discusses Jyeshtha's negative connotations too. For non-
binary revisions of that view, see Nagarajan,
"Threshold Designs," 100–101; Zeiler, "Female
Danger." On positive regard for her in the Pallava period, see Francis, Gillet, and Schmid,
"Chronique des études Pallava II," 467–70,
and "Chronique des études Pallava III," 301.

Nicolas Cane finds that inscriptions of the
revered Chola queen Shembiyan Mahadevi
describe her as a Jyeshtha. Cane, "Cempiyan-Mahādevī," 472, n. 1167. Francis regards
Jyeshtha as exceptional among terrifying,
celibate goddesses facing north. Francis, "Le
discours royal," 396, n. 389.

31 Tryna Lyons stresses the importance of this
distinction in the worship of Durga. So does
Frédérique Apffel-Marglin. Lyons, "The Simla
Devī Māhātmya Illustrations," 36; Apffel-Marglin, "Female Sexuality," 44.

32 Perceiving that the south-facing imagery is
also about power forced me to recognize my
own twenty-first-century anxieties about
female domesticity as failure and imprison-
ment. See Orr, "Domesticity and Difference."

33 My iconographic sources call this subject
variously Umaprasada, Umamaheshvara, and
Alingana-Chandrashekhara (Alingana-Can-
draśekhara), but it differs from most other
Shiva and Uma compositions in that the figures are not both seated and frontal or both
standing, and their arms are not around each
other's backs or shoulders.

34 The two lumps above her shoulder, however,
look altered because they are so awkward. The
lime layer fashions both into Shiva's hands, but
they are at odd distances and odd angles to the
rest of his body.

35 For other examples of this kind of fecund
asymmetry between married deities, see
Apffel-Marglin, "Types of Sexual Union," on
Shri and Vishnu in Orissan songs and pictures;
and Narayanan, "Śrī," 92–98, on Shri Vaishnava imagery. Glenn E. Yocum perceives in the
Tamil tradition that marriage to a god tames
other deities. Yocum, "Comments: The Divine
Consort," 281.

36 For a cautionary example against assuming
that goddesses and their sexuality express feminist power, see Menon and Shweder, "Power
in Its Place."

37 This relief is closest to the iconographic
category of Umasahita-Sukhasana, which
Adicéam sees as deriving from Somaskanda
imagery. Adicéam, "Les images de Śiva dans
l'Inde du Sud: XII, XIII, XIV." Some iconographers call this Umamaheshvara, but others
reserve this term for the couple embracing.
It is distinct from later Umasahita groups in
that Devi does not hold the blue lotus bud or

the *kunda* flower, and Shiva holds the crescent moon in his upper left hand instead of wearing it in his hair. It seems early in the evolution of this iconographic type. Lockwood et al. date the composition as later than Somaskanda panels carved for Rajasimha's immediate predecessor, Parameshvara (Parameśvara) I, but earlier than the majority of Somaskandas carved for Rajasimha himself. Lockwood, Siromoney, and Dayanandan, *Mahabalipuram Studies*, 21–23. Uma's back still abuts the edge of the relief frame (as it does in the panel carved under Parameshvara in the Dharmaraja Ratha), though her shoulders twist toward frontality and her foremost arm already rests on the throne. Her face is not yet fully frontal, nor does she share a footstool with Shiva as she will in the Shore Temple relief. Shiva's posture already shows the left leg pendant and a hand resting palm up in his lap (*dhyana mudra / dhyāna mudrā*), but that hand does not yet rest on his ankle. His footstool here is, uncanonically, a seated *gana*.

38 She holds two lotuses when she is lustrated by a pair of elephants in sculptures at nearby Mamallapuram. For photos, see Schmid, "La Prospérité," figs. 7, 9; K. R. Srinivasan, *Cave Temples of the Pallavas*, plates 42, 54a.

39 In Tamil culture, Lakshmi was already a symbol of wifely duty as she was in Orissa. Apffel-Marglin, "Types of Sexual Union"; Leslie, "Śrī and Jyeṣṭhā," 109–13.

40 Francis sees things differently, finding death symbolism in Dakshinamurti's image. Francis, "Le discours royal," 394, n. 380. Pratapaditya Pal argues that "Dakshinamurti" derives from the term for knowledge or grace. Pal, "The Image of Grace and Wisdom," 253–55.

41 But R. K. K. Rajarajan sees this figure as assimilating Vishnu imagery. Rajarajan, "Dakṣiṇāmūrti."

42 Francis, Gillet, and Schmid, "Chronique des études 'Pallava' I," 594–95. Gillet cites passages to this effect from the *Mṛgendrāgama* (Kr. 8.213–214a) and the *Somaśambhupaddhati* (vv. 21–23), though she also notes that the *Lingapurana* (1.21.60 b) explains the torch simply through Shiva's association with the charnel ground. Gillet, *La création d'une iconographie*, 100–103.

43 Parlier-Renault sees the yogic figures of Dakshinamurti and Shiva as the Yogi destroying

Jalandhara as exceptions to the meanings she proposes for the monument's north/south pattern. Parlier-Renault, *Temples de l'Inde méridionale*, 163, 185–87, 218.

44 Francis et al. noticed the connection. Francis, Gillet, and Schmid, "Chronique des études 'Pallava' I," 594–95. They see fire as a divine manifestation to humans, noting the Amaravati Buddha in his column of flame.

45 The crescent moon in Shiva's matted hair, his ax, the serpents, his smiling countenance, the forward-facing palm of reassurance (*abhaya mudra*), and his hand resting near his thigh all match descriptions of Lingodbhava found in *agama*s and *shilpa shastra*, texts that delineate iconography, perhaps for artists. The domical top of the cylinder clarifies the cylinder's identity as a *linga*. Other unusual features include Shiva's eight arms (instead of two or four); the trident; the noose, or *rudrakshamala* (*rudrākṣamāla*); the conch-like object in the upper right; and the open-palmed *pataka mudra* (*pataka mudrā*) (perhaps), though these do not point strongly in the direction of any other iconographic identification. Other sources on his iconography include Filliozat, "Les images de Śiva dans l'Inde du Sud: I"; and Chandrakumar, "Iconography of Liṅgodbhavamūrti."

46 Some texts emphasize Vishnu's and Brahma's ignorance by opening this narrative with a scene of these two squabbling for primacy. In some recensions, Brahma lies that he has found the *linga*'s top. For this, Shiva curses Brahma that no temples shall be built to him. See Filliozat, "Les images de Śiva dans l'Inde du Sud: I," 46–49.

47 Compare Heston's similar findings that at the *gopuram* at Ellora's Kailasanatha temple, a complementary dyad organizes sculptural narratives on the south and north flanks of the entryway. Stories on the south tell of knowledge conferred through Shiva's grace. Those on the north tell of knowledge arduously won through conflict. Heston, "Iconographic Themes."

48 Rea, *Pallava Architecture*, 40.

49 Some identify this figure of Shiva as Ardhanarishvara (half woman) playing a *vina* (Vinadhara). Lockwood, Siromoney, and Dayanandan, *Mahabalipuram Studies*, 234–37; Hawley, "The Boston Vīṇādhara Śiva";

Schmid, personal communication on-site, 2013. I agree about the *vina* but not Ardhanarishvara. His headdress, locks of hair, and earrings do differ on the left and right sides of his head, but such asymmetries are common on various manifestations of Shiva. What others read as Ardhanarishvara's single breast, I read as the upper gourd of the *vina*. A distinct ridge is visible around the lip of the gourd. Breasts of goddess figures at the Kailasanatha show no such sharp edges delineating the breast from the torso. Nor have I seen any image of Ardhanarishvara in which Shiva fondles his own breast. He fondles Devi's left breast often enough in sculpture but only when it is not attached to his own body. The hand he spreads around this hemisphere reads, to me, as holding the *vina* and pressing down its strings.

A comparable hemisphere is certainly a gourd and not a breast on a similar figure of Shiva on Rajasimha's *prakara* (fig. 2.13, no. 48). There, Shiva holds the gourd too close to the centerline of his body for anyone to read it as a breast. I regard this as one of the many cases in which figures on this *prakara* reiterate figures on Rajasimha's *vimana* and, therefore, as evidence that sculptors of the *prakara* carved the *vimana* figure as a male playing a *vina* and not as Ardhanarishvara. Gillet may agree. She identifies the *prakara* figure as simply "Shiva musicien." Gillet, *La création d'une iconographie*, no. 72 on ground plan in flyleaf pocket.

50 Suggested to me by Himanshu Prabha Ray, personal communication, 2010.

51 On *agama*s and later *vastushastra* identifying Bhutas or *gana*s as warriors helping Shiva battle the three cities (Tripura), see Dhaky, "Bhūtas and Bhūtanāyakas," 251, n. 52.

52 M. A. Dhaky finds that the twelfth to thirteenth centuries' *Viśvakarmīyāvāstushastra* associates *gana*s and Bhutas with the compass points and with elements of the cosmos. Ibid., 245. They are creations of the creator, Shiva, and they reflect the qualities he manifests. In this text, moreover, north is *durmukha* (unsightly) and correlates with air, which can be "generative of terrifying cyclonic furies with limitless power of destruction." Ibid., 245.

Kamal Giri notes the frieze of *gana*s on this building's lowest sandstone molding, the one that rests on the shallow granite layer now abutted by the courtyard paving slabs. Giri describes them as either playing music and "in a delightful mood" or making war and "in a furious mood." Giri, "Gaṇas," 90–91. These friezes, however, have been so extensively damaged and replaced that we cannot be confident that those figures making war face only to the north and those playing music face only to the south.

53 In this kind of looking, I take inspiration from Francis et al., who looked closely enough to see that the reliefs lining the *prakara* wall of the Vaikuntha Perumal temple had been incorrectly reassembled on every wall but the south one. Francis, Gillet, and Schmid, "Chronique des études 'Pallava' I," 597–98.

54 On these and other identifications of subject matter in the sculptures of the *prakara*, see Gillet, *La création d'une iconographie*, 285–320.

55 In this complicated section of the *prakara* around Vishnu's shrine, extra sculpture fills side walls that face east and west. Lakshmi is on one of these, facing west. The key to Gillet's plan seems to identify a figure of Saraswati on this spot, but the giant petals beneath the figure's seat suggest Lakshmi's lotus throne. Sandstone emerging from the stucco in the upper right reveals an elephant's trunk and a pot of water. Stucco on the upper left masks under a remarkably bushy fly whisk what I presume to be the other elephant and pot. Stucco has apparently misled iconographers for years.

56 *Matrika* sculptures in the Tamil region do not hold babies. To the north, they often do. The Kailasanatha figures are the earliest known *matrika*s in the Tamil region, and their postures are unusually varied and energetic. On *matrika* iconography more broadly, see Panikkar, *Saptamatrka Worship and Sculptures*; Meister, "Regional Variations in Mātṛka Conventions"; Mani, *Saptamātṛkas in Indian Religion and Art*; Arunachalam, "The Sapta Mātā Cult."

57 Schmid observes that the story of the sages' wives and Shiva Bhikshatana is on the surface of Rajasimha's *vimana* that is directly opposite these *matrika*s, setting up a complementarity between fierce *matrika*s and seduced wives who all inherit the older mythology of Skanda. Schmid, "Bhakti in Its Infancy."

58 Nagaswamy calls them the Ekādasa Rudras (Eleven Rudras). Nagaswamy, *Tantric Cult of South India*, 24. Gillet calls them "Onze Rudra." Gillet, *La création d'une iconographie*, plan 1. Perhaps as heavenly bodies, these expanded on Shiva's solar aspect. On that aspect, see Mallmann, *Les enseignements iconographiques*. Only six of these figures have legs. The other five are just heads peering between their companions' heads and may have been inserted at a later date to suit changing iconographic preferences. Animals fill the bottom register, vehicles or familiars perhaps of the ancient deities above?

59 On the name Alakshmi for Jyeshtha, see Schmid, "La Prospérité." On the Pallava taste for pairing Jyeshtha and Lakshmi, see Francis, Gillet, and Schmid, "Chronique des études Pallava II," 467–71.

60 That is, I continue to read them as I did in 2005. Francis, too, reads them as women in mountain scenes. Francis, "Le discours royal," 394, n. 378. Nagaswamy reads them as Uma. Nagaswamy, *Tantric Cult of South India*, 158–60. Srinivasan calls them "Parvati in the Himalayas." K. R. Srinivasan, "Pallavas of Kāñcī," 63–64. Schmid, too, reads these as Parvati. Schmid, "Bhakti in Its Infancy," 128–30.

61 See Hatley, "The Brahmayāmalatantra," 9, 13. The term *yogini* has signified a wide variety of female beings. Its simplest meaning is "a female practitioner of yoga," a human woman who has renounced family and possessions to wander in the wilderness practicing and teaching the yogic path toward enlightenment. Dehejia finds no visual representation of such yoginis before the seventeenth century. Dehejia, *Yoginī, Cult and Temples*, 11–19. On human women in recent times who are ascetics and renunciants, see Denton, "Varieties of Hindu Female Asceticism"; and Ojha, "Feminine Asceticism in Hinduism."

62 Others who read them as royal include Francis, "Le discours royal," 397, n. 394; Francis, Gillet, and Schmid, "Chronique des études Pallava II," 456, n. 78; Lockwood, Siromoney, and Dayanandan, *Mahabalipuram Studies*, 30; Mahalingam, *Kāñcīpuram in Early South Indian History*, 126. Frederick Asher and C. Minakshi note that in the Vaikuntha Perumal temple, reliefs narrating the history of the Pallava royal succession occupy positions closely comparable to the reliefs lining the inner face of the Kailasanatha's *prakara*. Asher, "Historical and Political Allegory"; Minakshi, *The Historical Sculptures at the Vaikuṇṭhaperumāḷ Temple*, 52. Asher sees this as analogizing kings and gods. Minakshi sees in this echoing a comparison between the political events depicted at the Vaikuntha Perumal and the divine acts depicted at the Kailasanatha. I would add that the younger temple's reliefs narrating the history of the royal dynasty from divine origins through mythic time up to the reign of the monument's patron also echo the inscription encircling Rajasimha's *vimana* in the Kailasanatha (see appendix 2).

63 For example, see Hudson, *The Body of God*, 107. George L. Hart notes that north is the direction kings face when fasting to death in the rite called *vadakiruttal* (*vaṭakiruttal*). So the king sits in the relative south, and the south is still the place of death. Hart, *The Poems of Ancient Tamil*, 88. Parlier-Renault was concerned to find "love" expressed in the monument's south because she associated south with the abode of death in the Vedas. Parlier-Renault, *Temples de l'Inde méridionale*, 219. See ibid., 14–30, for her analysis of the Vedic evidence. Francis puzzles over these orientations, too. Francis, "Le discours royal" 394, n. 380.

64 Lockwood, Siromoney, and Dayanandan, *Mahabalipuram Studies*, 35.

65 Francis, Gillet, and Schmid, "Chronique des études 'Pallava' I," 591–93, 596–97, 606. They framed their observations as preliminary and called for further study.

66 Gillet, *La création d'une iconographie*, 318–19. Her understanding of the gift draws from Schmid, *Le Don de voir*.

67 Francis, "Le discours royal," 393–98, citing Schmid, "Au seuil du monde divin," 78–84; Schmid, "Bhakti in Its Infancy," 109.

68 Francis, "Le discours royal," 433–34. See also note 19 above.

69 Schmid, "La Prospérité."

70 Parlier-Renault, *Temples de l'Inde méridionale*, 7, 215. She mapped the pairs as married/benevolent versus solitary/war. Less convincingly, she identified the two categories as Conflict facing north and Love facing south, and Shiva as the lord of the North marrying the South, which is Devi's land. Ibid., 146–87,

219. This required her to posit a strong iconographic presence for Kama and Kamakshi, who were not yet significant deities in local religion, nor are their iconographic signs apparent on this monument. Francis, Gillet, and Schmid, "Chronique des études Pallava III," 269–78.

71 Parlier-Renault, *Temples de l'Inde méridionale*, 216. Isabelle Clark-Decès made a similar suggestion to me in personal communication in 2011.

72 Hart, *The Poems of Ancient Tamil*, 32. In the poems there is "over and over the metamorphosis of the gruesome objects of battle into beautiful or productive things associated with peace, especially things connected with agriculture." Hart cites *Pur*, 19, 26, 370, 372. For more on *akam* and *puram*, see also Hart, *Poets of the Tamil Anthologies*, 3. See also Ramanujan, *Poems of Love and War*.

73 The sources from which I piece together my understanding of those terms include Apffel-Marglin, "Types of Sexual Union"; Apffel-Marglin, "Female Sexuality"; Apffel-Marglin, "Types of Oppositions"; Apffel-Marglin, introduction to *Purity and Auspiciousness*; Hart, *The Poems of Ancient Tamil*; Hiltebeitel, "Purity and Auspiciousness"; Inden, "Kings and Omens"; Nagarajan, "Hosting the Divine"; Nagarajan, "Threshold Designs," 100–102; Narayanan, "The Two Levels of Auspiciousness."

74 Here I rely heavily on Apffel-Marglin's words. See Apffel-Marglin, "Types of Oppositions."

75 Hart, *Poets of the Tamil Anthologies*, 6.

76 Light has auspicious connotations in contemporary Tamil culture. Markali is the *mangalam* time of year, the gods' daytime. Dark winter is the *amangalam* season, the gods' nighttime. Nagarajan, "Threshold Designs." This does not match up, however, with the *mangalam* categories Apffel-Marglin finds in Odisha. There light can be associated with heat and aridity, which discourage growth. Apffel-Marglin, "Female Sexuality," 54. Pallava culture seems to have aligned light and fecundity more along Tamil lines. Pallava inscriptions express time in terms of bright and dark fortnights. See Mahalingam, *Inscriptions of the Pallavas*, cxxxi.

77 On the meaning of Shri, see Narayanan, "Śrī," 92–94. Elsewhere she is associated with wealth, abundant food, and procreative sexuality. Apffel-Marglin, "Types of Oppositions," 74–75.

78 Compare Lisa N. Owen's reading of themes of expansion, movement, and fecundity in the "rich curls of foliage and cascades of water, . . . *makaras* [fantastic, crocodilian beasts that symbolize water], . . . [and] semi-human aquatic beings" of the Chota Kailasa temple in Ellora. Owen, "Absence and Presence," 106. Michael Yonan argues that eighteenth-century people experiencing rococo architecture similarly perceived the immanence of the sacred in plants and creatures flowing, bursting, and transforming in what we once called architectural ornament. Yonan, *The Wieskirche*; Yonan, "Material Transformations."

79 On pairing Lakshmi with Durga, see Schmid, "La Prospérité"; Divakaran, "Durgā, the Great Goddess"; Nagaswamy, *Tantric Cult of South India*, 160.

80 Schmid, "La Prospérité." Compare Hatley's use of the term *polythetic* to characterize the same phenomenon of goddesses variously sharing attributes in his multiple sources on yoginis: no two are identical, no element they share may be shared by all of them, but all are bound together by this web of shared options. Hatley, "The Brahmayāmalatantra," 10. The worship of South Asian goddesses at other sites, too, emphasizes their integration of *mangalam* and *amangalam*. See Craddock, "Reconstructing the Split Goddess"; Harman, "Introduction: Fierce Goddess"; Zeiler, "Female Danger."

81 Hart, introduction to *The Four Hundred Songs*, xix. On the king's responsibility for the health and productivity of the kingdom, see also Ali, "Royal Eulogy"; Lockwood, Siromoney, and Dayanandan, *Mahabalipuram Studies*, 32; Shulman, "On South Indian Bandits and Kings."

82 "Your good country has the prosperity of great victories." Hart, *Poets of the Tamil Anthologies*, 114.

83 Other South Asian temples bear iconographic programs that align *amangalam* subjects with the north and *mangalam* subjects with the south. Mary Beth Heston finds gentle, grace-conferring aspects of Shiva on the south side of the *gopuram* of the Kailasanatha temple in Ellora and fierce, combative forms of him on the north side. She also finds the two categories resolving into one truth for visitors over

the course of their journey through the site. Heston, "Iconographic Themes," 223–26, 235. Further inside that monument, reliefs facing north tell the grim war epic *Mahabharata*, which ends with its ideal kings abdicating and going off to the forest. On the opposite walls, reliefs narrate the *Ramayana* epic, ending with the king restored to his throne. John S. Hawley notes the counterpositions. Hawley, "Scenes from the Childhood of Kṛṣṇa." Both stories are about ideal kings who fight bravely and successfully to protect their kingdoms and families. Kirsti Evans finds *Mahabharata* reliefs facing north and *Ramayana* reliefs facing south on Hoyshala temples. Evans, *Epic Narratives in the Hoysaḷa Temples*, 14. On the Brahmapurishvara (Brahmapurīśvara) temple in Pullamangai, David T. Sanford finds *Ramayana* panels positioned so that episodes of increasing happiness face the sun as it waxes in the months approaching summer, and episodes of mounting sorrow face the waning sun in the months approaching winter. Sanford, "Miniature Relief Sculptures," 279.

CHAPTER 3.
LOOKING EAST AND WEST,
WITH AND WITHOUT SONS

1 Lockwood et al. find forty Somaskanda reliefs from Rajasimha's time and only two from before that. Lockwood et al., *Pallava Art*, 21–45. They appear at every project associated with Rajasimha. Gabriel Jouveau-Dubreuil reports they are not present at Ellora or Badami, cities of the rival Chalukya dynasty. Jouveau-Dubreuil, *Iconography of Southern India*, 33. Schmid finds the analogy between Shiva's family and the Pallava family to be new with Rajasimha rather than preceding him. Schmid, "Bhakti in Its Infancy," 93–96 and n. 11. Soundara Rajan floated the possibility that Somaskanda sculptures were the only cult objects in Rajasimha's temples. Soundara Rajan, "'Cult' in the Pallava Temples." Francis, Schmid, and Gillet find the Somaskanda theme still being used by local authorities who governed under and after the Pallavas. Francis, Gillet, and Schmid, "Chronique des études Pallava II," 454–57. It seems still to have carried associations with power.

The simile appears in the inscription around the granite basement molding of Rajasimha's temple at Panaimalai. Rangacharya, *EI*, 19, No. 18; Francis, "Le discours royal," 184, 670, *inscription royale* (hereafter IR) 43; Hultzsch, *SII*, 1.31. An inscription for the same king at the Adiranachanda cave in Saluvankuppam celebrates Skanda/Guha and Parvati as part of Shiva's family. Hultzsch, *SII*, 1.21–23; Hultzsch, *EI*, 1.F, No. 23; Francis, "Le discours royal," 679, IR 68. In the Vēlūrpāḷaiyam grant, the simile describes a later Pallava king's birth. Francis, "Le discours royal," 687, IR 88; H. K. Sastri, *SII*, 2.5.98. For other inscriptions that make the analogy, see Champakalakshmi, "Iconographic Programme and Political Imagery," 223–25. T. V. Mahalingam notes the double entendre in these inscriptions. Mahalingam, *Kāñcīpuram in Early South Indian History*, 121. See also L'Hernault, *L'iconographie de Subrahmanya*, 52–57; Lockwood et al., *Pallava Art*, 53–65.

2 As many scholars have pointed out. Asher, "Historical and Political Allegory"; Schmid, "Bhakti in Its Infancy"; Lockwood et al., *Pallava Art*, 21–52. Francis reads Somaskanda images as a Pallava solution to resolving the tension between the king's spiritual search and his duties to reign and make war. Francis, "Le discours royal," 433–34, figs. 260–76. Gillet thinks the monument's whole program is about kings. Gillet, *La création d'une iconographie*, 338, 594.

Parlier-Renault sees the king as being modeled on the god. Parlier-Renault, *Temples de l'Inde méridionale*, 220. Hart, by contrast, saw ancient kings as the starting point of that flow: "Most of the Hindu gods in South India were modeled after kings, and then later kings partly modeled themselves on Hindu gods." Hart, introduction to *The Four Hundred Songs*, xviii.

3 R. Champakalakshmi proposes reading the figures of Uma and Skanda as Kotravai and Murugan, the ancient Tamil gods of the dry (*pālai*) and hilly (*kuriñci*) zones. The Pallavas, outsiders to the Tamil region, bring in their god, Shiva, and place him in this family relationship that subordinates the earlier gods of the area. She finds the Somaskanda theme significant at Rajaraja I Chola's temple in Tanjavur too. Champakalakshmi, "Iconographic

Programme and Political Imagery," 223–25.

4 On Mahendra predeceasing Rajasimha, see Mahalingam, *Kāñcīpuram in Early South Indian History*, 133; Mahalingam, *Readings in South Indian History*, 31–32; K. R. Srinivasan, *Cave Temples of the Pallavas*, 8–9; Schmid, "Bhakti in Its Infancy," 120; Francis, "Le discours royal," 645.

5 There is no longer any sculpture in or on temple A, which was completely disassembled and rebuilt in 2000, but Rea reports seeing inside it the decayed traces of seated figures of Shiva, Parvati, and others, looking like the reliefs inside the other seven structures in this row. Rea, *Pallava Architecture*, 22.

6 Schmid suspects that most did contain paintings of Somaskanda. Schmid, "Bhakti in Its Infancy," 109. On the painting fragments of Somaskanda and other Shiva manifestations in other cells of this *prakara*, see Champakalakshmi, "South Indian Paintings," 698–99; Krishna, "The Paintings of Kanchi," 49–50; Lockwood et al., *Pallava Art*, 32.

7 I could not obtain permission to photograph this item, but I was permitted to see it in 2013. The relief was heavily stuccoed. Lockwood et al. report a Somaskanda there in the mid-twentieth century. Lockwood, Siromoney, and Dayanandan, *Mahabalipuram Studies*, 27. But at the start of the twentieth century, Rea does not list a baby among the figures in that relief. Rea, *Pallava Architecture*, 28. In 1931, A. H. Longhurst states that this shrine carries its Somaskanda on the outside instead of the inside. Longhurst, *Pallava Architecture*, pt. 3, 13–14. He provides no photographic evidence of the interior, however. Perhaps the renovations of that era omitted the baby.

8 Some scholars think the relief was a Somaskanda and the baby was worn away. Francis, Gillet, and Schmid, "Chronique des études Pallava II," 456, n. 78; Francis, "Le discours royal," 730 and fig. 266. Longhurst in 1931 presumed the exterior relief was a Somaskanda, but the photo he cites reveals that Uma's arm and thigh were visible even then, and not covered by a figure of baby Skanda. Longhurst, *Pallava Architecture*, pt. 3, 13–14 and plate 6(b). That photo is easier to read in Rea, *Pallava Architecture*, plate 5.

Schmid is convinced there was never a baby in this relief. Schmid, "Bhakti in Its Infancy,"

118–19. Rea reports no baby in that relief either. Rea, *Pallava Architecture*, 27–28.

9 See, by contrast, her leg lowered and behind the baby in Somaskanda reliefs at Mamallapuram's Shore Temples, Dharmaraja Ratha, and Mahishasuramardini cave and at four eighth-century temples in Kanchi. Lockwood et al., *Pallava Art*, 25–26, 33; K. R. Srinivasan, *Cave Temples of the Pallavas*, plate 47.

The relief inside Rajasimha's *vimana* shows Skanda as well as Uma's right thigh and arm, but it places Skanda above Uma's thigh.

10 Schmid, too, notes the female attendants. Schmid, "Bhakti in Its Infancy," 109. Similar-looking women attend in a later Somaskanda-like panel in Taccur in which Schmid and her colleagues read the Uma figure as an emblem of the local Bana queen. See Francis, Gillet, and Schmid, "Chronique des études Pallava II," 455–57.

Lockwood et al. believe that plaster in the east and west cells of Rajasimha's *prakara* conceals the presence of Brahma and Vishnu behind the seated couple. Lockwood et al., *Pallava Art*, 32.

11 R. Nagaswamy reads this and other sculptures at the monument as portraits of Rajasimha and his queen. Nagaswamy, "New Light on Mamallapuram," 30; Nagaswamy, *Tantric Cult of South India*, 56. So does T. G. Aravamuthan in his *Portrait Sculpture*, 26.

I am equally unconvinced by Mahalingam that sculptures "in small shrines around the sanctum sanctorum" are portraits of Rajasimha or by Lockwood et al. that Pallava Somaskanda reliefs were portraits of specific Pallavas. Mahalingam, *Kāñcīpuram in Early South Indian History*, 126; Lockwood et al., *Pallava Art*, 49–51.

12 Francis et al. move away from an exclusive identification of the large tableau on Mahendra's *vimana* as a Somaskanda or a royal group. Francis, Gillet, and Schmid, "Chronique des études Pallava II," 456, n. 78. In his dissertation, Francis emphasizes instead what gods and kings shared, and the significance of this image as the god's "human homologue, the royal patron whose deeds have those of the god as their model." Francis, "Le discours royal," 398.

13 Here I build on the work of Schmid, who reads the addorsing of Somaskandas with royal

couples as "symbiosis" or linked "stages" in the process of transformation from one to the other and alternation as inviting comparison, as a means to distinguish and equate Pallava kings and their gods, and as a reminder of the importance of lineage continuity to royal discourse. To her, the frequency of Skanda imagery there renders the specific idea of "filiation" as *the* theme of the monument, whereas I am proposing it is one very important theme that joins others in a mapping of multiple royal ideals. Schmid, "Bhakti in Its Infancy," 96–98, 118–19. Gillet, too, notes the alternation of these two kinds of couples, concluding the ones without children are likely to be royal. Gillet, *La création d'une iconographie*, 285.

14 Schmid, "Bhakti in Its Infancy," 106–10. See chapter 2, note 58.

15 Schmid also observes these repeated mentions of the father-son link, and particularly in verse 2 through the Shiva/Guha analogy it carries over from verse 5 of Rajasimha's inscription. She finds this echo on Mahendra's shrine by correcting Hultzsch's original translation of *guhagaṇa* in verse 2 ("the troops of his attendants") to mean "a troop led by Skanda." Ibid., 115–16.

Mahendra's inscription links to Rajasimha's *prakara* inscription too. Verse 1 repeats the *biruda ūrjita* to describe Mahendra's father. The same *biruda* is inscribed on cell 2 of the large *prakara*. Hultzsch, *SII*, 1.27, n. 1.

16 For further interpretation of the verse on Rajasimha's *vimana*, see chapter 5.

17 Schmid hypothesizes that perpendicularity is the angle of interaction for royalty and for visitors to interact with the divine. Schmid, " La Prospérité," 509–11.

18 "The triad of Somaskandamūrti has shaped the architectural plan." Schmid, "Bhakti in Its Infancy," 119. Schmid compares Mahendra's contribution to the *khila*, or introductory portion, of a text, the addition of which transforms the text's previous meaning. She, however, would have architectural counterpart to Uma be the open *mandapam*.

19 Hardy, *The Temple Architecture of India*, 37–43. See the discussion on Hardy's formulation in my introductory chapter.

20 Crispin Branfoot makes this point with special clarity. Branfoot, *Gods on the Move*, 54.

21 Schmid, "Bhakti in its Infancy," 120.

22 Francis, "Le discours royal," 390; Schmid, "Bhakti in Its Infancy," 114.

23 Architecture for goddesses can have male door guardians. See the temple to yoginis at Hirapur. Kaimal, *Scattered Goddesses*, 112.

24 On biological reductionism, see Ochshorn, "Goddesses and the Lives of Women," 387.

25 On these codings, see Meister, "Juncture and Conjunction." Nagaswamy may allude to those when he reads the male principle in this *vimana* and the female principle in this *mandapam*. Nagaswamy, *Tantric Cult of South India*, 158.

See Tryna Lyons on the increasing sexualization of the Goddess from sixth- to sixteenth-century portrayals of goddesses in one illuminated manuscript of the *Devi Mahatmya*. Lyons, "The Simla *Devī Māhātmya* Illustrations."

26 See chapter 1, on the inscriptions of the open *mandapam*.

27 On problems produced by conflating goddesses with living women, see the critique of Marija Gimbutas's work in Ochshorn, "Goddesses and the Lives of Women," 387; Goodison and Morris, introduction to *Ancient Goddesses*, 16; Torjesen, introduction to *Women and Goddess Traditions*; Tringham and Conkey, "Rethinking Figurines."

28 Kaimal, "Learning to See the Goddess."

29 See the useful critiques of my article in Francis, "Le discours royal," 390, n. 357; Francis, Gillet, and Schmid, "Chronique des études 'Pallava' I." I accept Francis's point that there were no more than fifty-eight cells in Rajasimha's *prakara*, falling short of the number often associated with yoginis, which is sixty-four. The space at the northeast corner between cells 55 and 56 probably never held a cell but was organized as the southeast corner is.

30 Early examples surviving from the Pallava kingdom are rock-cut monoliths of the seventh century, the Arjuna Ratha and Dharmaraja Ratha in Mamallapuram.

31 K. R. Srinivasan perceives the structures along the *prakara*'s inner face as shrines dedicated to Shiva. K. R. Srinivasan, "Temples of the Later Pallavas," 222. He calls the cells *dēvakulikā*, meaning "small house of a deity." K. R. Srinivasan, "Pallavas of Kāñcī," 63–64.

32 Stein sees sitting in cells of the *prakara* as a practice suitable to Shaiva Siddhanta, as a

means of getting closer to Shiva. Stein, "All Streets Lead to Temples," 58. Dennis Hudson found that he could fit his six-foot frame inside, seated, cross-legged, facing the single entrance. Hudson, personal communication, 1995.

33 P. R. Srinivasan proposed that this *prakara* "has for its prototype the form of the monasteries, especially of Nāgārjunakoṇḍa . . . [and] Taxila also." P. R. Srinivasan, *South Indian Temple Architecture*, 29–30. According to L. K. Tripathi, Stella Kramrisch saw this *prakara* still carrying the "impress" of *vihara*s and perhaps Jaina caves as it also signaled forward in time as a precursor to yogini temples. Tripathi, "Causaṭha Yoginī Temple," 39. Rea found unconvincing an earlier theory that these cells, and especially those that face east and flank the compound entrance, indicate Jain usage. Rea, *Pallava Architecture*, 18. On the persistence of Jaina and Buddhist worship in Kanchi under the Pallavas, see my introductory chapter, note 12.

34 See, for example, a recently excavated row of *vihara*s at Nalanda. Rajani, "Archaeological Remains at Nalanda," fig. 1.

35 *Parivaralaya* shrines survive in the Tamil countryside at Erumbur, Tirukkattalai, Nangavaram, Kodumbalur (Muvarkoyil and Mucukundeshvara), Tiruvishalur, Cittur, Andanallur, Tiruccendurai, Visalur, Malaiyatipatti, and Nartthamalai. See Venkatarama Ayyar, *A Manual of the Pudukkottai State*, vol. 2, pt. 2, 1073; Balasubrahmanyam, "Early Choḷa Sculptures of Erumbur"; Balasubrahmanyam, *Early Chola Temples*, 327–29; K. A. N. Sastri, *The Cōḷas*, 699; Soundara Rajan, "Muttaraiyars of Nēmam and Sēndalai," 130; Soundara Rajan, "Irrukuvēḷs of Koḍumbāḷūr," 213; Soundara Rajan, *Rock-Cut Temple Styles*, 104.

Because at least parts of these sets survive at so many sites, I am inclined to agree with S. R. Balasubrahmanyam that building such shrines was a common practice in the eighth to tenth centuries. Balasubrahmanyam, *Early Chola Temples*, 327–29; contra Dhaky, "Cōlas of Tañjāvūr," 150.

36 Stein, "All Streets Lead to Temples," 91. On the *digvijaya* concept as a goal of the Pallavas, see Francis, "Le discours royal," 498. Gerd J. R. Mevissen proposes that royal temples positioned images of Shiva Tripurantaka to face in all directions, as they do at the Rajarajeshvara temple in Tanjavur, to characterize the royal patron as *digvijaya*. Mevissen, "Political Geography"; Mevissen, "Three Royal Temple Foundations." Reading across many kinds of medieval South Asian texts, Daud Ali finds the "conquest of the four quarters" central to the goals of medieval South Asian kings. Ali, "Royal Eulogy," 197. See also Lisa N. Owen on *sarvatobhadra* images that face in all the directions to show the radiating body of the Jina. She notes these are close analogs of four-faced images of Shiva (Sadashiva) and that *sarvatobhadra* images receive *abhisheka*. Owen, "Absence and Presence," 115–18.

Nagaswamy identifies guardians of the directions (*dikpalas*) at the Kailasanatha. Nagaswamy, "Innovative Emperor and His Personal Chapel," 53. Champakalakshmi agrees that *dikpala* shrines are present at the cardinal points in the *prakara* surrounding the Rajarajeshvara temple too. Champakalakshmi, "Iconographic Programme and Political Imagery."

37 I have made that argument for this reading of their brethren framing the great cliff and Krishna Govardhana relief at Mamallapuram, heraldic, rigid figures that contrast sharply with the soft, naturalistic forms of animals in the middle of each relief. Kaimal, "Playful Ambiguity," figs. 16, 23.

38 Composite leonine creatures, sometimes called *yali*, became common on temples in southern India and may then have had no specific reference to kings. Branfoot explains their frequent use in composite pillars to express dynamism and "expanding form." He notes they are usually ithyphallic, as are all the rearing lions at the Kailasanatha. Branfoot, *Gods on the Move*, 181–86.

39 Dancers and musicians escorted the king into battle and warrior chieftains of ancient Tamil Nadu performed a leaping victory dance on the battlefield over the bodies of their defeated enemies, according to Zvelebil, *Ananda-Tāṇḍava*, 45. In poetry of the Sangam period (ca. early centuries CE), dance was closely associated with war. Hart, *The Poems of Ancient Tamil*, 23–24. In those poems, dance can be read as a means for controlling disorder. Hart, *The Poems of Ancient Tamil*, 135.

On these two visualizations of Shiva's dance carrying on early Tamil associations between dance, war, and the king's performance on the battlefield, see Gillet, *La création d'une iconographie*, 300–301, figs. 214–17. Mevissen notes that the *Mayamata*, composed circa ninth to twelfth centuries, promises that worship of Dancing Shiva and Shiva Tripurantaka can bring about the immediate death of an enemy. Mevissen, "Political Geography," 489.

40 Gillet, *La création d'une iconographie*, chap. 3. For Gillet, this pose captures the royal side of Shiva's identity into which he transforms from his "savage" aspect, which manifests in his dance on folded legs. Where she sees transformation, I see interconnections. I do not see "savagery."

I too have found no examples of this posture earlier than the Kailasanatha sculptures and only two examples from the following centuries. These two are an eleventh-century bronze from Tiruvalangadu and a twelfth-century stone relief from Kulittalai. See Sivaramamurti, *Nataraja in Art*, 251–52, figs. 108–9. C. Sivaramamurti reads the same posture in a mural fragment at Panaimalai (ibid., 201, fig. 49), but there I perceive only the raised arm (also apparent in the *urdhvatandava* figures on the Kailasanatha's east wall) and not the raised leg. Note that this pose is distinct from the pose Sivaramamurti labels *urdhvajanu* (*ūrdhvajānu*), in which both legs bend at the knee and turn out, the weight-bearing foot flat to the ground and the other foot suspended just above and perpendicular to the ground. Ibid., 197, fig. 42. *Urdhvajanu* images are not as rare.

41 T. A. Gopinatha Rao identifies the Kailasanatha pose as *lalatātilakam*, a dance in which Shiva uses his toe to mark the tilak on his forehead. Gopinatha Rao, *Elements of Hindu Iconography*, vol. 2, pt. 1, 264–66, plate 64.2. This is the only example he illustrates of this pose in which the raised leg passes behind the shoulder, which would make it considerably more difficult for the foot to touch the forehead. Srinivasan calls this figure the Urdhva-tandava-murti, noting a dancing *gana* below on the west wall. K. R. Srinivasan, "Pallavas of Kāñcī," 62. The only surviving *gana* there is fluting, however.

42 David Shulman identifies this scene with the dance contest on the basis of Shiva's pose and Devi's presence as witness. He reads this *urdhvatandava* pose as involving a sexual display of the male organ (the *urdhva linga*) and thus of male power. These sculptures at the Kailasanatha are his only evidence that the story might be as old as the eighth century. Shulman, *Tamil Temple Myths*, 213–19; 401, n. 6.

Kapila Vatsyayan finds that the Kailasanatha figure makes of this posture something especially "massive, impressive and aggressive." Vatsyayan, *Classical Indian Dance*, 326.

43 Gillet, *La création d'une iconographie*, 143–72. Francis adds that fire can signal the fire sacrifice and thus war. Francis, "La discours royal," 395. Nagaswamy calls this Samhara Tandava, or "dance of destruction." Nagaswamy, *The Kailasanatha Temple*, 15. Gopinatha Rao cannot link this pose to any of the 108 *karana*s (dance postures) listed in Bharata's *Natya Shastra*, he illustrates no similar images, and he does not associate the figure with any narratives. Gopinatha Rao, *Elements of Hindu Iconography*, vol. 2, pt. 1, 269–70; plate 70. He mentions that term only once in reference to a very differently posed Vṛṣabhahanamurti bronze. Gopinatha Rao, *Elements of Hindu Iconography*, vol. 2, pt. 1, 355; plate 109. Sivaramamurti, who conflates this pose with *alidha* (in which one foot rests flat and the other rests on the toes), presents no examples of this pose before the Kailasanatha. He presents one comparable figure in a seventeenth-century mural at Tiruvalañjuli and a sculpture from the National Museum at Khajuraho. I suspect that one relief in the Kailasanatha *prakara* (see fig. 2.12, no. 14) replicates this pose: the upraised arm and the extended thigh are visible, though the lower half of the figure is obscured by plaster. Sivaramamurti, *Nataraja in Art*, 199, 277, 339, 43; figs. 46, 144, 233, 197. Srinivasan labels this figure "Sandhyānṛttāmurti," "the twilight dance form." K. R. Srinivasan, "Pallavas of Kāñcī," 62. Anne-Marie Gaston uses that term for Shiva's dance of gay abandon for Parvati in the Himalayas at evening. She classifies the Kanchi figures, however, as Natarajas instead. Gaston, *Śiva in Dance*, 48–49.

44 For publications of this inscription, see note 1 above.

45 Francis, "Le discours royal," 493; IR 82. The text is published as Hultzsch, *SII*, 2.3.73, 342–61, lines 34–36. Like the inscription around

Rajasimha's *vimana* at the Kailasanatha complex, this also traces the Pallava lineage back to Brahma, by way of Ashvatthaman.

46 On Ganga's and the Pallavas' shared role as mediators between earth and sky, bringing prosperity, see Francis, "Le discours royal," 396–97, 415–16, 545–46; and Gillet, *La création d'une iconographie*, 247. Francis notes two aspects of these images that emphasize the idea of prosperity delivered: that the goddess shows no jealousy and that the figure of Shiva resembles Buddhist *chakravartin* imagery.

On an emphasis on purity and the Gangadhara theme as marking the descent of the Pallavas into the southern regions, see Francis, Gillet, and Schmid, "Chronique des études Pallava II," 432–34; Gillet, *La création d'une iconographie*, 264–65. On Ganga embodying royal qualities for the Pallavas, see Lockwood et al., *Pallava Art*, 47–52. On Gangadhara as purification by flood, see Parlier-Renault, *Temples de l'Inde méridionale*, 200. Ilavenil Ramiah proposes that the meaning of the Gangadhara relief in Mahendra's cave on the Trichy Rock Fort is the king "presenting himself as a ruler who was willing and able to promote agricultural development, especially through investment in water management, and as a necessary and plausible arbiter in a contentious religious and political climate." Ramiah, "Gods and Kings," 156.

47 Ali, "Royal Eulogy," 185.

48 Francis, Gillet, and Schmid, "Chronique des études 'Pallava' I," 433, 585–86; Gillet, *La création d'une iconographie*, 264–65; Schmid, "La Prospérité"; Francis, "Le discours royal," 414–17.

49 On Somaskanda images continuing the theme of Shiva catching Ganga, see Lockwood et al., *Pallava Art*, 53–65. On the Pallavas interweaving the stories of Skanda and of Ganga's descent, see Francis, "Le discours royal," 186–87; Francis, "The Genealogy of the Pallavas."

50 Others have noted that this aspect of Shiva faces both directions. Lockwood et al. suggest this subject "can be considered both as a terrific form as well as a grace-bestowing form of Shiva," as Ganga's rage at being compelled to earth evoked his violent side. Lockwood et al., *Pallava Art*, 47. On the west wall, too, he is terrifying with fangs bared and his mouth open.

51 Others see this wall as a space of transition between the south and north walls. Francis, "Le discours royal," 395; Francis, Gillet, and Schmid, "Chronique des études 'Pallava' I," 591–92; Gillet, *La création d'une iconographie*, 320. Parlier-Renault uses the terms *pivot* and *synthesis*. Parlier-Renault, *Temples de l'Inde méridionale*, 199, 259. Francis and Schmid see Gangadhara belonging at the center of the *vimana*'s west wall because it articulates the role of the king as mediator between heaven and earth. Francis, "Le discours royal," 416, citing a conference paper delivered by Schmid in 2006.

CHAPTER 4.
CIRCUMAMBULATING
THIS WAY AND THAT

1 On a clockwise approach being standard, see, for example, Branfoot, *Gods on the Move*, 44.

2 Dominic Goodall shared with me (by personal communication) and translated two passages enjoining people with heavy injunctions from crossing the *pranala* (*praṇāla*), the channel draining the effluent from ritual ablutions in the sanctum, which one must do in counterclockwise circumambulation. One is from a twelfth-century work, the *Prāyaścittasamuccaya*, edited by Dr. R. Sathyanarayanan:

laṅghane śivanirmālyapraṇālasyāyutaṃ japet
(v. 207ab)
If one should step over the spout (that carries away) what has been offered to Shiva, one should recite (the Aghora-mantra) ten thousand times. (Goodall's translation)

The other is from an earlier or contemporary North Indian work of HṛdayaShiva and consists in quotations of whole chapters of tantras. The translation in Śaiva Rites of Expiation, edited by R. Sathyanarayanan, reads:

athavaa śivanirmālyam praṇālam vā pralaṃ ghayeti (v. 40:2)
japtvāyutatrayaṃ datvā gaḍḍukānāṃ satāṣṭakaṃ kāmatas tu tadā suddhir akāmād ayutadvayaṃ (v. 40:3)
Now if he steps over offerings that have been made to Shiva, or over the conduit (that

carries away offerings that have been poured over the *linga*),

he should recite thirty thousand (repetitions of an unspecified mantra) and give 108 (repetitions of the mantra over) pots. (If he did so) deliberately, then purification (will be regained in this way); if involuntarily, (then he need only recite) twenty thousand.

3 On Sanchi's Stupa I, the Tale of Prince Vessantara (Vessantara *jataka*) wraps this way on the inner face of the north gateway (*torana*). Williams, "On Viewing Sāñcī," 94. Sculptural narratives at Deogarh do too. Williams, *The Art of Gupta India*. Charles D. Collins and Stella Kramrisch believe the sculptures in Cave 1 at Elephanta were to be seen in a counterclockwise sequence. Collins, *The Iconography and Ritual*; Kramrisch, "The Great Cave Temple of Śiva in Elephanta." Devangana Desai finds *matrika* sculptures arrayed in counterclockwise sequence at the Kandariya Mahadeva temple in Khajuraho and interprets this to mean that they are circumambulating in a clockwise order, ahead of the visitor. Desai, "Temple as an Ordered Whole," 53. At Pattadakkal, Julie Romain found inscriptions as well as scenes from the epics wrapping the Papanatha temple in that direction. Romain, personal communication, Los Angeles, 2013. On the narrative sculptures leading counterclockwise at the Virupaksha temple in Pattadakkal, see also Wechsler, "Royal Legitimation."

4 See Parlier-Renault, *Temples de l'Inde méridionale*, 216; Soundara Rajan, "'Cult' in the Pallava Temples," 144–45.

5 Francis et al. propose that whereas the Kailasanatha and Shore Temples privilege orientation, the Vaikuntha Perumal privileges circumambulatory sequence. Francis, Gillet, and Schmid, "Chronique des études 'Pallava' I," 606. I am proposing that circumambulatory sequence also mattered at the Kailasanatha.

6 The map was drawn in 1980 by Mr. Durairaj and Mr. Ganesan for the École française d'Extrême-Orient in Pondicherry, where it is filed as no. PY523, échelle 1/6667. Staff at the institute kindly shared a copy with me when I visited in 1985.

On the temple's distance from the city center, see Srivatsan, "Kanchipuram, Temple Town Structure," 102–3; Raman, "Archaeological Excavations in Kanchipuram," 61–66.

7 Beyond the densely urbanized section of what is now called "Big Kanchi," the city stretched outward as a series of small, dense settlements separated by open spaces but linked by pathways from one another and the center. Champakalakshmi, "Urban Configurations"; Heitzman, "Urbanization and Political Economy"; Raman, "Archaeological Excavations in Kanchipuram," 67–68. James Heitzman finds that inscriptions make "frequent references to irrigation channels, fields and gardens." Heitzman, "Urbanization and Political Economy," 126.

8 The city's center shifted eastward under the Cholas and starting in the middle of the eighth century. Stein, "All Streets Lead to Temples," 91, 97–101. For Stein's latest thoughts on the location of the Pallava palace, see the introduction to this book, note 14.

9 Royal chapels are adjacent to palaces later in India. See, for example, Padmanabhapuram. Heston, "The Nexus of Divine and Earthly Rule."

10 There are no hills for ten miles. Raman, *Sri Varadarajaswami Temple*, 3. Kanchi sits on a long slab of earth that slopes east from the Western Ghats to the Bay of Bengal.

11 Heitzman, "Secondary Cities," 312; Nagaswamy, *The Kailasanatha Temple*, 17.

12 The city, too, had once been walled, though that wall was gone by the Pallava period. Heitzman, "Secondary Cities," 311.

13 Hudson cited Shaiva Siddhanta *agama*s as advocating worship of Candikeshvara at the end of circumambulation. Hudson, "How to Worship at Śiva's Temple," 316.

14 There are no *biruda*s on the three cells embedded in the southeast, southwest, and northwest corners, because they have no surface opening onto the courtyard.

15 Eugen Hultzsch judged the inscription on the third tier to be the oldest of the four because it is written in the same alphabet used for the *vimana* inscription. The other three he saw as copies of that tier, made within two generations or so, presumably as the first inscription began to erode. Hultzsch, *SII*, 1.24, 10.

16 Leslie Orr, personal communication, 2011.

17 See Summers, "*Figure come fratelli*." David Summers finds this effect produced by artists using the same drawing front and back.

18 The sample of Bhikshatana sculptures Gillet assembles from later eighth-century Pallava temples further suggests flexibility about his orientation. See the photos in Gillet, *La création d'une iconographie*, 118–31. He faces left and clockwise at the Olakkanatha in Mamallapuram, as he does on temple B in the eastern row of temples at the Kailasanatha complex. He faces right and counterclockwise at the Airavatesvara and Muktesvara temples. He faces right to walk toward the *linga* shrine from inside the porch at the Piravatesvara and at Mahendra's shrine in the Kailasanatha complex.

19 Gillet presumes each tableau represents a single narrative moment. Ibid., 20. Dehejia classifies such images as monoscenic. Dehejia, "Visual Narration in Early Buddhist Art."

20 Azaryahu and Foote, "Historical Space," 180, regarding history presented in landscapes. I am grateful to my student Huaiyao Chen for teaching me about this source.

21 Francis, Gillet, and Schmid, "Chronique des études 'Pallava' I," 597–602. Schmid walked through these sequences on-site for the "Archaeology of Bhakti" workshop in 2011.

22 Narratives leading both directions are common in India and beyond. For example, Anna Seastrand found scenes ordered clockwise on the Alwar Tirunakkari temple. Other murals also wrap in clockwise order. Seastrand, "Tracing a Line." I note that the narrative imagery Meister traces at Didwana leads in a clockwise direction. Meister, "Gaurīsikhara." Viewers would need to move counterclockwise to follow the war narrative on Trajan's column. Davies, "The Politics of Perpetuation." In Catholic churches, paintings or stained glass windows depicting the thirteen Stations of the Cross follow a clockwise sequence.

23 Gillet notes that Tamil and Sanskrit texts as well as four other Pallava-period temples in Kanchi (the Iravatesvara, Piravatesvara, Muktesvara, and Matangesvara) and Mahendra's shrine at the Kailasanatha all juxtapose these two episodes, *and in either sequence*. Gillet, *La création d'une iconographie*, 139–42.

24 See ibid., 139, n. 271. On the *Chidambaram Mahatmya* as a late reworking of older stories, see Kaimal, "Shiva Nataraja," 406.

25 This reading is given by Parlier-Renault, citing the *Shiva Purana* I (Vidyesvara), chaps. 6–8. Parlier-Renault, *Temples de l'Inde méridionale*, 193–98. Francis et al. suggest a narrative link in the juxtaposition of Lingodbhava and Bhikshatana. Francis, Gillet, and Schmid, "Chronique des études Pallava III," 296, n. 103. So does Gillet, but she quite reasonably struggles with the sequencing. Gillet, *La création d'une iconographie*, 140–41, 282.

26 Francis suggests that Shiva's torch-bearing and bent-legged figure on the west wall might continue the theme of fire from Dakshinamurti's torch on the south wall. That dance may be the dance in the charnel ground that follows Bhikshatana's interaction with the sages and their wives. Francis, "Le discours royal," 395.

27 On the relevance of this Sanskrit text to this Tamil building, see chapter 2.

28 Divakaran, "Durgā, the Great Goddess," 286. On the human-buffalo hybrid in the National Museum in New Delhi, see Agrawala, "A Rare Mahiṣamardinī Relief."

29 On this story, see Granoff, "Mahiṣāsuramardinī," 143–49. Granoff reads those intestines in the ropey form across the buffalo's body in a relief from Udayagiri. In that relief, however, Harle reads the object above the Goddess's hair as the lotus garland given by Ocean at Durga's birth. Harle, "On a Disputed Element."

30 Granoff, "Mahiṣāsuramardinī," 148. Granoff finds this way of telling the story distinctive to the *Devi Mahatmya*.

31 Chance, "Investigation of the Goddess' Ascetic Emanations," 33–35; Coburn, *Encountering the Goddess*, 69, vv. 8.8, 9.18.

32 For example, Gopinatha Rao, *Elements of Hindu Iconography*, vol. 1, pt. 1, 109–10; and Sivaramamurti, *Mahabalipuram*, 19. The version of this narrative at the Vishnu temple in Deogarh provides a precedent for showing the weapons personified.

33 See Lyons on the Goddess creating these states of mind in Vishnu and the demons. Lyons, "The Simla *Devī Māhātmya* Illustrations," 33. Nagaswamy argues that she is to be understood within Vishnu's sleeping form in this relief because she is that sleep, Yoganidra. This form is subtle and cannot be depicted through physical representations of her body. Nagaswamy, *Tantric Cult of South India*, 152–54. Srinivasan, too, sees this relief as linked

to the *Devi Mahatmya* tradition, and he adds that she will issue "in her full form from Vishnu's eyes, mouth, nose, arms, heart and chest enabling him to wake up and perceive Madhu and Kaitabha." K. R. Srinivasan, *Cave Temples of the Pallavas*, 155.

34 Other Pallava monuments pair these episodes too. At the Shore Temples in Mamallapuram, these subjects are carved close together and among the few elements cut into the granite bedrock on the shore. Tartakov and Dehejia, "Sharing, Intrusion, and Influence," 333. A mile south, the so-called Five Rathas place the Draupadi Ratha (holding the Goddess who stands on the buffalo head) next to the Bhima Ratha, where the unfinished interior holds the outlines of a reclining Vishnu. On both subjects recurring at Malaiadipatti, see Nagaswamy, *Tantric Cult of South India*, 154. I do not see them as equals there, however. Reclining Vishnu is the central and featured climax of one cave temple. Shiva is the star of the adjacent and later cave temple; the goddess who kills the buffalo stands to one side of him.

35 Lyons, "The Simla *Devī Māhātmya* Illustrations," 39. Compare Schmid, who remarks on how different the goddesses of the *Devi Mahatmya*'s four hymns are. Schmid, "La Prospérité," 477.

36 Srinivasan and Nagaswamy see the pairing of these two subjects as a deliberate device in sculpture as in the *Devi Mahatmya* for articulating the supremacy of the Goddess. Nagaswamy, *Tantric Cult of South India*, 154; K. R. Srinivasan, *Cave Temples of the Pallavas*, 155.

37 On the *Devi Mahatmya*'s goddess as existing outside Time as eternal embodiment of Triumph itself, see Lyons, "The Simla *Devī Māhātmya* Illustrations." Cynthia Ann Humes reads in the *Devi Mahatmya* a deliberate resistance to gender binaries. Humes, "Is the *Devi Mahatmya* a Feminist Scripture?"

38 This object looks even more like a shield in the open *mandapam*'s relief of this figure (see fig. 1.3b, no. 3), though its heavy plastering makes that relief a difficult source to rely on. There the shield is tilted slightly, revealing its circular form and revealing that the strip passing through her hand is a narrower shape attached within that circle.

39 Tartakov and Dehejia, "Sharing, Intrusion, and Influence," 331.

40 Here I see the same visual strategy at work that I perceived at the great cliff in Mamallapuram. Kaimal, "Playful Ambiguity." The purposeful omission of widely recognized signs can enable imagery to signify beyond a single narrative. Francis, too, suggests that Mahisha's absence lets this image function as a more general symbol of victory itself. See discussion in chapter 2, at note 12.

41 Dehejia and Tartakov see all iconographic signs of this and other Durgas of the period as interchangeable. Tartakov and Dehejia, "Sharing, Intrusion, and Influence," 330–32.

42 Death and Time are translated by the same word in Sanskrit: *kāla*. Tamil uses the same term. Nor are these separate or divergent meanings that happen to have clustered in the same signifier. Philosophy unites them. Time and death are the same thing: when time happens to people, they die; when death happens to people, it is a function of time.

43 Francis, "Le discours royal," 394–96.

44 Gillet, *La création d'une iconographie*, 283.

45 With Francis, I acknowledge that audiences could have taken from the monument's very form and the basic elements of the inscription a message of the dharmic king's power and privileged access to the divine. Francis, "Le discours royal," 141–47.

CHAPTER 5.
WORD-IMAGE TANGO

An earlier version of this chapter was published as Padma Kaimal, "Word-Image Tango: Telling Stories with Words and Sculptures at the Kailāsanātha Temple Complex in Kāñcīpuram," in *The Archaeology of Bhakti II: Royal Bhakti, Local Bhakti*, ed. Emmanuel Francis and Charlotte Schmid, Collection Indologie, no. 132 (Pondicherry: École française d'Extrême Orient and Institut français de Pondichéry, 2016), 159–207.

1 Probably the king approved of these praises, and perhaps he had some part in framing them, but I cannot agree with scholars who assume that these inscriptions represent the royal voice enough to assume the king is boasting, an assumption that seems apparent in, for example, Mahalingam, *Inscriptions of the Pallavas*, 173–75; Nagaswamy, *Tantric*

Cult of South India, 38; and K. R. Srinivasan, "Pallavas of Kāñcī," 38. On the particular character of Pallava panegyric, see Francis, "The Genealogy of the Pallavas"; and Francis, "Le discours royal," 291–306.

2   My understanding of narrativity and multiplicity in text/image dynamics derives from Barthes, "Structural Analysis of Narratives"; Becker, *Shifting Stones*; Brown, "Narrative as Icon"; Meister, "Gaurīśikhara"; Mostert, "Reading Images and Texts"; Williams, "On Viewing Sāñcī"; McCloud, *Understanding Comics*; Colgate colleagues Georgia Frank and Elizabeth Marlowe; and the students in my 2012 and 2013 "Sculpture and Narrative" seminars.

3   I agree with Francis that the temple also addressed itself to audiences that included the gods, Brahmins, other kings, rivals, and subordinates, to proclaim the exclusive dharmic status of its transmitter. Francis, "Le discours royal," 141–47. These other people surely had access to the exoteric layers of meaning I have laid out in the preceding chapters.

4   We can reconstruct where verse 1 begins even though it is now covered by the closed *mandapam* that abuts the *vimana* façade. On that reconstruction, see Sankaranarayanan, "A Pallava Inscriptional Poem," 72. In 1892, with the first publication of this inscription, Eugen Hultzsch explains: "By the temporary removal of some slabs, my assistant succeeded in preparing fac-similes of the greater part of the first verse and of a few additional letters at the beginning of the second verse." Hultzsch, *SII*, 1.24, 9. In the building's present state, the text emerges from that later construction at the last letter of "aṅgirās" in verse 2.

The foundation inscription on the same king's Shiva temple at Panaimalai also begins on the doorjamb just to the right of the sanctum door. As Francis puts it, Pallava foundation inscriptions begin where circumambulation finishes. Francis, "Le discours royal," 142, n. 475. On the inscription on the Panaimalai temple, see chapter 3, note 1.

5   Martha Ann Selby wonders if the course's placement is a gesture toward the visitor's heart. Personal communication, October 2013.

6   Leslie Orr, personal communication, 2011.

7   According to Dominic Goodall and Martha Ann Selby, personal communication, 2013.

8   Francis identifies this meter as Aryagiti (Āryāgīti). S. Sankaranarayanan calls it Samavritta (Samavṛtta). Francis otherwise confirms all of Sankaranarayanan's meter identifications.

9   When Hultzsch uncovered the first verses of the inscription, some letters were already lost. Hultzsch, *SII*, 1.24, 8–13. Sankaranarayanan specifies that these were the first seventeen letters and the last five letters of verse 1, as well as the first six letters of verse 2. Sankaranarayanan, "A Pallava Inscriptional Poem," 72.

10   On those connotations of Ganga to the Pallavas, see chapter 3.

11   McCloud, *Understanding Comics*, 60–92.

12   Contrast this with the dynastic history of the Pallavas carved at the Vaikuntha Perumal temple. Minakshi, *The Historical Sculptures at the Vaikuṇṭhaperumāḷ Temple*.

13   Bynum, *Jesus as Mother*, 139–43; Hiltebeitel and Erndl, "Introduction: Writing Goddesses, Goddesses Writing."

14   Ali, "Royal Eulogy," 169–83.

15   On this pattern operating in the eighth century, see ibid., 183. On the *yuga*s and their connections to the epics, see ibid., 180. I use Ali's English translations for the names of these *yuga*s.

16   Ibid.

17   Hawley, "Scenes from the Childhood of Kṛṣṇa," 78. Lawrence A. Babb finds temples modeling time much as Ali's texts do. Babb, "Time and Temples." Michael W. Meister argues that use of the *vastumandala* (a planning diagram that aligns a building with ideas about the cosmos) in the temple at Indore marks the temple as a chronogram. Meister, "Analysis of Temple Plans." J. McKim Malville views Hindu temples generally as chronograms in which walking into them returns the visitor to the primordial chaos of the *garbha griha* and passing back out moves time forward once again. Malville, "Astrophysics, Cosmology."

18   Mahendravarman's shrine at the Kailasanatha temple complex might present the same text-image collusion around that analogy, but with the Skanda-like son having grown into an adult.

19   The actual corner of the building is at the second of the three right angles that cluster at each corner of this building. The two right angles on either side of it are created by offset projections on each of the adjoining walls.

20 Ali, "Royal Eulogy," 183–86, 210.

21 Ibid., 183–86. For the king Rajendra I Chola, possessing Ganga was a way of claiming he had unified the earth. Ibid., 210.

22 Orr finds that *meykkirti*s, panegyric passages in Tamil inscriptions, also express the ideal that kings could bring back the past. Orr, "Transposing Royal Glory."

23 The texts Daud Ali synthesizes also identify the paramount sovereign as the repository of light when the *krita yuga* returns. Ali, "Royal Eulogy," 203. Rajendra I Chola's monuments contribute to his fame and light. Ibid., 205. To paraphrase Ali closely: in this world view, light emanates from a king who is favored by heaven and who can therefore restore the *krita yuga*. His fame is light and sparkles like jewels in his orders, acts, gifts, monuments, and institutions. When the Age of Completeness resumes, light drawn from above illuminates the world.

24 Ibid., 194.

25 Ibid., 211–12.

26 Granoff, "Heaven on Earth"; Meister, "The Hindu Temple"; Nagaswamy, "The Brahadiśvara as Paramākāśa."

27 Gillet, *La création d'une iconographie*, 282.

28 Francis, "Le discours royal," 36, n. 159; 405, n. 431; 428, n. 563.

29 The text on the wall actually reads "Śivacūḍāmaṇi." See appendix 2, v. 12, note 4.

30 Orr, preface to *Pondicherry Inscriptions*, pt. 1, iii, xvi; Schopen, "What's in a Name," 72.

31 Francis, "Le discours royal," 395; Gillet, *La création d'une iconographie*, 170–71.

32 The presence of words can in other contexts undercut the operation of iconicity in sculpture, however. See Janice Leoshko on the inscription of words working against narrativity on *bhumisparśa* (earth-touching) Buddha figures. Leoshko, "About Looking at Buddha Images."

33 Becker, *Shifting Stones*, 29, 42–59. Becker argues that even when visual narrative was not linear or thorough in laying out sequential events, its visuality was meant for the faithful to engage with and to comprehend. Narrative was what the Buddha did and how he taught, so sculptures that narrate were bringing the Buddha himself back into the presence of the viewer. Becker disagrees, as do I, with Robert L. Brown's claim that the purpose of visual narratives excludes narrative, that the Buddha is "not present to tell stories at all." Ibid., 34; Brown, "Narrative as Icon," 65.

34 Leoshko notes that partial narrativity can indicate audience familiarity. Leoshko, "About Looking at Buddha Images." On less thorough, or "weaker" in Werner Wolf's terminology, narrative being appropriate for well-versed viewers, see Becker, *Shifting Stones*, 86–87; Wolf, "Narrative and Narrativity."

35 Walter Smith argues that the Kailasanatha at Ellora aimed to re-create and transport Mount Kailasa from the Himalayas to the patron's own kingdom in the Western Ghats. W. Smith, "Architectural and Mythic Space."

36 See Roland Barthes's "reality effect." Barthes, "Structural Analysis of Narratives." Meister argues that multiple narratives cascading like an ocean over the surface of a temple can have a convincing effect on visitors. Meister, "Gaurīśikhara." Cynthia Talbot uses the term *facticity* to describe the phenomenon in inscriptions. Talbot, "Parameters of Poetic Praise."

37 As Francis, Gillet, and Schmid observe, the Shore Temples place deities around the Shiva sanctuary and kings around the large enclosure west of that, and the Vaikuntha Perumal wraps an enclosure wall lined with royal sculptures around a temple covered with deities. They see the Kailasanatha as having no sculptures that are specifically royal such as portraits or royal narratives. Francis, Gillet, and Schmid, "Chronique des études 'Pallava' I," 605. I agree and note that the royal presence there comes in the words of Rajasimha's inscription rather than sculptures, but once again in a girdling shape.

CONCLUSIONS

1 Sanderson, "History through Textual Criticism," 8–10, n. 6; Sanderson, "The Impact of Inscriptions," 234. Alexis Sanderson finds that by the sixth century, ascetics from this and other sects were initiating kings into their esoteric worlds. He identifies two earlier kings, the Chalukya Vikramaditya I and the Eastern Ganga Devendravarman, as having taken this initiation, but the inscriptions marking that do not use the phrase "Shaiva Siddhanta."

Many scholars agree that Rajasimha took Tantric initiation into Shaiva Siddhanta. See Davis, *Ritual in an Oscillating Universe*, 12; Francis, "Le discours royal," 438, n. 613; Gillet, *La création d'une iconographie*, 75, n. 168. Dominic Goodall sees the epithets in verse 5 as thus having a level of meaning specific to the king gaining knowledge of Shaiva Siddhanta doctrine and conquering *internal* enemies. Goodall, *The Parākhyatantra*, xix, n. 17.

Devangana Desai believes that the Kandariya Mahadeva temple in Khajuraho also had associations with the central Indian school of Shaiva Siddhanta. She finds a Sadashiva sculpture inscribed with a dedication by an *acharya* she identifies as a Shaiva Siddhanta. Desai, "Temple as an Ordered Whole," 40, 45–48.

2 Thus I am proposing a revision of Gillet's deduction that Shaiva Siddhanta did not shape temples until the eleventh century. Gillet, *La création d'une iconographie*, 74–75. She deduces this from the gap Hélène Brunner finds between sculptures and *agamas* before the eleventh century.

3 Davis, *Ritual in an Oscillating Universe*, 60.

4 Ibid., 46–49. Dennis Hudson finds that nineteenth-century Shaiva Siddhanta literature associates counterclockwise movement and the path of renunciation, setting them in counterpoint with clockwise movement for those who seek the auspicious path of emanation. He, too, posits two different forms of experience for visitors, one secret and one public, at the Vaikuntha Perumal temple. Hudson, *The Body of God*, 309. Francis et al. offer the important clarification that for the Pallavas there would be continuity rather than opposition between these two pathways. Francis, Gillet, and Schmid, "Chronique des études 'Pallava' I," 603.

Colleagues have shared with me their observations of contemporary practice of counterclockwise movement carrying connotations of renunciation and release. Joanne P. Waghorne and Martha Ann Selby, personal communication, 2013.

5 Davis, *Ritual in an Oscillating Universe*, 47, 52–60.

6 Goodall, *The Parākhyatantra*, xxvi–xxvii; Sankaranarayanan, "A Pallava Inscriptional Poem," 87.

7 Davis, *Ritual in an Oscillating Universe*, 9.

8 Ibid., 69–71.

9 Ibid., 47.

10 Ibid., 9.

APPENDIX 1. INSCRIPTIONS ON RAJASIMHA'S *PRAKARA*

Hultzsch, *SII*, 1.25. Other publications of the inscription include Francis, "Le discours royal," 668; Lockwood et al., *Pallava Art*, 173–85; Nagaswamy, "New Light on Mamallapuram." For the incomplete list of titles written in the large, ornamental script on the lowest molding, see Hultzsch, *SII*, 1.26.

1 All are in Sanskrit. The texts on the top and bottom tiers are in *nagari* script. The texts on tiers 2 and 3 are in Pallava-*grantha*.

APPENDIX 2. THE FOUNDATION INSCRIPTION OF THE RAJASIMHESHVARA

This appendix presents a simplified version of Francis's new edition and translation published as Francis, "Appendix," 195–203. For previous publications of the inscription, see Sankaranarayanan, "A Pallava Inscriptional Poem," 71; Francis, "Le discours royal," 667–68; Hultzsch, *SII*, 1.24, 9–12; Mahalingam, *Inscriptions of the Pallavas*, 173; and Nagaswamy, "New Light on Mamallapuram," 35–38.

1 *Amrita* is the elixir the gods consume.

2 *Varga* means "category."

3 That is, "the (temple of) Īshvara built by Rajasimhapallava" or "the (temple) of the Lord of the Pallavas built by Rajasimha."

4 This is a list of *birudas* of Narasimhavarman II, which mean, respectively, "he who is a lion among kings," "he who is victorious in battle," "he who bears fortune," "he whose bow is marvelous," "he who is an unequaled warrior," and "he who wears Shiva as his crest-jewel."

APPENDIX 3. THE FOUNDATION INSCRIPTION OF THE MAHENDRAVARMESHVARA

This translation is derived from Francis, "Le discours royal," 406–9, 671, *inscription royale* (hereafter IR) 46; Hultzsch, *SII*, 1.27; Mahalingam, *Inscriptions of the Pallavas*, no. 69; Nagaswamy, "New Light on Mamallapuram," 39–40; Schmid, "Bhakti in Its Infancy," 115–16.

1   Schmid, following Sylvain Brocquet, prefers "surrounded by a troop led by Skanda" to Hultzsch's "together with the troops of his attendants, the Guhas." Schmid, "Bhakti in Its Infancy," 116. Schmid notes that the foundation inscription emphasizes the father-son link repeatedly, and particularly in verse 2 through the Shiva/Guha analogy it carries over from verse 5 of Rajasimha's inscription. Ibid., 115.

2   Or as Francis puts it, "Mahendra III a pour aïeul Lokāditya, 'le Soleil des mondes dont la chaleur assécha la boue de l'armée de Raṇarasika' [B] (IR 46:2: *lokādityāt pras to raṇarasikacam pa kaśoṣipratāpād*)." Francis, "La discours royal," 409, n. 456.

3   "Narasiṃha II est 'créateur d'un autre âge d'or (*kritayuga*) grâce à ses vertus détournées du péché' (IR 46:3: *vrittair amhonivrittai kritayugam aparan nirmmimāṇo*)." Ibid., 407, n. 444.

4   Ibid., 681, IR 74; fig. 34; Francis, Gillet, and Schmid, "Chronique des études 'Pallava' I," 584.

5   Emmanuel Francis, lecture on-site, 2011.

6   Francis, "La discours royal," 680, IR 73; fig. 33.

7   Ibid., 671, IR 47.

8   Ibid., 681, IR 76.

APPENDIX 4.
THE FOUNDATION INSCRIPTIONS
AROUND *VIMANA*S C, E, AND G

I have compiled these translations from Francis, "Le discours royal," 391–92, nn. 361–63; Hultzsch, *SII*, 1.28–30; Lockwood et al., *Pallava Art*, 152; Mahalingam, *Inscriptions of the Pallavas*, 192–95, nos. 57–59.

1   Francis, "Le discours royal," 361–63. Francis suggests that the phrase including Kalakala was a later addition to the inscription. Ibid., 391, n. 363.

2   Lockwood et al., *Pallava Art*, 152.

3   Francis, "Le discours royal," 391, n. 362.

4   Lockwood et al., *Pallava Art*, 152.

5   Francis, "Le discours royal," 392, n. 366. Francis sees this as the fourth verse of the inscription.

6   Lockwood et al., *Pallava Art*, 152.

7   Francis reports that preceding verse 3 are at least fourteen *akṣara* (syllables) that seem to have been part of a supplementary strophe. Francis, "Le discours royal," 392, n. 365.

8   Ibid., 85; 391, n. 364. Francis sees this as the third verse of this inscription

9   Lockwood et al., *Pallava Art*, 152. Lockwood sees this as the third and final verse of this inscription.

10 Francis, "Le discours royal," 392, n. 366. Francis sees this as the fourth verse of the inscription.

11 Lockwood et al., *Pallava Art*, 152. Lockwood sees this as the second verse of the inscription.

BIBLIOGRAPHY

Adicéam, Marguerite E. "Les images de Śiva dans l'Inde du Sud: III et IV, Bhikṣāṭanamūrti et Kaṅkālamūrti." *Arts Asiatiques* 12 (1965): 85–91.

———. "Les images de Śiva dans l'Inde du Sud: II–XV." *Arts Asiatiques* 12–32 (1965–76).

———. "Les images de Śiva dans l'Inde du Sud: VIII, IX, X, Kevala-, Umāsahita- et Aliṅgana-Candraśekharamūrti." *Arts Asiatiques* 21 (1970): 40–49.

———. "Les images de Śiva dans l'Inde du Sud: XII, XIII, XIV, Sukhāsana, Umāsahitasukhāsana, Umāmaheśvaramūrti." *Arts Asiatiques* 28 (1973): 63–101.

———. "Les images de Śiva dans l'Inde du Sud: XV, Gaṅgādharamūrti." *Arts Asiatiques* 32 (1976): 99–138.

Agrawala, R. C. "A Rare Mahiṣamardinī Relief in the National Museum, New Delhi." *East and West* 16 (1966): 109–11.

Aitken, Molly Emma. *The Intelligence of Tradition in Rajput Court Painting*. New Haven, CT: Yale University Press, 2010.

Ali, Daud. "Royal Eulogy as World History: Rethinking Copper-Plate Inscriptions in Cōḻa India." In *Querying the Medieval: Texts and the History of Practices in South Asia*, by Ronald Inden, Jonathan S. Walters, and Daud Ali, 165–229. New York: Oxford University Press, 2000.

Apffel-Marglin, Frédérique. "Kings and Wives: The Separation of Status and Royal Power." *Contributions to Indian Sociology* 15, no. 1–2 (January 1981): 155–81.

———. "Types of Sexual Union and Their Implicit Meanings." In *The Divine Consort: Rādhā and the Goddesses of India*, edited by John S. Hawley and Donna M. Wulff, 298–315. Berkeley, CA: Graduate Theological Union, 1982.

———. "Female Sexuality in the Hindu World." In *Immaculate and Powerful: The Female in Sacred Image and Social Reality*, edited by Clarissa W. Atkinson, Constance H. Buchanan, and Margaret R. Miles, 39–60. Boston: Beacon Press, 1985.

———. Introduction to *Purity and Auspiciousness in Indian Society*, edited by John B. Carman and Frédérique Apffel-Marglin, 1–10. Leiden: E. J. Brill, 1985.

———. "Types of Oppositions in Hindu Culture." In *Purity and Auspiciousness in Indian Society*, edited by John B. Carman and Frédérique Apffel-Marglin, 65–83. Leiden: E. J. Brill, 1985.

Aravamuthan T. G. *Portrait Sculpture in South India*. New Delhi: Asian Educational Services, 1992. Originally published 1930, Madras.

Arunachalam, B. C. M. "The Sapta Mātā Cult." *Bulletin of the Institute of Traditional Cultures*, 1979, 1–24.

Asher, Frederick. "Historical and Political Allegory in Gupta Art." In *Essays on Gupta Culture*, edited by Bardwell Smith, 53–66. Delhi: Motilal Banarsidass, 1983.

Ataç, Mehmet-Ali. "'Time and Eternity' in the Northwest Palace of Ashurnasirpal II at Nimrud." In *Assyrian Reliefs from the Palace of Ashurnasirpal II: A Cultural Biography*, edited by Ada Cohen and Steven E. Kangas, 159–80, 234–39. Hanover, NH: Hood Museum of Art, Dartmouth College, and University Press of New England, 2010.

Azaryahu, Maoz, and Kenneth E. Foote. "Historical Space as Narrative Medium: On the Configuration of Spatial Narratives of Time at Historical Sites." *GeoJournal* 73, no. 3 (2008): 179–94.

Babb, Lawrence A. "Time and Temples: On Social and Metrical Antiquity." In *Ethnography and Personhood: Notes from the Field*, edited by Michael W. Meister, 193–221. New Delhi: Rawat Publications, 2000.

Badhreenath, Sathyabhama. Śāluvankuppam Excavations 2005–*07*. Memoirs of the Archaeological Survey of India. New Delhi: Director General, Archaeological Survey of India, 2015.

Bafna, Sonit. "On the Idea of the Mandala as a Governing Device in Indian Architectural Tradition." *Journal of the Society of Architectural Historians* 59, no. 1 (2000): 26–49.

Balasubrahmanyam, S. R. "Three Dated Early Choḷa Sculptures of Erumbur." *Lalit Kalā* 13 (1939): 16–21.

———. *Early Chola Temples*. New Delhi: Orient Longman, 1971.

Banerjea, J. N. *The Development of Hindu Iconography*. Calcutta: University of Calcutta Press, 1941.

Barthes, Roland. "Introduction to the Structural Analysis of Narratives." In *Image, Music, Text*, 79–124. New York: Hill and Wang, 1977.

Baxandall, Michael. *Painting and Experience in Fifteenth-Century Italy*. New York: Oxford University Press, 1972.

Becker, Catherine. *Shifting Stones, Shaping the Past: Sculpture from the Buddhist Stūpas of Andhra Pradesh*. New York: Oxford University Press, 2015.

Bois, Yve-Alain Bois. "Materialist Formalism." Lecture, Institute for Advanced Study, Princeton, NJ, 2011.

Brancaccio, Pia. "The Cave as a Palace and the Forest as a Garden: Buddhist Caves and Natural Landscape in the Western Deccan." Paper presented at the colloquium "Landscape and Sacred Architecture in Pre-modern South Asia," Dumbarton Oaks, Washington, DC, November 14, 2014.

Branfoot, Crispin. *Gods on the Move: Architecture and Ritual in the South Indian Temple*. London: Society for South Asian Studies, British Academy, 2007.

———. "Remaking the Past: Tamil Sacred Landscape and Temple Renovations." *Bulletin of the School of Oriental and African Studies* 76, no. 1 (2013): 21–47.

Brocquet, Sylvain. "Les inscriptions sanskrites des Pallava: Poésie, rituel, idéologie." Thèse de doctorat, Université de Paris III, 1997.

Brown, Robert L. "Narrative as Icon: The Jataka Stories in Ancient Indian and Southeast Asian Architecture." In *Sacred Biography in the Buddhist Traditions of South and Southeast Asia*, edited by Juliane Schober, 64–109. Honolulu: University of Hawai'i Press, 1997.

Brunner, Hélène. "Jñāna and Kriyā: Relation between Theory and Practice in the Śaivāgamas." In *Ritual and Speculation in Early Tantrism: Studies in Honor of André Padoux*, edited by Teun Goudriaan, 1–60. Albany: State University of New York Press, 1992.

Bynum, Caroline Walker. *Jesus as Mother: Studies in the Spirituality of the High Middle Ages*. Berkeley: University of California Press, 1982.

———. "Introduction: The Complexity of Symbols." In *Gender and Religion: On the Complexity of Symbols*, edited by Caroline Walker Bynum, Stevan Harrell, and Paula Richman, 1–20. Boston: Beacon Press, 1986.

Cane, Nicolas. "Cempiyan-Mahādevī, reine et dévote: Un 'personnage épigraphique' du Xe siècle." Thèse de doctorat, Université de recherche Paris Sciences et Lettres, 2017.

Champakalakshmi, R. "South Indian Paintings: A Survey." In *South Indian Studies (Dr. T. V. Mahalingam Commemoration Volume)*, 696–714. Mysore: Geetha Book House, 1990.

———. "The Urban Configurations of Toṇḍaimaṇḍalam: The Kāñcīpuram Region, c. A.D. 600–1300." In *Urban Form and Meaning in South Asia: The Shaping of Cities from Prehistoric to Precolonial Times*, edited by Howard Spodek and Doris Meth Srinivasan, 185–207. Studies in the History of Art, vol. 31. Washington, DC: National Gallery of Art, 1993.

———. "Iconographic Programme and Political Imagery in Early Medieval Tamiḻakam: The Rājasiṃheśvara and the Rājarājeśvara." In *Indian Art: Forms, Concerns and Development in Historical Perspective*, edited by B. N. Goswamy and Kavita Singh, 217–43. New Delhi: Munshiram Manoharlal Publishers, 2000.

Chance, Stacey Lynn. "Investigation of the Goddess' Ascetic Emanations: A Yogini Set from Tamilnadu." Master's thesis, University of Missouri, 2000.

Chanchani, Nachiket, and Tamara I. Sears. Introduction to "Transmission of Architectural Knowledge in Medieval South Asia," edited by Nachiket Chanchani and Tamara I. Sears. Special issue, *Ars Orientalis* 45 (2015): 7–13.

Chandrakumar, T. "Iconography of Liṅgodbhavamūrti in South India: A Probe into Stylistic Evolution." *East and West* 41 (1991): 153–72.

Coburn, Thomas B. *Encountering the Goddess: A Translation of the Devī-Māhātmya and a Study of Its Interpretation*. SUNY Series in Hindu Studies, edited by Wendy Doniger. Albany: State University of New York Press, 1991.

Coleman, Tracy. "Dharma, Yoga, and Viraha-Bhakti in Buddhacarita and Kṛṣṇacarita." In *The Archaeology of Bhakti I: Mathurā and Maturai, Back and Forth*, edited by Emmanuel Francis and Charlotte Schmid, 35–59. Pondicherry: École française d'Extrême-Orient, 2014.

Collins, Charles D. *The Iconography and Ritual of Śiva at Elephanta*. Albany: State of University of New York Press, 1988.

Craddock, Elaine. "Reconstructing the Split Goddess as Śakti in a Tamil Village." In *Seeking Mahādevī: Constructing the Identities of the Hindu Great Goddess*, edited by Tracy Pintchman, 145–69. Albany: State University of New York Press, 2001.

Davies, Penelope J. E. "The Politics of Perpetuation: Trajan's Column and the Art of Commemoration." *American Journal of Archaeology* 101, no. 1 (1997): 41–65.

Davis, Richard H. *Ritual in an Oscillating Universe: Worshiping Śiva in Medieval India*. Princeton, NJ: Princeton University Press, 1991.

———. "Becoming a Śiva, and Acting as One in Śaiva Worship." In *Ritual and Speculation in Early Tantrism: Studies in Honor of André Padoux*, edited by Teun Goudriaan, 107–20. Albany: State University of New York Press, 1992.

———. "Indian Art Objects as Loot." *Journal of Asian Studies* 52, no. 1 (1993): 22–48.

———. "Hudson Rethinks Bhagavata Thoughts." *Journal of Vaishnava Studies* 11, no. 1 (2002): 27–43.

DeCaroli, Robert. "An Analysis of Daṇḍin's *Daśakumāracarita* and Its Implications for Both the Vākāṭaka and Pallava Courts." *Journal of the American Oriental Society* 115, no. 4 (1995): 671–78.

Dehejia, Vidya. *Yoginī, Cult and Temples: A Tantric Tradition*. New Delhi: National Museum, 1986.

———. "On Modes of Visual Narration in Early Buddhist Art." *Art Bulletin* 72 (1990): 374–92.

———. *Indian Art*. New York: Phaidon Press, 1997.

Dehejia, Vidya, and Richard H. Davis. "Addition, Erasure, and Adaptation: Interventions in the Rock-Cut Monuments of Māmallapuram." *Archives of Asian Art* 60 (2010): 1–18.

Denton, Lynn Teskey. "Varieties of Hindu Female Asceticism." In *Roles and Rituals for Hindu Women*, edited by Julia Leslie, 211–31. Rutherford, NJ: Fairleigh Dickinson University Press 1991.

Desai, Devangana. "The Location of Sculptures in the Architectural Scheme of the Kaṇḍāriya Mahādeva Temple of Khajuraho: Śāstra and Practice." In *Shastric Traditions in Indian Arts*, edited by Anna Libera Dallapiccola and Christine Walter-Mendy, 155–65. Stuttgart: Steiner, 1989.

———. "Temple as an Ordered Whole—the Iconic Scheme at Khajuraho." *Journal of the Asiatic Society of Bombay*, n.s., 70 (1995): 38–58.

———. "Textual Tradition and the Temples of Khajuraho." In *Archaeology and Text: The Temple in South Asia*, edited by Himanshu Prabha Ray, 59–76. New York: Oxford University Press, 2010.

Dessigane, R., P. Z. Pattabiramin, and Jean Filliozat. *Les légendes çivaïtes de Kāñcipuram: Analyse de textes et iconographie*. Pondicherry: Institut français d'indologie, 1964.

Dhaky, M. A. "Cōlas of Tañjāvūr." In *Encyclopaedia of Indian Temple Architecture*, edited by Michael W. Meister and M. A. Dhaky, vol. 1, pt. 1, *South India: Lower Dravidadesa, 200 BC–AD 1324*, 145–98. New Delhi: American Institute of Indian Studies and Oxford University Press, 1983.

———. "Bhūtas and Bhūtanāyakas: Elementals and Their Captains." In *Discourses on Śiva: Proceedings of a Symposium on the Nature of Religious Imagery*, edited by Michael W. Meister, 240–56; figs. 203–25. Philadelphia: University of Pennsylvania Press, 1984.

Divakaran, Odile. "Durgā, the Great Goddess: Meanings and Forms in the Early Period." In *Discourses on Śiva: Proceedings of a Symposium on the Nature of Religious Imagery*, edited by Michael W. Meister, 271–88; figs. 237–57. Philadelphia: University of Pennsylvania Press, 1984.

Duggan, Lawrence G. "Reflections on 'Was Art Really the "Book of the Illiterate"?'" In *Reading Images and Texts: Medieval Images and Texts as Forms of Communication; Papers from the Third Utrecht Symposium on Medieval Literacy, Utrecht, 7–9 December 2000*, edited by Mariëlle Hageman and Marco Mostert, 109–19. Turnhout, Belgium: Brepols, 2005.

———. "Was Art Really the 'Book of the Illiterate'?" In *Reading Images and Texts: Medieval Images and Texts as Forms of Communication; Papers from the Third Utrecht Symposium on Medieval Literacy, Utrecht, 7–9 December 2000*, edited by Mariëlle Hageman and Marco Mostert, 63–107. Turnhout, Belgium: Brepols, 2005.

Dumarçay, Jacques, and Françoise L'Hernault. *Temples Pallava construits*. Paris: École française d'Extrême-Orient, A. Maisonneuve, 1975.

Eck, Diana L. *Darśan, Seeing the Divine Image in India*. 2nd ed. Chambersburg, PA: Anima Books, 1985.

Etter, Anne-Julie. "Antiquarian Knowledge and Preservation of Indian Monuments at the Beginning of the Nineteenth Century." In *Knowledge Production, Pedagogy and Institutions in Colonial India*, edited by Indra Sengupta and Daud Ali, 75–95. New York: Palgrave Macmillan, 2011.

Evans, Kirsti. *Epic Narratives in the Hoysaḷa Temples: The Rāmāyaṇa, Mahābhārata, and Bhāgavata Purāṇa*. Studies in the History of Religions, vol. 74, edited by H. G. Kippenberg and E. T. Lawson. Leiden: E. J. Brill, 1997.

Ferro-Luzzi, Gabriella Eichinger. "The Female *Liṅgam*: Interchangeable Symbols and Paradoxical Associations of Hindu Gods and Goddesses." *Current Anthropology* 21 (1980): 45–68.

Filliozat, Jean. "Les images de Śiva dans l'Inde du Sud: I, L'image se l'origine du liṅga (Liṅgodbhavamūrti)." *Arts Asiatiques* 8, no. 1 (1961): 43–56.

Francis, Emmanuel. "Le discours royal: Inscriptions et monuments Pallava (IVème–IXème siècles)." Thèse de doctorat, Université Catholique de Louvain, 2009.

———. "The Genealogy of the Pallavas: From Brahmins to Kings." *Religions of South Asia* 5, no. 1 (2011): 339–63.

———. "Appendix: The Foundation Inscription of the Rājasiṃheśvara." In "Word-Image Tango: Telling Stories with Words and Sculptures at the Kailāsanātha Temple Complex in Kāñcīpuram," by Padma Kaimal, 195–203. Chap. 4 of *The Archaeology of Bhakti II: Royal Bhakti, Local Bhakti*, edited by Emmanuel Francis and Charlotte Schmid. Collection Indologie, no. 132. Pondicherry: École française d'Extrême Orient and Institut français de Pondichéry, 2016.

Francis, Emmanuel, Valérie Gillet, and Charlotte Schmid. "L'eau et le feu: Chronique des études 'Pallava' I." *Bulletin de l'École française d'Extrême-Orient* (Paris) 92 (2005): 581–611.

———. "Trésors inédits du pays tamoul: Chronique des études Pallava II. Vestiges Pallava autour de Mahābalipuram et à Taccūr." *Bulletin de l'École française d'Extrême-Orient* (Paris) 93 (2006): 431–81.

———. "*De loin, de près*: Chronique des études Pallava III." *Bulletin de l'École française d'Extrême-Orient* (Paris) 94 (2007): 253–317.

Francis, Emmanuel, and Charlotte Schmid. Preface to *Pondicherry Inscriptions*, pt. 2, *Translation, Appendices, Glossary and Phrases*, edited by G. Vijayavenugopal, v–xlviii. Pondicherry: Institut français de Pondichéry and École française d'Extrême-Orient, 2010.

Gaston, Anne-Marie. *Śiva in Dance, Myth, and Iconography*. New York: Oxford University Press, 1982.

Gillet, Valérie. *La création d'une iconographie śivaïte narrative: Incarnations du dieu dans les temples pallava construits*. Collection Indologie, no. 113. Pondicherry: Institute français de Pondichéry; Paris: École français d'Extrême-Orient, 2010.

Giri, Kamal. "Gaṇas and Their Representation in the Kailāśanātha Temple, Kāñcîpuram." *Vishveshvaranand Indological Journal* (Hoshiarpur) 21, no. 1–2 (1983): 85–93.

Goodall, Dominic. *The Parākhyatantra, a Scripture of the Śaiva Siddhānta*. Collection Indologie, no. 98. Pondicherry: Institut français de Pondichéry and École française d'Extrême-Orient, 2004.

Goodison, Lucy, and Christine Morris. "Beyond the 'Great Mother': The Sacred World of the Minoans." In *Ancient Goddesses: The Myths and the Evidence*, edited by Lucy Goodison and Christine Morris, 113–32. Madison: University of Wisconsin Press, 1999.

———. Introduction to *Ancient Goddesses: The Myths and the Evidence*, edited by Lucy Goodison and Christine Morris, 6–21. Madison: University of Wisconsin Press, 1999.

Gopalan, R. *History of the Pallavas of Kanchi*. Madras: University of Madras, 1928.

Gopinatha Rao, T. A. *Elements of Hindu Iconography*. 2nd ed. 2 vols. in four parts. Madras, 1914. Reprint, Delhi, 1985.

Granoff, Phyllis. "Mahiṣāsuramardinī: An Analysis of the Myths." *East and West* 29 (1979): 139–51.

———. "Heaven on Earth: Temples and Temple Cities of Medieval India." In *India and Beyond: Aspects of Literature, Meaning, Ritual and Thought; Essays in Honour of Frits Staal*, edited by Dick van der Meij, 170–93. London: Kegan Paul International, 1997.

Guha, Kamalesh, and Gabriella Eichinger Ferro-Luzzi. "More on the Idea of the Female *Liṅgam*." *Current Anthropology* 24 (1983): 407–8.

Hardy, Adam. *The Temple Architecture of India*. Hoboken, NJ: Wiley, 2007.

———. *Theory and Practice of Temple Architecture in Medieval India: Bhoja's Samarāṅgaṇasūtradhāra and the Bhojpur Line Drawings*. With translations from the Sanskrit by Mattia Salvini. New Delhi: Indira Gandhi National Centre for the Arts, 2015.

Harle, James C. "On a Disputed Element in the Iconography of Early Mahiṣāsuramardinī Images." *Ars Orientalis* 8 (1970): 147–53.

———. *Temple Gateways in South India*. 2nd rev. ed. New Delhi: Munshiram Manoharlal Publishers, 1995. Originally published 1963 by Bruno Cassirer (Oxford, UK).

Harman, William. "Introduction: Fierce Goddess of South Asia." *Nidān: International Journal for the Study of Hinduism* 24 (2012): i–iii.

Hart, George L. *Poets of the Tamil Anthologies: Ancient Poems of Love and War*. Princeton, NJ: Princeton University Press, 1979.

———. Introduction to *The Four Hundred Songs of War and Wisdom: An Anthology of Poems from Classical Tamil, the Puṟanāṉūṟu*. Edited and translated by George L. Hart and Hank Heifetz, xv–xxxvii. New York: Columbia University Press, 1999.

———. *The Poems of Ancient Tamil: Their Milieu and Their Sanskrit Counterparts*. New Delhi: Oxford University Press, 1999.

Hatley, Shaman. "The Brahmayāmalatantra and Early Śaiva Cult of Yoginīs." Ph.D. dissertation, University of Pennsylvania, 2007.

Hawley, John S. "Scenes from the Childhood of Kṛṣṇa on the Kailāsanātha Temple, Ellora." *Archives of Asian Art* 34 (1981): 74–90.

———. "The Boston Vīṇādhara Śiva." *Journal of the Oriental Institute* (M. S. University of Baroda) 33, no. 1–2 (1983): 141–45.

Heitzman, James. "Urbanization and Political Economy in Early South India: Kāñcīpuram during the Cōla Period." In *Structure and Society in Early South India: Essays in Honour of Noboru Karashima*, edited by Kenneth R. Hall, 117–56. New York: Oxford University Press, 2001.

———. "Secondary Cities and Spatial Templates in South India, 1300–1800." In *Secondary Cities and Urban Networking in the Indian Ocean Realm, c. 1400–1800*, edited by Kenneth R. Hall, 303–34. New York: Lexington Books, 2008.

Heston, Mary Beth. "Iconographic Themes of the *Gopura* of the Kailāsanātha Temple at Ellorā." *Artibus Asiae* 43, no. 3 (1981–82): 219–35.

———. "The Nexus of Divine and Earthly Rule: Padmanābhapuram Palace and Traditions of Architecture and Kingship in South Asia." *Ars Orientalis* 26 (1996): 81–106.

Hiltebeitel, Alf. "Purity and Auspiciousness in the Sanskrit Epics." In *Purity and Auspiciousness in Indian Society*, edited by John B. Carman and Frédérique Apffel-Marglin, 41–54. Leiden: E. J. Brill, 1985.

Hiltebeitel, Alf, and Kathleen M. Erndl. "Introduction: Writing Goddesses, Goddesses Writing, and Other Scholarly Concerns." In *Is the Goddess a Feminist? The Politics of South Asian Goddesses*, edited by Alf Hiltebeitel and Kathleen M. Erndl, 11–23. New York: New York University Press, 2000.

Hudson, Dennis. "Kanchipuram." In *Temple Towns of Tamil Nadu*, edited by George Michell, 18–39. Mumbai: Marg Publications, 1993.

———. "How to Worship at Śiva's Temple." In *Religions of India in Practice*, edited by Donald S. Lopez, 304–20. Princeton, NJ: Princeton University Press, 1995.

———. "Interpreting the Kailasanatha Temple in Kanchipuram: Thoughts on an Approach." Symposium of the American Council on Southern Asian Art, Minneapolis, 1996.

———. *The Body of God: An Emperor's Palace for Krishna in Eighth-Century Kanchipuram*. Edited by Margaret H. Case. New York: Oxford University Press, 2008.

Hultzsch, Eugen. "No. 48. Kanchi Inscription of Vikramaditya." *Epigraphia Indica* 3 (1884–85): 359–60.

———. "Nos. 21–23. Inscriptions on the Atiraṇachaṇḍeśvara Temple, Śaluvaṅkuppam." In *South Indian Inscriptions*, edited by Eugen Hultzsch, vol. 1, 6–8. New Delhi: Archaeological Survey of India, 1890.

———. "No. 24. The Pallava Inscriptions on the Kailāsanātha Temple at Kāñcîpuram: Round the Outside of the Shrine of Rājasiṁheśvara." In *South Indian Inscriptions*, edited by Eugen Hultzsch, vol. 1, 8–14. New Delhi: Archaeological Survey of India, 1890.

———. "No. 25. Round the Inside of the Enclosure of the Rājasiṁheśvara Temple, First Tier." In *South Indian Inscriptions*, edited by Eugen Hultzsch, vol. 1, 14–21. New Delhi: Archaeological Survey of India, 1890.

———. "No. 26. Round the Inside of the Enclosure of the Rājasiṁheśvara Temple, Fourth Tier." In *South Indian Inscriptions*, edited by Eugen Hultzsch, vol. 1, 21–22. New Delhi: Archaeological Survey of India, 1890.

———. "No. 27. The Pallava Inscriptions on the Kailāsanātha Temple at Kāñcîpuram: Round the Outside of the Shrine of Mahendravarmeśvara." In *South Indian Inscriptions*, edited by Eugen Hultzsch, vol. 1, 22–23. New Delhi: Archaeological Survey of India, 1890.

———. "Nos. 28–30. The Pallava Inscriptions on the Kailāsanātha Temple at Kāñcîpuram." In *South Indian Inscriptions*, edited by Eugen Hultzsch, vol. 1, 23–24. New Delhi: Archaeological Survey of India, 1890.

———. "No. 31. A Pallava Inscription in a Cave-Temple near Panamalai." In *South Indian Inscriptions*, edited by Eugen Hultzsch, vol. 1, 24. New Delhi: Archaeological Survey of India, 1890.

———. "No. 151. A Pallava Grant from Kūram." In *South Indian Inscriptions*, edited by Eugen Hultzsch, vol. 1, 144–55. New Delhi: Archaeological Survey of India, 1890.

———. "VI. Inscriptions of the Kailāsānatha Temple at Kāñchīpuram." In *South Indian Inscriptions*, edited by Eugen Hultzsch, vol. 1, 110–25. New Delhi: Archaeological Survey of India, 1890.

———. "No. 73. Kasakudi Plates of Nandivarman Pallavamalla." In *South Indian Inscriptions*, edited by Eugen Hultzsch, vol. 2, pt. 3, 342–61. New Delhi: Archaeological Survey of India, 1895.

———. "No. 1. The Pallava Inscriptions of the Seven Pagodas: F—Inscriptions on the Cave-Temple at Sāḷuvaṅguppam; No. 23." *Epigraphia Indica* 10 (1910): 12–13.

———. *South Indian Inscriptions*. Vol. 2. Madras: Archaeological Survey of India, 1895. Reprint, New Delhi: Archaeological Survey of India, 2001.

Humes, Cynthia Ann. "Is the *Devi Mahatmya* a Feminist Scripture?" In *Is the Goddess a Feminist? The Politics of South Asian Goddesses*, edited by Alf Hiltebeitel and Kathleen M. Erndl, 123–50. New York: New York University Press, 2000.

Huntington, Susan L., and John C. Huntington. *The Art of Ancient India: Buddhist, Hindu, Jain*. New York: Weatherhill, 1985.

Inden, Ronald. "Kings and Omens." In *Purity and Auspiciousness in Indian Society*, edited by John B. Carman and Frédérique Apffel-Marglin, 30–40. Leiden: E. J. Brill, 1985.

Indian Archaeology 1978–79: A Review. Edited by B. K. Thapar. New Delhi: Archaeological Survey of India, Government of India, 1981.

Indian Archaeology 1994–95: A Review. Edited by S. B. Mathur. New Delhi: Archaeological Survey of India, Government of India, 2000.

Jamwal, R. S. "Lime Mortars for Historical Buildings." *Conservation of Cultural Property in India* 29 (1996): 158–63.

Jouveau-Dubreuil, Gabriel. *Ancient History of the Deccan*. Translated by V. S. Swaminadha Dikshitar. 1920. Reprint, New Delhi: Classical Publications, 1979.

———. *Iconography of Southern India*. Translated by A. C. Martin. Paris: P. Geuthner, 1937. Reprint, New Delhi: Cosmo, 2001.

Kaimal, Padma. "Playful Ambiguity and Political Authority in the Large Relief at Mamallapuram." *Ars Orientalis* 24 (1994): 1–27.

———. "Shiva Nataraja: Shifting Meanings of an Icon." *Art Bulletin* 81 (1999): 390–419.

———. "Learning to See the Goddess." *Journal of the American Academy of Religion* 73, no. 1 (2005): 45–87.

———. *Scattered Goddesses: Travels with the Yoginīs*. Ann Arbor, MI: Association for Asian Studies, 2013.

———. "Word-Image Tango: Telling Stories with Words and Sculptures at the Kailāsanātha Temple Complex in Kāñcīpuram." In *The Archaeology of Bhakti II: Royal Bhakti, Local Bhakti*, edited by Emmanuel Francis and Charlotte Schmid, 159–207. Collection Indologie, no. 132. Pondicherry: École française d'Extrême Orient and Institut français de Pondichéry, 2016.

———. "Loved, Unloved, Changed: Afterlives of the Kailasanatha Temple in Kanchipuram." *Artibus Asiae* 81.2 (2021).

Kalidos, Raju. "Iconography of Mahiṣāsuramardiṇī. A Probe into Stylistic Evolution." *Acta Orientalia* (Copenhagen) 50 (1989): 7–48.

Kanaganayagam, Chelva. "Reading the Pallava Period through Its Religious and Secular Texts." Paper presented at "Kālam," Sixth Tamil Chair Conference, University of California, Berkeley, April 2010.

Kramrisch, Stella. "The Great Cave Temple of Śiva in Elephanta: Levels of Meaning and Their Form." In *Discourses on Śiva: Proceedings of a Symposium on the Nature of Religious Imagery*, edited by Michael W. Meister, 1–11. Philadelphia: University of Pennsylvania Press, 1984.

Krishna, Nanditha, ed. *Kanchi, a Heritage of Art and Religion*. Madras: C. P. Ramaswami Aiyar Institute of Indological Research, C. P. Ramaswami Aiyar Foundation, 1992.

———. "The Paintings of Kanchi." In *Kanchi, a Heritage of Art and Religion*, edited by Nanditha Krishna, 49–55. Madras: C. P. Ramaswami Aiyar Institute of Indological Research, C. P. Ramaswami Aiyar Foundation, 1992.

Kuppusamy, Bahour S. *Pondicherry Inscriptions*. Pt. 2, *Translation, Appendices, Glossary and Phrases*, edited and translated by G. Viyayavenugopal. Pondicherry: Institute français de Pondichéry and École française d'Extrême-Orient, 2010.

Leoshko, Janice. "About Looking at Buddha Images in Eastern India." *Archives of Asian Art* 52 (2000–2001): 63–82.

Leslie, Julia. "Śrī and Jyeṣṭhā: Ambivalent Role Models for Women." In *Roles and Rituals for Hindu Women*, edited by Julia Leslie, 107–27. Rutherford, NJ: Fairleigh Dickinson University Press, 1991.

L'Hernault, Françoise. *L'iconographie de Subrahmanya au Tamilnad*. Pondicherry: Institut français d'indologie, 1978.

Lockwood, Michael, A. Vishnu Bhat, and Gift Siromoney. "Dhvani in Epigraphy and Stone." In *Pallava Art*, by Michael Lockwood, A. Vishnu Bhat, Gift Siromoney, and P. Dayanandan, 146. Madras: Tambaram Research Associates, 2001.

———. "A Mystery Dog in Sculpture." In *Pallava Art*, by Michael Lockwood, A. Vishnu Bhat, Gift Siromoney, and P. Dayanandan, 142–44. Madras: Tambaram Research Associates, 2001.

Lockwood, Michael, A. Vishnu Bhat, Gift Siromoney, and P. Dayanandan. *Mamallapuram and the Pallavas*. Madras: Christian Literature Society, 1982.

———. *Pallava Art*. Madras: Tambaram Research Associates, 2001.

Lockwood, Michael, Gift Siromoney, and P. Dayanandan. *Mahabalipuram Studies*. Madras: Christian Literature Society, 1974.

Longhurst, A. H. *Pallava Architecture*. Pt. 3, *The Later or Rājasimha Period*. Memoirs of the Archaeological Survey of India. New Delhi: Cosmo Publications, 1982. Originally published 1930 by Archaeological Survey of India (Calcutta).

Lorenzen, David. "A Parody of the Kāpālikas in the Mattavilāsa." In *Tantra in Practice*, edited by David Gordon White, 81–96. Princeton, NJ: Princeton University Press, 2000.

Lyons, Tryna. "The Simla *Devī Māhātmya* Illustrations: A Reappraisal of Content." *Archives of Asian Art* 45 (1992): 29–41.

Mahalingam, T. V. *Kāñcīpuram in Early South Indian History*. New York: Asia Publishing House, 1969.

———. *Readings in South Indian History*. Delhi: B. R. Publishing Corporation, 1977.

———. *Inscriptions of the Pallavas*. New Delhi: Indian Council of Historical Research; Delhi: Agam Prakashan, 1988.

Mallmann, Marie-Thérèse de. *Les enseignements iconographiques de l'Agni-Purana*. Ministère d'état, Annales du Musée Guimet, Bibliothèque d'études, vol. 67. Paris: Presses universitaires de France, 1963.

Malville, J. McKim. "Astrophysics, Cosmology, and the Interior Space of Indian Myths and Temples." In *Concepts of Space, Ancient and Modern*, edited by Kapila Vatsyayan, 123–44. New Delhi: Indira Gandhi National Centre for the Arts and Abhinav Publications, 1991.

Mani, V. R. *Saptamātṛkas in Indian Religion and Art*. New Delhi: Mittal Publishers, 1995.

McCloud, Scott. *Understanding Comics: The Invisible Art*. New York: HarperPerennial, 1994.

Meister, Michael W. "Juncture and Conjunction: Punning and Temple Architecture." *Artibus Asiae* 41, no. 2/3 (1979): 226–34.

———. "Forest and Cave: Temples at Candrabhāgā and Kansuāñ." *Archives of Asian Art* 34 (1981): 56–73.

———. "Analysis of Temple Plans: Indor." *Artibus Asiae* 43, no. 4 (1981–82): 302–20.

———. "Symbol and Surface: Masonic and Pillared Wall-Structures in North India." *Artibus Asiae* 46, no. 1/2 (1985): 129–48.

———. "Regional Variations in Mātṛka Conventions." *Artibus Asiae* 47, no. 3/4 (1986): 233–62.

———. "Prāsāda as Palace: Kutina Origins of the Nāgara Temple." *Artibus Asiae* 49, no. 3/4 (1988–89): 254–80.

———. "The Hindu Temple: Axis of Access." In *Concepts of Space, Ancient and Modern*, edited by Kapila Vatsyayan, 269–80. New Delhi: Indira Gandhi National Centre for the Arts and Abhinav Publications, 1991.

———, ed. *Ethnography and Personhood: Notes from the Field*. New Delhi: Rawat Publications, 2000.

———. "Navigating Hudson." *Journal of Vaishnava Studies* 11, no. 1 (2002): 45–49.

———. "Vāstupuruṣamaṇḍalas: Planning in the Image of Man." In *Mandalas and Yantras in the Hindu Traditions*, edited by Gudrun Bühnemann, 251–70. Leiden: E. J. Brill, 2003.

———. "Gaurīśikhara: Temple as an Ocean of Story." *Artibus Asiae* 69, no. 2 (2009): 295–315.

Meister, Michael W., and Ananda K. Coomaraswamy. "Early Indian Architecture: IV. Huts and Related Temple Types." *Anthropology and Aesthetics* 15 (1988): 5–26.

Meister, Michael W., and M. A. Dhaky, eds. *Encyclopaedia of Indian Temple Architecture*. Vol. 1, pt. 1, *South India: Lower Dravidadesa, 200 BC–AD 1324*. New Delhi: American Institute of Indian Studies and Oxford University Press, 1983.

Meister, Michael W., and Joseph Rykwert. "Adam's House and Hermits' Huts: A Conversation." *Anthropology and Aesthetics* 15 (1988): 27–33.

Menon, Usha, and Richard A. Shweder. "Power in Its Place: Is the Great Goddess of Hinduism a Feminist?" In *Is the Goddess a Feminist? The Politics of South Asian Goddesses*, edited by Alf Hiltebeitel and Kathleen M. Erndl, 151–65. New York: New York University Press, 2000.

Mevissen, Gerd J. R. "Political Geography as a Determinant in South Indian Temple Art? A Case Study of Tripurantakamurti." In *South Asian Archaeology 1993: Proceedings of the Twelfth International Conference of the European Association of South Asian Archaeologists Held in Helsinki University, 5–9 July 1993*, edited by Asko Parpola and Petteri Koskikallio, vol. 2, 483–95. Helsinki: Suomalainen Tiedeakatemia, 1994.

———. "Three Royal Temple Foundations in South India: Tripurāntaka Imagery as a Statement of Political Power." In *Temple Architecture and Imagery of South and Southeast Asia: Prāsānidhi—Papers Presented to Professor M. A. Dhaky*, edited by Parul Pandya Dhar and Gerd J. R. Mevissen, 169–88. New Delhi: Aryan Books International, 2016.

Michell, George. Review of *Temples de l'Inde méridionale (VIe–VIIIe siècles): La mise en scène des mythes*, by Édith Parlier-Renault. *Bulletin of the School of Oriental and African Studies* 71, no. 1 (2008): 129–30.

Minakshi, C. *The Historical Sculptures at the Vaikuṇṭhaperumāḷ Temple, Kāñcī*. Memoirs of the Archaeological Survey of India. Delhi: Government of India, 1941.

Mitchell, W. J. T. *What Do Pictures Want?* Chicago: University of Chicago Press, 2005.

Mitterwallner, Gritli von. "The Kuṣāṇa Type of the Goddess Mahiṣāsuramardinī as Compared to the Gupta and Mediaeval Types." In *German Scholars on India*, 196–213. Bombay: Nachiketa Publications, 1978.

Mosteller, John F. "The Problem of Proportion and Style in Indian Art History: Or Why All Buddhas in Fact Do Not Look Alike." *Art Journal* 49, no. 4 (1990): 388–94.

Mostert, Marco. "Reading Images and Texts: Some Preliminary Observations." In *Reading Images and Texts: Medieval Images and Texts as Forms of Communication; Papers from the Third Utrecht Symposium on Medieval Literacy, Utrecht, 7–9 December 2000*, edited by Mariëlle Hageman and Marco Mostert, 1–7. Turnhout, Belgium: Brepols, 2005.

Nagarajan, Vijaya Rettakudi. "Hosting the Divine: The *Kolam* in Tamilnadu." In *Mud, Mirror and Thread: Folk Traditions of Rural India*, edited by Nora Fisher, 192–201. Ahmedabad: Mapin; Middletown, NJ: Grantha Corporation; Santa Fe, NM: in association with Museum of New Mexico Press, 1993.

———. "Threshold Designs, Forehead Dots, and Menstruation Rituals: Exploring Time and Space in Tamil *Kolam*s." In *Women's Lives, Women's Rituals in the Hindu Tradition*, edited by Tracy Pintchman, 85–105. New York: Oxford University Press, 2007.

Nagaswamy, R. "New Light on Mamallapuram." In *Transactions of the Archaeological Society of South India Transactions, 1960–62*, 1–50. Madras: Archaeological Society of South India, 1962.

———. *The Kailasanatha Temple (A Guide)*. Tamilnadu Department of Archaeology. Madras: State Department of Archaeology, Government of Tamilnadu, 1969.

———. *Tantric Cult of South India*. New Delhi: Agam Kala Prakashan, 1982.

———. "Innovative Emperor and His Personal Chapel: Eighth Century Kanchipuram." In *Royal Patrons and Great Temple Arts*, edited by Vidya Dehejia, 37–60. Bombay: Marg Publications, 1988.

———. "The Brihadiśvara as Paramākāśa." In *Concepts of Space, Ancient and Modern*, edited by Kapila Vatsyayan, 299–310. New Delhi: Indira Gandhi National Centre for the Arts and Abhinav Publications, 1991.

Narayanan, Vasudha. "The Two Levels of Auspiciousness in Śrīvaiṣṇava Ritual and Literature." In *Purity and Auspiciousness in Indian Society*, edited by John B. Carman and Frédérique Apffel-Marglin, 55–64. Leiden: E. J. Brill, 1985.

———. "Śrī: Giver of Fortune, Bestower of Grace." In *Devī: Goddesses of India*, edited by John S. Hawley and Donna M. Wulff, 87–108. Comparative Studies in Religion and Society. Berkeley: University of California Press, 1996.

Ochshorn, Judith. "Goddesses and the Lives of Women." In *Women and Goddess Traditions: In Antiquity and Today*, edited by Karen L. King, 377–405. Minneapolis: Fortress Press, 1997.

Ojha, Catherine. "Feminine Asceticism in Hinduism: Its Tradition and Present Condition." *Man in India* 61, no. 3 (1981): 254–85.

Orr, Leslie C. "Gods and Worshippers on South Indian Sacred Ground." In *The World in the Year 1000*, edited by James Heitzman and Wolfgang Schenkluhn, 225–54. Lanham, MD: University Press of America, 2004.

———. "Identity and Divinity: Boundary-Crossing Goddesses in Medieval South India." *Journal of the American Academy of Religion* 73, no. 1 (2005): 9–43.

———. Preface to *Pondicherry Inscriptions*, pt. 1, *Introduction with Texts and Notes*, edited by G. Vijayavenugopal, iii–xxvii. Pondicherry: Institut français de Pondichéry and École française d'Extrême-Orient, 2006.

———. "Domesticity and Difference / Women and Men: Religious Life in Medieval Tamilnadu." In *Women's Lives, Women's Rituals in the Hindu Tradition*, edited by Tracy Pintchman, 109–29. New York: Oxford University Press, 2007.

———. "Transposing Royal Glory: Texts, Temples, and the Tenkasi Pandyas." Paper presented at the Annual Conference on South Asia, University of Wisconsin–Madison, October 2013.

Owen, Lisa N. "Absence and Presence: Worshipping the Jina at Ellora." In *Archaeology and Text: The Temple in South Asia*, edited by Himanshu Prabha Ray, 96–123. New York: Oxford University Press, 2010.

Pal, Pratapaditya. "The Image of Grace and Wisdom: Dakṣiṇāmūrti of Śiva." *Oriental Art* 28, no. 4 (1982): 244–56.

Pallava, King Mahendravikramavarma. *Mattavilāsa Prahasana*. Edited and translated by Michael Lockwood and A. Vishnu Bhat. Madras: Christian Literature Society, 1981.

Panikkar, S. *Saptamatrka Worship and Sculptures: An Iconological Interpretation of Conflicts and Resolutions in the Storied Brahmanical Icons.* New Delhi: D. K. Printworld, 1997.

Paramasivan, S. "Technique of the Painting Process in the Kailasanatha and Vaikunthaperumal Temples at Kanchipuram." *Nature*, no. 3599 (October 22, 1938): 757.

Parker, Samuel K. "Text and Practice in South Asian Art: An Ethnographic Perspective." *Artibus Asiae* 63, no. 1 (2003): 5–34.

Parlier-Renault, Édith. *Temples de l'Inde méridionale (VIe–VIIIe siècles): La mise en scène des mythes.* Paris: Presses de l'Université Paris-Sorbonne, 2006.

Pattabiramin, P. Z. 1971. *Sanctuaires rupestres de l'Inde du Sud.* Vol. 42. Pondicherry: Institut français d'indologie.

Presler, Franklin A. "The Structure and Consequences of Temple Policy in Tamil Nadu, 1967–81." *Pacific Affairs* 56, no. 2 (1983): 232–46.

Preston, James J. *Cult of the Goddess: Social and Religious Change in a Hindu Temple.* Prospect Heights, IL: Waveland Press, 1985.

Rajani, M. B. "The Expanse of Archaeological Remains at Nalanda." *Archives of Asian Art* 66, no. 1 (2016): 1–23.

Rajarajan, R. K. K. "Dakṣiṇāmūrti on *Vimānas* of Viṣṇu Temples in the Far South." *South Asian Studies* 27, no. 2 (2011): 131–44.

Ramachandra Rao, S. K. *Mandalas in Temple Worship*. Yantras and Mandalas in Temple Worship, vol. 1, edited by Daivajna K. N. Somayaji. Bangalore: Kalpatharu Research Academy, 1988.

Raman, K. V. *The Dharmarāja Ratha and Its Sculptures*. New Delhi: Abhinav Publications, 1975.

———. *Srī Varadarājaswami Temple—Kāñchī: A Study of Its History, Art and Architecture*. New Delhi: Abhinav Publications, 1975.

———. "Archaeological Excavations in Kanchipuram." *Tamil Civilization* 5, no. 1–2 (1987): 61–72.

Ramanujan, A. K. *Poems of Love and War from the Eight Anthologies and the Ten Long Poems of Classical Tamil*. Delhi: Oxford University Press, 1985.

Ramiah, Ilavenil. "Gods and Kings: Meaning in the Śiva Gaṅgādhara Relief at Thiruchirapalli." *Artibus Asiae* 75, no. 2 (2015): 155–78.

Rangacharya, V. "No. 18. Two Inscriptions of the Pallava King Rajasimha-Narasimhavarman II: A—the Mahābalipuram Inscription; B—the Panamalai Inscription." *Epigraphia Indica* 19 (1927–28): 109–15.

Rea, Alexander. *Pallava Architecture*. Archaeological Survey of India, New Imperial Series. Madras: Superintendent, Government Press, 1909. Reprint, Varanasi: Indological Book House, 1970.

Rice, Lewis. "The Chalukyas and Pallavas." *Indian Antiquary* 8 (1879): 23–29.

Sanderson, Alexis. "History through Textual Criticism in the Study of Śaivism, the Pañcarātra and the Buddhist Yoginītantras." In *Les sources et le temp (Sources and Time): A Colloquium, Pondicherry, 11–13 January 1997*, edited by François Grimal, 1–47. Pondicherry: Institut français de Pondichéry and École française d'Extrême-Orient, 2001.

———. "The Impact of Inscriptions on the Interpretation of Early Śaiva Literature." *Indo-Iranian Journal* 56 (2013): 211–44.

Sanford, David T. "Miniature Relief Sculptures at the Pullamangai Śiva Temple, with Special Reference to the Ramayana Sequence." In *Kusumāñjali: New Interpretation of Indian Art and Culture; Sh. C. Sivaramamurti Commemoration Volume*, edited by M. S. Nagaraja Rao, 277–87. Delhi: Agam Kala Prakashan, 1987.

Sankaranarayanan, S. "A Pallava Inscriptional Poem in Sanskrit." *Adyar Library Bulletin* 55 (1991): 71–90.

Sarma, I. K. "Beginnings of Temple Architecture at Kanchipuram: Raw Materials and Religious Impacts." In *Archaeology and History: Essays in Memory of Shri A. Ghosh*, vol. 2, 545–51. Delhi: Agam Kala Prakashan, 1987.

Sastri, H. Krishna. "No. 98. The Velurpalaiyam Plates of Vijaya-Nandivarman (III)." In *South Indian Inscriptions*, vol. 2, pt. 5, 501–17. Madras: Superintendent, Government Press, 1916.

Sastri, K. A. Nilakanta. *The Cōḷas*. Madras: University of Madras, 1955.

Sathyanarayanan, R., ed. *Śaiva Rites of Expiation: A First Edition and Translation of Trilocanaśiva's Twelfth-Century Prāyaścittasamuccaya*. With an introduction by Dominic Goodall. Collection Indologie, no. 127. Pondicherry: Institut français de Pondichéry and École française d'Extrême-Orient, 2015.

Schmid, Charlotte. "Á propos des premières images de la Tueuse de buffle: Déesses et krishnaïsme ancien." *Bulletin de l'École française d'Extrême-Orient* (Paris) 90–91 (2003): 7–67.

———. "Au seuil du monde divin: Reflets et passages du dieu d'Alanturai á Puḷḷamaṅkai." *Bulletin de l'École française d'Extrême-Orient* (Paris) 92 (2005): 39–152.

———. "Mahābalipuram: La Prospérité au double visage." *Journal Asiatique* (Paris) 293, no. 2 (2005): 459–527.

———. *Le Don de voir: Premières représentations krishnaïtes de la région de Mathurā*. Monographies 193. Paris: École française d'Extrême-Orient, 2010.

———. "Bhakti in Its Infancy: Genealogy Matters in the Kailāsanātha of Kāñcīpuram." In *The Archaeology of Bhakti I: Mathurā and Maturai, Back and Forth*, edited by Emmanuel Francis and Charlotte Schmid, 89–141. Pondicherry: École française d'Extrême-Orient, 2014.

Schopen, Gregory. "What's in a Name: The Religious Function of the Early Donative Inscriptions." In *Unseen Presence*, edited by Vidya Dehejia, 58–73. Mumbai: Marg Publications, 1996.

Seastrand, Anna. "Tracing a Line: Guruparamparā in the Murals of Alvar Tirunakari." *Journal of Vaishnava Studies* 22 (2013): 43–63.

Sheikh, Samira. "Taming the Goddess in Late Mughal Gujarat." Paper delivered at the Annual Meeting of the American Historical Association, Boston, January 2011.

Shulman, David. "The Murderous Bride: Tamil Versions of the Myth of Devī and the Buffalo Demon." *History of Religions* 16, no. 2 (1976): 120–47.

———. "On South Indian Bandits and Kings." *Indian Economic and Social History Review* 17, no. 3 (1980): 283–306.

———. *Tamil Temple Myths: Sacrifice and Divine Marriage in the South Indian Śaiva Tradition.* Princeton, NJ: Princeton University Press, 1980.

———. "Notes on the Kālantaka Myth at Tirukkadavur." In *Śrīnidhih: Perspectives in Indian Archaeology, Art and Culture (Shri K. R. Srinivasan Festschrift)*, edited by K. V. Raman et al., 267–74. Madras: New Era Publications, 1983.

Singh, M. "Studies on Weathering of Kailasanatha Temple, Kancheepuram." *Current Science* 64, no. 8 (April 25, 1993): 559–65.

Siromoney, Gift, M. Bagavandas, and S. Govindaraju. "An Application of Component Analysis to the Study of South Indian Sculptures." *Computers and the Humanities* 14, no. 1 (June 1980): 29–37.

Sivaramamurti, C. *Mahabalipuram.* New Delhi: Director General, Archaeological Survey of India, 1972.

———. *Nataraja in Art, Thought, and Literature.* New Delhi: National Museum, 1974.

Smith, David. *The Dance of* Śiva*: Religion, Art and Poetry in South India.* Cambridge: Cambridge University Press, 1996.

Smith, Walter. "Architectural and Mythic Space at Ellora." *Oriental Art* 42 (Summer 1996): 13–21.

Soundara Rajan, K. V. "'Cult' in the Pallava Temples." In *Transactions of the Archaeological Society of South India, 1962–65*, 143–62. Madras: Archaeological Society of South India, 1969.

———. "Rajasimha's Temples in Toṇḍaimaṇḍalam." In *Transactions of the Archaeological Society of South India, 1962–65*, 169–200. Madras: Archaeological Society of South India, 1969.

———. "Irrukuvēḷs of Koḍumbāḷūr." In *Encyclopaedia of Indian Temple Architecture*, edited by Michael W. Meister and M. A. Dhaky, vol. 1, pt. 1, *South India: Lower Dravidadesa, 200 BC–AD 1324*, 199–214. New Delhi: American Institute of Indian Studies and Oxford University Press, 1983.

———. "Muttaraiyars of Nēmam and Sēndalai." In *Encyclopaedia of Indian Temple Architecture*, edited by Michael W. Meister and M. A. Dhaky, vol. 1, pt. 1, *South India: Lower Dravidadesa, 200 BC–AD 1324*, 125–44. New Delhi: American Institute of Indian Studies and Oxford University Press, 1983.

———. *Rock-Cut Temple Styles: Early Pandyan Art and the Ellora Shrines.* Mumbai: Somaiya Publications, 1998.

Srinivasan, C. R. *Kanchipuram through the Ages.* Delhi: Agam Kala Prakashan, 1979.

Srinivasan, K. R. "Some Aspects of Religion as Revealed by Early Monuments and Literature of the South." *Journal of the Madras University* 32, no. 1 (1960): 131–98.

———. *Cave Temples of the Pallavas.* New Delhi: Archaeological Survey of India, 1964.

————. "Temples of the Later Pallavas." In *Studies in Indian Temple Architecture*, edited by Pramod Chandra, 197–239. New Delhi: American Institute of Indian Studies, 1975.

————. "Pallavas of Kāñcī: Phase I." In *Encyclopaedia of Indian Temple Architecture*, edited by Michael W. Meister and M. A. Dhaky, vol. 1, pt. 1, *South India: Lower Dravidadesa, 200 BC–AD 1324*, 23–80. New Delhi: American Institute of Indian Studies and Oxford University Press, 1983.

Srinivasan, P. R. *Beginnings of the Traditions of South Indian Temple Architecture*. Bulletin of the Madras Government Museum, vol. 7, no. 4. Madras: Printed by the Rathnam Press, for the Controller of Stationery and Printing, 1959.

————. "Gangadharashtakam in Pallava Inscription from Tiruchirapalli." In *Śrīnidhih: Perspectives in Indian Archaeology, Art and Culture (Shri K. R. Srinivasan Festschrift)*, edited by K. V. Raman et al., 431–35. Madras: New Era Publications, 1983.

Srivatsan, A. "Kanchipuram, Temple Town Structure—the Past and the Present." In *Kanchi, a Heritage of Art and Religion*, edited by Nanditha Krishna, 102–4. Madras: C. P. Ramaswami Aiyar Institute of Indological Research, C. P. Ramaswami Aiyar Foundation, 1992.

Stein, Emma Natalya. "All Streets Lead to Temples: Mapping Monumental Histories in Kanchipuram, ca. 8th–12th Centuries CE." Ph.D. dissertation, Yale University, 2017.

Subbaraman, S. "Conservation of Shore Temple, Mahabalipuram and Kailasanatha Temple, Kancheepuram." In *Proceedings of the 5th International Congress on Deterioration and Conservation of Stone*, vol. 2, 1025–34. Lausanne, Switzerland: Presses Polytechniques Romandes, 1985.

Subramanian, T. S. "A Restoration Feat." *Frontline* 20, no. 1 (January 18–31, 2003).

Summers, David. "*Figure come fratelli*: A Transformation of Symmetry in Italian Renaissance Painting." *Art Quarterly* 1 (1977): 59–88.

Talbot, Cynthia. "Parameters of Poetic Praise in Mughal India: Comparing Eulogies of Rana Raj Singh." Paper presented at the Annual Conference on South Asia, University of Wisconsin–Madison, October 2013.

Tartakov, Gary Michael, and Vidya Dehejia. "Sharing, Intrusion, and Influence: The Mahiṣāsuramardinī Imagery of the Calukyas and the Pallavas." *Artibus Asiae* 45, no. 4 (1984): 287–345.

Thakur, Laxman S. "Application of Vāstupuruṣamaṇḍala in the Indian Temple Architecture: An Analysis of the Nāgara Temple Plans of Himachal Pradesh." *Artibus Asiae* 50, no. 3/4 (1990): 263–84.

Torjesen, Karen Jo. Introduction to *Women and Goddess Traditions: In Antiquity and Today*, edited by Karen L. King, 1–3. Minneapolis: Fortress Press, 1997.

Tringham, Ruth, and Margaret Conkey. "Rethinking Figurines." In *Ancient Goddesses: The Myths and the Evidence*, edited by Lucy Goodison and Christine Morris, 2–45. Madison: University of Wisconsin Press, 1999.

Tripathi, L. K. "Causaṭha Yoginī Temple, Khajuraho." *Journal of the Indian Society of Oriental Art*, n.s., 6 (1974–75): 33–42.

Vatsyayan, Kapila. *Classical Indian Dance in Literature and the Arts*. New Delhi: Sangeet Natak Akademi, 1977.

Venkatarama Ayyar, K. R., ed. *A Manual of the Pudukkottai State*. 2nd rev. ed. Vol. 2, pt. 2. Pudukkottai: Sri Brihadamba State Press, 1944.

Wechsler, Helen J. "Royal Legitimation: Rāmāyaṇa Reliefs on the Papanātha Temple at Pattadakal." In *The Legend of Rāma: Artistic Visions*, edited by Vidya Dehejia, 27–42. Bombay: Marg Publications, 1994.

Williams, Joanna G. *The Art of Gupta India*. Princeton, NJ: Princeton University Press, 1982.

————. "On Viewing Sāñcī." *Archives of Asian Art* 50 (1997–98): 93–98.

Wolf, Werner. "Narrative and Narrativity: A Narratological Reconceptualization and Its Applicability to the Visual Arts." *Word and Image* 19, no. 3 (2003): 180–97.

Yocum, Glenn E. "Comments: The Divine Consort in South India." In *The Divine Consort: Rādhā and the Goddesses of India*, edited by John S. Hawley and Donna M. Wulff, 278–81. Berkeley, CA: Graduate Theological Union, 1982.

Yonan, Michael. "The Wieskirche: Movement, Perception, and Salvation in the Bavarian Rococo." *Studies in Eighteenth-Century Culture* 41 (2012): 1–25.

———. "Material Transformations: Thinking about Objects and Spaces at the Wieskirche." *Journal of Art Historiography* 9 (2013): 1–13.

Zeiler, Xenia. "Female Danger: 'Evil,' Inauspiciousness, and Their Symbols in Representations of South Asian Goddesses." *Nidān: International Journal for the Study of Hinduism* 24 (2012): 100–116.

Zvelebil, Kamil V. *Ananda-Tāṇḍava of Śiva-Sadanṛttamūrti*. Madras: Institute of Asian Studies, 1985.